SELECTED WORKS

OF

HULDREICH ZWINGLI,
(1484-1531)

THE REFORMER OF GERMAN SWITZERLAND.

TRANSLATED FOR THE FIRST TIME FROM THE ORIGINALS.

The German Works by Lawrence A. McLouth, Professor of German in New York University, and the Latin by Henry Preble, New York City, and Professor George W. Gilmore, Meadville, Pennsylvania.

EDITED

WITH GENERAL AND SPECIAL INTRODUCTIONS AND OCCASIONAL NOTES

BY

SAMUEL MACAULEY JACKSON,

PROFESSOR OF CHURCH HISTORY IN NEW YORK UNIVERSITY; EDITOR OF "THE HEROES OF THE REFORMATION," AND AUTHOR IN THAT SERIES OF THE LIFE OF HULDREICH ZWINGLI.

WIPF & STOCK · Eugene, Oregon

Wipf and Stock Publishers
199 W 8th Ave, Suite 3
Eugene, OR 97401

Selected Works of Huldreich Zwingli
The Reformer of German Switzerland (1484-1531)
By Zwingli, Ulrich and Jackson, Samuel Macauley
Softcover ISBN-13: 978-1-7252-6552-3
Hardcover ISBN-13: 978-1-7252-6554-7
eBook ISBN-13: 978-1-7252-6553-0
Publication date 2/4/2020
Previously published by Longmans, Green & Co., 1901

PREFACE.

THIS volume presents a selection from the contents of the eight volumes in which the works of Huldreich Zwingli, the Reformer of German Switzerland, are preserved in the only edition now accessible, namely, that published in Zurich between 1828 and 1842, with a supplement in 1861. Egli and Finsler's edition in the *Corpus Reformatorum* is announced but will not be finished for at least ten years. The selection has been made purposely from those papers which had never been translated —at least not in their entirety—into modern German or English. These papers have been arranged in chronological order, and when read consecutively present a documentary history of several phases of the Zurich Reformation. They have been utilized in my biography of Zwingli, published by G. P. Putnam's Sons, New York city, in the series of "Heroes of the Reformation," and are here printed in full by the courtesy of the publishers of the series. As appears, the translations from the Latin were made by Mr. Henry Preble, of this city, and by Prof. George W. Gilmore, and those from the Zurich German by Mr. Lawrence A. McLouth, Professor of German in the New York University. They will be found accurate and spirited, and I am very proud to be able to put into the hands of the English reader for the first time matter of so interesting and important a character. My highest ambition is that Huldreich Zwingli may win in this way a large number of friends. My own part in this new volume is a very modest one. I have made the selections, supplied some introductory matter, and a few notes. Those who would like to read more of the writings of Zwingli I refer to my biography alluded to above, in which will be found Professor McLouth's translation in full of the sermon upon fasting, preached in the spring of 1522, which was the first published reformation document in Switzerland; and the Confession of Faith presented by Zwingli at the Diet of Augsburg, 1530, translated by Rev. Henry E. Jacobs, D. D., LL. D., Professor in the Evangelical Lutheran Seminary, Philadelphia, Pa.; reprinted by permission, from Dr. Jacobs' edition of the *Book of Concord*, Philadelphia, the best edition of that important collection and its accompanying documents. Also, I would say that in 1899, in Collegeville, Pa., there appeared a translation of Zwingli's "Christian Education of Youth," by Professor Reichenbach, of Ursinus College, Philadelphia. I am not aware that there are any other accessible English translations of Zwingli's prose writings, but in my biography appear in English many extracts from Zwingli's correspondence and from documents bearing upon him.

SAMUEL MACAULEY JACKSON.

NEW YORK CITY, *April 8, 1901.*

INTRODUCTION.

HULDREICH ZWINGLI was born in the outskirts of the village of Wildhaus, forty miles east by south of Zurich, in Switzerland, on the first of January, 1484. His family on both sides were peasants, but persons of more or less prominence and of high character. His father was the village magistrate and his father's brother the village priest. This uncle was in 1487 transferred to a higher position at Wesen, upon the Lake of Walenstadt, twelve miles to the southwest of Wildhaus, and took Zwingli with him. So there the child received his first book learning, and then he was sent by his uncle, who was providentially a friend of the New Learning, to Bern, Vienna and Basel for school and university training. In 1506 Zwingli, who had just taken the degree of Master of Arts at the University of Basel, became the priest of the parish of Glarus, about seven miles south of Wesen. There he remained ten years, and would have stayed much longer, probably, had it not been that his very vigorous attacks upon the mercenary military service of the Swiss, which service he recognized as a disgrace to his country and a sure and swift means of their moral ruin, awakened so much opposition on the part of the principal families in the Canton, who were interested in hiring out these mercenaries, that he was compelled to leave. He next appears as preacher in the famous monastery of Einsiedeln, in which is the Chapel of Meinrad, containing the wonder-working wooden image of the Virgin and Child. Thousands of pilgrims have every year for a millennium visited this sacred spot, and among them have been the most distinguished in the Church. When Zwingli went there he was already a fine scholar, an admired preacher and a recognized patriot. He inspired high and low with respect, and easily made the acquaintance of the cardinals and bishops and learned men who came in a continuous stream to the shrine. He also read diligently the books he found in the remarkably rich library of the monastery. Thus was he prepared for the prominent part he was destined to play. After two years he was called to the principal church of Zurich, and there he maintained himself as preacher and reformer and author for the rest of his life.

When he began his preaching in Zurich he had apparently no profound spiritual conceptions. He was an extremely pleasant, witty and agreeable man, and had a host of friends, for whose advantage he was ready at any time to do his best, so that he fastened them to himself as with hooks of steel. He was moreover a friend of the New Learning and felt the breath of the new era. He had been taught by Wyttenbach and Erasmus that the traditional church theology had very small basis in the Bible; had also come to the conclusion that the Bible was the great source of theology, so had been reading attentively the New Testament in the original Greek, and had even begun the study of Hebrew in order that he might get at the meaning of the Old Testament at first hand. In his zeal to drink in the water of life from the fountain he even had gone so far as to commit to memory the Epistles of St. Paul in Greek. From the beginning of his Zurich ministry he showed himself well acquainted with the text of Scripture, and able to quote it at pleasure. He began his preaching in Zurich with a continuous exposition of the Gospel of Matthew, and went on to expound other New Testament books in the same way. Living thus in the hearing of the divine oracles, thinking much upon their utterances, he was one of the first upon whom the vision of the purer, more unshackled, less hide-bound church fell. And without passing through any profound spiritual experience, entering rather as a devout scholar than as a religious enthusiast into the temple of God, he arrived at those conceptions of the truth which bear the name of Protestant. It was his exposure of the unbiblical character of much of the teachings and ceremonies of the Roman Church which roused the people of Zurich into open revolt against that church, and it was the distressing rumor of the probable defection of the Zurich people which was the occasion of the visit of the delegation from the Bishop of Constance, which is described in the first paper in this volume.

In this volume Zwingli is exhibited in various relations as leader in reform and the defense of reform. Thus the earnest petition (1522) which Zwingli wrote, to allow priests to marry, showed how enforced celibacy hindered holy living. The First Disputation (1523) showed the popularity of the proposed reforms. The Marriage Ordinance (1525) is a contribution to the history of the times. The reply to the Baptist arguments and exposure of their social disorders (1527), for the Baptists were the disturbers of the standing order in Zurich and fomenters of no one end of trouble for the Reformers there and in Germany, and the treatment they received, showed how far the Reformers were from being ready to grant to others the freedom of speech they exercised themselves. Still the Baptists were attacked on grounds of state polity rather than religiously.

The busy life of Zwingli, on whom fell the burden of directing the churches which received his leadership, was cut short by a violent death. He was involved in the struggle between the Forest cantons (Uri, Schwyz, Unterwalden, Luzern, Zug) up amid the mountains of Northern Switzerland, which were intensely Old Church, and the Reformed cantons (chiefly Zurich and Bern). The former would not grant freedom to gospel preaching, so the latter in punishment cut them off from necessary supplies, as they could do, since they commanded the commerce of the country. This brought matters to a crisis, and the opposing cantons met at Cappel, only 10 miles south of Zurich, October 11, 1531. Zwingli, as chief city pastor, went to the field as a non-combatant, although armed for defense, and perished the same day. He was a good man, a valiant fighter for the truth as he conceived it, and the Reformed churches, as contrasted with the Lutheran churches, look to him as one of their great founders.

TABLE OF CONTENTS.

	PAGE
PREFACE	3
INTRODUCTION	5
I. VISIT OF THE EPISCOPAL DELEGATION TO ZURICH, APRIL, 1522	9
II. THE PETITION OF ELEVEN PRIESTS TO BE ALLOWED TO MARRY, JULY, 1522	25
III. THE ACTS OF THE FIRST ZURICH DISPUTATION, JANUARY, 1523	40
IV. ZURICH MARRIAGE ORDINANCE, 1525	118
V. REFUTATION OF THE TRICKS OF THE CATABAPTISTS, 1527 *	123

* This is the literal rendering of the title of the Treatise, but as the Baptists are meant called them so on p. 123. Subsequent reflection led me to think it would have been better to have kept the original form, but the book being printed from type I was not able to restore the correct title in this edition.]

ZWINGLI SELECTIONS.

I. LETTER OF HULDREICH ZWINGLI TO ERASMUS FABRICIUS ABOUT THE PROCEEDINGS, ON THE 7TH, 8TH AND 9TH OF APRIL, 1522, OF THE DELEGATES SENT TO ZURICH BY THE BISHOP OF CONSTANCE.*

How the Reverend Lord Bishop of Constance, through his delegates, the suffragan Melchior [Wattli], John Wanner (who, however, I know took part in the affair against his will), and N[icholas] Brendlin, dealt with Huldreich Zwingli, preacher at Zurich, before the Board of Ecclesiastics and the Senate † on the 7th, 8th and 9th days of April.

ZWINGLI TO ERASMUS FABRICIUS.

On the seventh day of April the before mentioned Fathers came to our city pretty early, and I, knowing that they were coming, was trying to discover what their design was, and yet could not until late at night, when our beloved deacon, Henry Lutius, came and gave me warning that the clerk, as they call him, was getting together the whole body of priests for a meeting

---

* Zwingli's Works, ed. Schuler u. Schulthess, iii., 7–16. Translated from the original Latin by Mr. Henry Preble, New York city.

† I. e., City Council, hence the members in it are called councillors, but the Latin form Zwingli used has been allowed to stand. This body was in two parts, the Small Council, which contained only 50 members, and only half of these were on duty at any one time, and the Great Council, also called the Council of the Two Hundred, which included the Small Council. The Great Council was the deciding body on all legislative matters of importance, the Small was the exeutive committee, and both were representative bodies. The chief officer was the burgomaster, here called the President of the Senate. See my biography of Zwingli, pp. 42–44.

early next morning at the usual place of assembly of the canons. I regarded it as a happy omen that the thing had been thus neatly set on foot by a courier both lame and without grace, and began to consider in my mind how they were likely to begin their job. At length I understood, as I thought, and when day dawned and we had come together the suffragan began in the fashion that will follow when I come to describe how the matter was carried on before the Senate. His whole speech was violent and full of rage and arrogance, though he took pains to hide the fact that he had any quarrel with me. For he avoided mentioning my name as scrupulously as if it were sacred, though meanwhile there was nothing that he didn't say against me. When the tragedian had finished shrieking out his part, I stepped forward, feeling that it was unbecoming and disgraceful to allow a speech which might do so much damage to go unrebutted, especially as I saw from their sighs and their pale and silent faces that some of the feebler priests who had recently been won for Christ had been troubled by the tirade. Therefore I made answer upon the spur of the moment to the words of the suffragan, with what spirit or feeling the good men who heard me may judge. The general gist of what I said, however, you shall hear when we come to the proceedings before the Senate. The delegates abandoned this wing as routed and put to flight, and hurried quickly to another, to the Senate, namely, where, as I have learned from Senators, the same harangue was delivered and my name was avoided in the same way, and the Senate was persuaded not to have me summoned. For they said they had no concern whatever with me. After this the opinions varied for some time, but finally they decided that the Commons (that is, two hundred men, called the Greater Senate), should meet in full assembly on the following day, and that the bishops* of the city, of whom there are three

---

* Zwingli uses this term of the people's priests or preachers of the three parish churches in Zurich, viz., the Great Minster, Minster of our Lady, and St. Peter's. He explains it below.

of us, should be warned not to be present. For nothing was going to be said in reply to our friends, no one could contradict so sound a speech, and so on. When I discovered this, I devoted all my energy to getting us admitted to the meeting of the Senate to be held on the following day. For a long time I turned every stone in vain, for the chief men of the Senate said it could not be done, inasmuch as the Senate had voted otherwise. Then I began to cease my efforts and to plead with sighs to him who heareth the groans of those in bondage not to abandon the truth, but to come to the defense of his gospel, which he had willed to have us preach. At length on the ninth the citizens assembled, and loudly vented their indignation at their bishops not being admitted, but they of the Senate which from its number is called the Less resisted because they had voted otherwise previously. The Greater Senate, however, compelled them against their will to put the matter to vote, and it was decided that their bishops should be present and hear everything, and if need be make answer. Thus, not, as Livy says, did the greater part prevail over the better; for here both the greater and the better part prevailed. And this I have allowed myself to write, not for the sake of laying any blame upon the Lesser Senate, but to show what plotting and underhand action can accomplish. For what else were the delegates of the Bishop of Constance after but to say without witnesses whatever came into their mouths before the simple minded commons? Thanks be to God. For when the delegates were brought into the Senate, we bishops of Zurich were also admitted, Henry Engelhard, LL.D., of the nunnery, Rudolph Röschlin, bishop of St. Peter's, and I, Huldreich Zwingli. * Then

* Henry Engelhard had been people's priest at the cathedral of Our Lady since 1496. He had also been a canon of the Great Minster, but in 1521 resigned so that Zwingli might be appointed. This act of disinterestedness shows what a fine character he was. He remained ever one of Zwingli's friends. He died in 1551, a very old man. Rudolph Röschlin, people's priest at St. Peter's, was very slow in accepting the Reformation, was at the time of this episcopal visit an old man, and a few weeks after it resigned his place and was succeeded by Zwingli's bosom friend, Leo Jud.

when they had been given permission to speak, and the suffragan had extended to the assembly greeting and blessing from his Most Illustrious Leader and Bishop (for this must now at least be admitted), he began with that wonderfully sweet voice of his, than which I have scarcely ever heard one sweeter in speech. Indeed, if his heart and brain were as good, you might say that he could excel Orpheus and Apollo in sweetness, Demosthenes and the Gracchi in persuasive power. I should like to set down his speech in its entirety, but I cannot, partly because he spoke in an involved and jumbled together style, without order, and partly because so long a speech could not, I think, be remembered even by a Porcius Latro. But since I had my note-book at hand and took down the main headings, in order to be able to meet and answer them more fitly, I will first put down these headings and then subjoin what I said in reply to each of them.

With the manner of a consummate tragedian he said that (1) certain persons were teaching new, obnoxious and seditious doctrines (wieder wärtig und aufrührig lehren, in German), to wit: that (2) no human prescriptions and no ceremonials ought to be regarded. If this doctrine prevailed, it would come to pass that not only the laws of the state but even the Christian faith would be done away with, although (3) ceremonies were a sort of *manuductio* or "leading by the hand" to the virtues (for he was pleased to use this word *manuductio* even before people who did not understand Latin, because, no doubt, the German term eine einleitung, "an introduction," did not seem to him strong enough (or, if you will, fine enough). Ceremonials were in fact, he said, a source of virtue (ein ursprung), though he afterwards had the boldness to deny before all those witnesses that he used the word; (4) they were also teaching that Lent ought not to be kept, for certain persons in this city had ventured to withdraw from other Christians and from the Christian Church, though this statement also he afterwards denied with as much shamelessness as stubbornness. My lord Brendlin bore witness that he had not used that expression, though the whole Senate still bears witness that he used it. So persistently do these people fancy that they are free to say off-hand whatever they please and to deny off-hand what they have said, almost at the moment of saying it. He said (5) that they had eaten meat in Lent to the scandal of the whole republic of Christ; though (6) this was evidently not permitted by the gospels, they yet ventured to declare that they might do it in accordance with the writings of the Evangelists and Apostles; they had violated (7) the decrees of the Holy Fathers and the councils, and (8) a most ancient custom which (9) we never could have kept so long if it had not emanated from the Holy Spirit. For Gamaliel in the Acts of the Apostles had said : " Let them alone ; for if this work is of God," etc. Then he urged the Senate (10) to remain with and in the Church, for outside of it no one had salvation. For (11) the things which were being taught so wrongheadedly were being taught without grounds. And not having satisfied himself in what he had said before about ceremonials, he fell (12) to speaking of them again, saying that they were the only means by which the humbler Christians were brought to the recognition of salvation, and that it belonged to the duties of the people's priests (for that is the way bishops and preachers are named now-a-days by those counterfeit bishops, to keep their name sacred) to teach the simple-minded populace that there were certain symbols which denoted certain things, and that it was their function to explain and set forth the meaning and value thereof. At length, after the above turn in his speech, he began to discourse (13) upon grounds of offence, not unlearnedly, I confess, only I wish that he had cited as happily the things against himself as those for him. He added that Christ enjoined with as much emphasis as he put upon any precept, that offences be avoided, for he added that most clear mark of indignation, " Woe !" " Woe to the world from offences !" Going back also to Paul, from whose epistles he had quoted many things before he discoursed upon

"Woe," he called to witness (14) that in order not to offend the Jews he had suffered Timothy to be circumcised. And what he ought to have said among his first remarks about seditious teachings, he talked on after everything else, saying (15) that no one ought to trust his own ideas; for that even Paul had been unwilling to depend upon his own notions, and had gone to Jerusalem to compare his gospel with the Apostles, etc. And after a very beautiful peroration to his remarks he rose, and was on the point of going away with his allies, when I addressed them in the following terms:

"My Lord suffragan" (and in this I made an indiscreet and ignorant enough blunder; for they tell me I should have said "most merciful Lord," but being unskilled in polished ways I take hold like a clophopper) "and fellow-ecclesiastics," I said "wait, I pray, until I make explanation in my own behalf." For that my fellow-bishops allowed me to do. To this he said: "It has not been enjoined upon us to engage in discussion with any one." "And I," said I, "have no intention of entering into discussion, but what I have thus far been teaching these excellent citizens I would willingly and gladly set forth to you who are both learned men and delegates sent here, so to speak, with full powers; that the greater faith may be had in my teachings if you shall have voted them right, and if not, that the opposite may take place." "We have said nothing," said he, "in opposition to you, and therefore there is no need for you to make explanation." But I said: "Though you have refrained from mentioning my name, yet all the force and power of your words were aimed and hurled at me. For, as a matter of fact, they were dealing with me in the style of the old gladitorial combats between Mirmillons and Gauls, wherein the Mirmillon cried: "It is not you I am aiming at, Gaul, it is the fish I am aiming at." So my name was kept out of sight and not mentioned, in order that most serious charges, if it please the gods, might be developed against me, whose name is Zwingli. While we were thus contending together,

M. Roest, President of the Senate, tried by entreaty to persuade the men of Constance to listen, to which entreaty the suffragan replied that he knew with whom he should have to deal if he listened. Huldreich Zwingli was too violent and choleric to make any duly and moderately carried on discussion possible with him. I answered: "What wrong have I ever done you? And what kind of a way of doing is this, to worry so harshly and bitterly a guiltless man who has done his duty by Christianity, and to refuse to hear any explanation? I have always felt myself bound to hope, unless I am mistaken (but perhaps I am mistaken), that if any one ever came forward to contradict the truth and teachings of the gospel, it would come to pass that the High Prelate of Constance would rush to its aid before all others and hear the whole case, and this by your help especially, whom he has even now employed as delegates because of your preëminent learning. For what would ye do if I wanted to go to him without your knowledge? If I feared to meet you? If I refused to have your opinion in the matter? Now, when I do nothing of the kind, but ask your presence in order to give an account of my faith and teachings, how have you the face to venture to refuse it? It could not have failed to rouse suspicion if I had allowed you to go away, even though you desired it; now when I appeal of my own accord to your judgment and justice, do you dare to abandon me?" Then said they: "Our Reverend Master did not wish us to enter into a dispute with any one, so it is impossible for us to hear you. If you wish to take any point of doctrine to the bishop you are free to do so; if you need anything apprize him of it." But I said: "I beg of you if you are not willing from any other consideration to vouchsafe me this favour, yet grant me this wish for the sake of our common faith, our common baptism, and for the sake of Christ, the giver of life and salvation, and if you may not listen as delegates, you still may as Christians." When I had thus adjured them the citizens began to murmur in their indignation, so that at last, driven by the urgent request of the president and the unworthiness of their course, they went back to their seats. Thereupon I began to speak in defence of the teachings of Christ to the best of my ability, and made answer to their main heads in about this fashion:

1. My lord suffragan has stated that certain persons were teaching seditious and obnoxious doctrines, but I cannot be persuaded that he means this to be taken of me, who for nearly four years now have been preaching the gospel of Christ and the teachings of the Apostles with so much energy. And yet it savors somewhat of this, inasmuch as he made the statement before the Senate. For what concern were it of mine if such teachings were preached elsewhere, provided they were not preached at Zurich? Therefore, since it is not likely that the suffragan spoke of the affairs of outsiders, it is clear that his remarks were aimed at me. However much they disguise it, it is evident that here is the David to whom this Nathan imputed the wrong. But as to the gospel, it is no wonder that in one place or another there should be differences between those who cling doggedly to ἐντάλωατα, that is, human prescriptions, and those who are unfriendly to the same. For Christ prophesied most clearly that this would come to pass, saying: "I came not to send peace on earth, but a sword. For I am come to set a man at variance against his father, and the daughter against her mother, and the daughter-in-law against her mother-in-law, and it shall come to pass that a man's foes shall be they of his own household." Yet there was no need of this answer either. For Zurich more than any other of the Swiss cantons is in peace and quiet, and this all good citizens put down to the credit of the gospel.

2. As to the reproach, in the next place, that it is taught that no human prescriptions nor ceremonials ought to be kept, I will acknowledge frankly that I desire to see a fair portion of the ceremonials and prescriptions done away with, because the things prescribed are in great part such as also Peter in the Acts says

can not be endured. Nor am I going to listen to those who say that Peter spoke of the old ceremonials and prescriptions. Be it understood, though, that if I should grant them this it is still clear that Peter was of opinion that Christians ought to be free from burdens and bitterness of the kind. But if Peter deprecated that old yoke so greatly, which was yet much lighter than that which we bear to-day, what think ye he would have done if there had been question of a heavier one? Now that the old yoke would have been more endurable to Christians than ours (to say nothing for the nonce of the decrees of the pontiffs, which are much more numerous and onerous than the commands of Moses,) is shown well enough by the excessive observation of fasts, the careful selection of foods, and the enforced leisure of feast days. For how trifling will the fasts of the Jews become which they ordained at times for those in great sorrow, if you compare them with these stated forty days' fasts of ours, institutions fit for serfs, and those that are ordained in a sort of unbroken and continuous row in honour of the saints! Furthermore, if you compare the selection of foods, its observation is more onerous among the Christians than among the Jews. They abstained from certain kinds of food, but not at a fixed period, with the exception of the Passover. We abstain from numerous kinds and for long seasons. And in the enforced leisure of feast days we surpass the Jews very greatly. But if Peter did not want the Christians worried by the lighter yoke much less would he approve the heavier. I denied, however, that I was of opinion that no human prescriptions at all ought to be kept or enacted. For who would not joyfully accept what was decided by the concurrent opinion of all Christians? But on the other hand, the decrees of certain most unholy spirits, who after the manner of the Pharisees would lay unbearable burdens upon the necks of men and not touch themselves even with the tip of their fingers, were an abomination. And as to his having said, with a view to rouse the Senate to anger, that we should fail to obey the laws of the state, I said this was not the spirit of Christ or of the Apostles. For Christ had said: "Render unto Cæsar the things that are Cæsar's," etc., and had paid the tribute or tax. Nay, at his birth his parents reported his name according to the proclamation of Cæsar; while the Apostles taught "Render unto all their due, tribute to whom tribute is due, etc., and obey them who are set in authority over you, and not only the good," etc. Hence it was evident that he had spoken more vigorously than truly, as would be made still clearer by an illustration. For all the peoples of the whole world had obeyed the laws most rigorously, even before the man Christ was born. Nay, Christianity was the most powerful instrument for the preservation of justice in general, and the faith of Christ could not be done away with even if all ceremonials were done away with altogether. Nay, ceremonials achieved nothing else than the cheating of Christ and his faithful followers and doing away with the teachings of the Spirit, calling men away from the unseen to the material things of this world, but this could not be described and explained in short compass.

3. Then I showed that the simple-minded people could be led to the recognition of the truth by other means than ceremonials, to wit, by those by which Christ and the Apostles had led them without any ceremonials as far as I had been able to learn through the sacred writings, and that there was no danger that the people were not capable of receiving the gospel, which he who believes can understand. They can believe, therefore they can also understand. Whatever takes place here is done by the inspiration of God, not by the reasoning of man, as Christ also thanked the Father, saying: "I thank thee, O, Father, etc., because thou hast hid these things from the wise and prudent, and hast revealed them unto babes. Even so, Father, for so it seemed good in thy sight." And Paul (1 Cor. 1) says that "God hath chosen the foolish things of the world to confound the wise."

4. I had nowhere taught that Lent ought not to be kept, though I could wish that it were not prescribed so imperiously, but were

left free to the individual. But he for whom Lent was not enough might fast for the rest of the year also; there would not be wanting men to advise fasting, and I presaged that they would be likely to effect more than those who thought that at the frown of their power and the threat of excommunication, everything would fall to pieces with a crash as at the frown of Jove.

5. Certain persons, and they by no means bad ones, had ventured to eat flesh, and they were not tainted, but since they had not been forbidden by the divine law to eat flesh, they seemed rather to have eaten it in witness of their faith than to any one's reproach. And this was clear from the fact that presently when told by me that they ought to take into account the possible cause of offence they stopped, so that there was no need of this fine delegation, inasmuch as the evil died out of itself, granting that it was an evil. Still I wondered exceedingly that I had been a minister of the gospel in the diocese of Constance for fifteen years and had thus far never known of the men of Constance having sent anywhere so magnificent a delegation to investigate how the affairs of the gospel were going on, but now when they had found a very trifling observance not broken as much as they seemed to wish, they filled everything with their lamentations, and accused the people of Zurich of being the only ones who had the effrontery to meditate withdrawing from the Christian communion. Yet when the suffragan denied that expression, as I have said, and Brendlin supported his denial, though the whole Senate cried out in rebuttal, I allowed their denial in somewhat these terms: Since you deny the expression, show that it escaped you unawares and I will easily pardon it; as far as I am concerned you shall be free to correct any utterances you please. But the Republic of Christ has suffered no offence and no disgrace if some few persons have failed to keep human tradition.

6. And I showed that it was an unsound contention that the gospel writings nowhere clearly allowed the eating of flesh. For Mark (ch. 7) speaks in this fashion: " There is nothing from

without a man that entering into him can defile him." Here I showed by the argument from the preceding (in the way they manipulated the sacred writings) that the argument of the following held good in this way: Therefore, whatever is outside of a man cannot by entering into him defile him. Words are signs to me. A general negative is no sign. If he had said "no food," he would have left out the category of drinks; if he had said "no drink," he would have left out that of food. Therefore, it pleased him who is the Truth to say "nothing." Then he added "cannot even defile." Hear! The Voice of Truth declares it cannot; man, who is a liar, for all men are liars, says it can. Here the man squirms and says these words are not so clear, and must be interpreted in this way, but the preceding words must be regarded and the words that follow, though this is what follows: "Do ye not perceive that whatsoever thing from without entereth into the man it cannot defile him, because it entereth not into his heart, but into the belly, and goeth out into the draught, purging all meats?" What can be said more clearly, if you please, even though you regard the preceding and the following?

7. They added the words "contrary to the decrees of the Holy Fathers and the councils." I answered that Engelhard, the ornament of our city, had carefully weighed with me those in which our friends placed greatest confidence, and that no such asseveration could be made from those which they treated as a sacred anchor. For the question was not whether Lent ought to be done away with, but whether it was permissible by the law of Christ to eat meat at that time. While I forbid no man's fasting, I leave it free to him.

8. They had also added: "and contrary to very ancient custom." Here I frankly granted that it was the custom, and not a bad one. But if it were the custom, why was a proclamation added? I promised that I would certainly see to it that the custom should not be wantonly interrupted.

9. And if this custom (he continued) had not been inspired by the divine spirit it would not have lasted so long, in accordance with the words of Gamaliel. I answered that this and other things which were not from the mind of God would be done away in their own good time. For "every plant," says Christ in Matthew, "which my heavenly Father hath not planted shall be rooted up." But selection of foods neither Christ nor the Apostles had prescribed. Therefore no one ought to be surprised if unhappy mortals are turning their eyes towards freedom, since Christ in his loving kindness has now illumined the world more brightly with his gospel by a sort of second revelation.

10. After this the weighty speaker made his turn to the Senate, appealing to them to stay with and in the Church, for outside of it none were saved. This I met thus: " Let not this exhortation move you, most excellent citizens, as if you had ever abandoned the Church of Christ. For I am persuaded of you that you hold in fresh remembrance what is said in the narrative of Matthew, that the foundation of the Church is that rock which gave his name to Peter the faithful confessor. No one lays other foundation than this, nor can do so. Nay, in every nation and place, every one who confesses the Lord Jesus with his tongue and believes in his heart that God raised him from the dead shall be saved, whether he be among the Indians or the Scythians, and it is fixed beyond controversy that outside of that Church none is saved, within which we all believe ourselves to be the more firmly as we glory the more certainly in the hope of the glory of the sons of God." Here I might have dragged the man forth and laid bare his notion of the Church, but I preferred to spare him, that he might repent at length of having said before the whole Senate that I was too rough spoken to make it possible to discuss with me. When he had thus made his exhortation I began to look to the end of his remarks, but things turned out differently from what I hoped. For he turned back to this other point and said:

11. That rubbish (for thus, if I mistake not, that crowd call the gospel teaching) was taught without foundation in Scripture. Here again I fled to the protection of the words of Mark vii., as a sort of Achilles' shield, and shot forth these shafts: Do you want clearer proofs presented to you? Is not Christ worthy of belief? Or Mark? I have gathered many passages together, but I abstain from giving the rest now in order not to nauseate the Fathers. Here my lord Englehard opportunely drew a New Testament from his pocket and bade me interpret the passage of Paul's Epistle to Timothy i. 4. I took the book and translated the passage into German, and it is wonderful how they all breathed a sigh of relief, recognizing the passage, most of them, from the exposition of that epistle that I had made the year before. So much difference does it make at what point things are said.

12. Immediately leaving these points, he brought the ceremonials out into battle line again, wounded however, and I attempted to rout them completely again thus: His point that it was the duty of the people's priests to set forth the meaning of the ceremonials I upset in this way. The gospel of Christ had been committed to me to preach assiduously; what the ceremonials indicated those would set forth who lived by them. I admit that I purposely, though quietly, meant to touch the man's sore point in this. For what else do those suburban bishops do but stuff their purses with illusions of consecrating things? But if any master of ceremonials ventured to preach other than the truth to the sheep entrusted to me, I declared I would not stand it.

13. Now what he had said about offences I should have approved in general, if all his words had not seemed to point toward keeping those who were weak always weak, though it is the duty of the stronger, as those fellows wish and ought to be regarded, προσλαμβάνεσθαι, that is, to take up and comfort and help the weak, that they may also be made strong. Yet this one thing I added: Since he had spoken much of the anxious care of

the High Prelate of Constance to avoid or guard against offence to the Church, had he no exhortation to his priests at last after Christ's fashion, bidding them to put their own immunity behind them and bear the general burdens with the rest of the Christian brethren, and to pay tax and tribute? For Christ, in order not to give ground of offence to those who exacted the tribute money, paid it and performed a miracle besides, but it could not be denied that all the people in every nation were complaining because the priests and monks and nuns were supported in idleness, contributing neither labour nor money for the uses of the State. They complained bitterly after they had left the Senate that this had been brought in outside the subject, as they say, but it seems to me that nothing could have been said more appropriately at this point, when they were talking of the High Prelate of Constance being so anxious about grounds of offence.

14. In the next place, though I was aware that Paul had suffered Timothy to be circumcised, yet I maintained that he could not be persuaded by any means to allow Titus to be circumcised, and I tried to give the reason for both acts, namely, that with Timothy, while Christianity was still in the green blade, he had suffered the Macedonians to be circumcised that no breach of the peace might arise, but after the new doctrine had grown somewhat more vigorous, and Paul had learned by his perception of this that Titus could be saved without any disturbance, he saved him. Here I put forth all my strength to persuade the Senators to abide by the ancient custom until either the bonds of that yoke were loosened for us or the world itself consented together more clearly for the taking up again of freedom.

15. Finally I said that those could rightfully be said to rely on their own notions and ideas who struggled against the accepted Scriptures and put human traditions before the teachings of heaven, not those who protected themselves by no other weapons or defences than the sacred writings, for the former trusted in flesh and blood, the latter in the truth of heaven alone, not one

jot of which could ever pass away. Though I was aware that Paul had compared his gospel with the Apostles finally, I also knew that he did not do it for fourteen years. And though I perceived what they were after with that illustration, their side was weakened rather than propped up by it. For I had insisted a little while before so obstinately that they should be present at my explanation for no other reason than that they might see clearly how I handled the sacred writings; nay, that I was ready to give an account of the faith that was in me before the dwellers in heaven, or on earth, or in hell. And finally, having begged the Senate to take in good part all that I had said, I stopped speaking, except that when the suffragan began to snap out something more and to drive it in vigorously, that it had been decreed by the Holy Fathers and the councils that meat should not be eaten in Lent, I also began to contend more recklessly and to deny that it had been decreed by any councils, at least by any general ones. At last when he had finished his appendix we adjourned the Senate.

These, dear Brother Erasmus, are the wounds I received and inflicted in the assembly of the Ecclesiastics and Senators; these the means with which I ran to the aid of the feeble. It has all been written down off hand as it was spoken, for the suffragan had brought a prepared speech with him, but I was forced to fight and defend myself as I stood. If I have said anything more briefly or more fully than it occurred, I think this should be attributed to human weakness, which hardly recognizes how little power it has in remembering. Yet the main drift of the proceedings in general I have touched upon, whether in the Senate or in the body of Ecclesiastics or in private discussion. For the evening after the morning they had spoken before the body of Ecclesiastics, I stumbled upon them by accident and talked much with them. Thus I learned just where their sore point was.

Good by, and if you write to my friend Oechsli, greet him for me.

II. PETITION OF CERTAIN PREACHERS OF SWITZERLAND TO THE MOST REVEREND LORD HUGO, BISHOP OF CONSTANCE, THAT HE WILL NOT SUFFER HIMSELF TO BE PERSUADED TO MAKE ANY PROCLAMATION TO THE INJURY OF THE GOSPEL, NOR ENDURE LONGER THE SCANDAL OF HARLOTRY, BUT ALLOW THE PRESBYTERS TO MARRY WIVES OR AT LEAST WOULD WINK AT THEIR MARRIAGES.*

To the Most Reverend Father and Lord in Christ, Hugo of Hohenlandenberg, Bishop of Constance, the undersigned offer obedient greeting.

Your Excellency will perhaps wonder, Most Reverend Father, what this unusual action of writing a letter to yourself means, and not without reason. For nature has ordained that the unexpected should create not only wonder, but at times even a feeling of dumfoundedness. Yet we would have you to be entirely free and undisturbed in regard to this matter which we are laying before you. For we do not come to your Excellency in regard to anything very troublesome, but to find help. For we are so sure that you are both a most pious lord and a most loving father that there is nothing we do not promise ourselves

* Zwingli's *Works*, iii. 17–25. Translated by Mr. Henry Preble from the original Latin.

This paper explains itself. The revelation it makes is curious. The signers had doubtless desire to preach the gospel as they understood it; but they had a much greater desire to be legally married. They must have known that their bishop had no authority to grant their requests. It should be remarked that when Zwingli and his 10 associates drew up the paper here given they were priests in good and regular standing, and had no idea of leaving the church. Their statements are to be believed. This frank, not to say naive, petition stands against all denials of the unchastity of most of the Swiss clergy. Simultaneously with its issuance Zwingli issued another, written in German (see his *Works*, i. 30–51), addressed to the government of the Confederacy, which also was a plea for the free course of the gospel, but particularly that if the bishop should allow the priests to marry the government would allow it and protect the married priests.

from you. And this the fact itself shows, for we should never have ventured to write to your Fatherhood unless we had had thorough confidence in it. We desire, therefore, humbly to beg you to listen kindly to what we are going to disclose a little later, to hear it graciously, and to take it in good part. This is demanded both by the matter itself which drives us to this appeal and by the office which you fill as a loving father. The matter itself, to come to it at last, is this: Your Most Reverend Fatherhood knows how for a long time the heavenly teachings which God, the Creator of all things, willed to have made plain unto the poor race of men by one no way inferior to himself, by his Son, in all things his equal, have, not without the utmost loss to the cause of salvation, been lying hidden through the ignorance, not to say evil intentions, of certain persons, and how rudely, when he had determined to recall and renew those teachings in our day by a sort of second revelation, certain persons attack or defend them. For all the efforts of these defenders are aimed at putting an end to the whole conflict by the first onset, and if they fail in this they collapse utterly, but the attacking party are so shamelessly persistent in their contention that though thrown upon their backs by the boss of the shield of Holy Writ and pierced by the sword of the Spirit, which is the word of God, they will not yield, but would rather contend against Christ than abandon their pretensions, until they be compelled to abandon both Christ and their own pretensions, after the fashion of the Jews of old, who having fought against the living Christ till they had slain him, pursued him even when dead, till they all likewise perished themselves. And though we do not by any means willingly predict this same ill-omened end for the present misguided lot, we cannot help fearing that it may come to pass sometime, and for that we are not without reasons. For as in the old days the Jews cast out in vain from the synagogue those who believed in Christ (for the faith grew more and more each day), so in these days of ours, if any continue to frighten away or even to destroy the real heralds of Christ, they will meet with the same result. Therefore must the words of Gamaliel be pounded into them often, that they may keep their hands off of those who bring us the commands of heaven. For if it be of God it cannot be destroyed, for it were folly for any to try to fight against God; but if it be of men it will perish of itself. Meanwhile most watchful care should be taken lest, as those poor wretches perished miserably in their doomed city, some disaster overwhelm us unawares. For the word of God has never been disregarded with safety. Therefore, Most Reverend Father, we beseech you by our Lord Jesus Christ, not to join those who aim at putting under a bushel, nay, at extinguishing, the light that came into the world to illumine all men, and who call evil good and good evil, turning sweet into bitter and light into darkness, but rather to join those who have this one desire, that the whole concourse of Christians return to their head, which is Christ, and form one body in him, and, having received the spirit of God, recognize the blessings bestowed upon them by God. And this we see is by no means the case with those who promise themselves some sort of peace, if human prescriptions be set before Christ even. In God we ought to be made one, for he himself is one. In man, who is constantly divided against himself, how is it possible that we be made one? Christ prayed to the Father to make us one in him, and shall man dare to promise us unity in him? In one God, in one faith, in one baptism we shall certainly be made one, for these are one. In some one man, when there are so many laws contradicting each other and such divergent opinions, so far are we from being made one that in no surer way can we be led astray into error and disagreement than in this. Nay, we see one and the same man often at variance with himself in these points. Those things that we set forth a little while ago and all other things that urge us to unity, whence can they be more clearly and purely got than from their very fountain head? He that draweth from that shall abound in the water that springs forth into everlasting life. But the well is deep, and we have nothing to draw with, unless he who is eager to be drawn brings us rope and bucket and windlass, and after the manner of Moses graciously opens a well for our feeble souls, at which the thirsty sheep may drink and be led back to the heavenly pastures, which surely are found in no other corner of the universe than in the Gospel. For what other fountain head is there than Christ himself, who invites us to himself freely, saying: "If any one thirsteth, let him come to me and drink." For he desires that we all receive of his abundance, we who are in need of all things. For we have neither silver nor gold wherewith to satisfy him, but he urges us to hasten to him with joyfulness, to drink freely. Who has ever shown himself so liberal an inn-keeper among men as to suffer his wine to be poured out and distributed without charge save Christ alone, who bestows his blessings free so plentifully? And if we shall not seize the favour that offers itself to us thus freely, what hope awaits us? What excuse, pray, shall we make? Of what tortures shall we not judge ourselves worthy if we repel from us him who desires to become so near a friend? We are aware that our life differs all too widely from the pattern of the Gospel, but is the Gospel on that account to be abolished and done away with? Ought we not rather to devote ourselves vigorously to correcting our faults according to its standard and to subduing our feebleness, since it is the one thing, could we only believe it, from the inspiration of which salvation will come to us, according to the command of Christ when he sent forth his Apostles to preach the Gospel with these words: "Preach the Gospel (not your own theories or decrees or the regulations which some chance shall happen to dictate) to every creature." And he added: "Whosoever believeth" (when the Gospel has been preached, of course), "and is baptized, shall be saved," and on the other hand, "Whosoever believeth not, shall be damned." Since therefore, as we have said, God, as of old he used to warn Israel time and again by the mouth of his prophets, now deigns in our day to illumine us with his Gospel, in order to renew his covenant which cannot be annulled, we have thought that this opportunity ought by no means to be neglected, nay, that we ought to strive with unremitting effort that as many as possible may share in the glory of this salvation. And inasmuch as meanwhile a report reaches us that by the wickedness of certain persons your heart has been so hardened that you mean shortly to put forth a proclamation warning us to turn aside from the Gospel if in any part it shall prove at variance with human tradition, though the report hardly deserves credence among us, yet we are moved somewhat, not indeed to hesitate in slothful fear, but to pity your lot, if things are as they are commonly reported, that this pestiferous class of men, who confound all things to serve their own purposes, has been able to extend their influence even to yourself. But heaven forbid! For we place such high hope in you that we doubt not we shall do a thing acceptable to you if we shall show the utmost faithfulness in the interests of the Gospel. For we cannot in any way be persuaded that you desire to see the duty that belongs peculiarly to your office neglected and abandoned. For Christ sent you not to baptize nor to anoint, but to preach the gospel. May heaven bless our undertaking! We have determined to spread abroad the knowledge of the Gospel with uninterrupted effort, and to do it so seasonably that none shall have a right to complain that we have done him any injury. But if we shall not attain a prosperous issue in this according to the judgment of men, there is no cause to wonder. For it is a rock of offence and a stumbling-block and a sign that is proving false. For he came unto his own, and his own received him not. For these reasons it is becoming that your Fatherhood should look with favour upon our vigorous efforts, which though perhaps uncommon are by no means unconsidered, and that you should not only permit but help and advance this business, which is Christ's, not ours. That will be above all things honourable and worthy of a bishop. Nay it will belong to you, not to take upon your shoulders some part merely of the work undertaken, but, like Moses, to lead the way and to beat back or destroy the obstacles, so far at least as you can; and you can by encouraging and urging men to this task, or, if that is too much, by approving and favouring it, and removing grounds of offence.

For among the things that threaten most to harm the budding teachings of Christ are grounds of offence. For how, by the everlasting God, will the simple-minded commons believe in him who even whiile he preaches the Gospel is thought by them to be licentious and a shameless dog? Can any thing happen more disastrous to our sacred calling? We beg you, therefore, to show yourself as indulgent towards the second part of our petition as we believe you to be. We think that your most Reverend Fatherhood is not unaware how unsuccessfully and scantily the prescriptions in regard to chastity that have come down to our times from our predecessors have been kept by the general run of priests, and oh, that they could have vouchsafed us strength to keep their commands as easily as they gave them! Yet God willed not that this be granted to man, that this gift of gods and angels might not be put down to the credit of man, but of God only. For this is plainly shown by the words of Christ (Matthew xix. 10–12) when, after much discussion had taken place between himself and the Pharisees with regard to marriage, and his disciples said that, if the case were such as the discussion showed, it were better not to marry, he answered that not all men were capable of chastity, but only those to whom it had been given, wishing to show that it was a gift of God, that was given to some men in such wise that they might recognize that the divine goodness and not their own strength was of avail in this thing. And this is evidently indicated by what follows a little later, when, having made particular mention of eunuchs, he leaves it free to every man to keep or not to keep the law of chastity, saying, "He that is able to receive it, let him receive it." He meant, no doubt, that they to whom it was granted from above were bound to keep the law. For otherwise none could hold out under it. We, then, having tried with little enough success alas! to obey the law (for the disease must be boldly disclosed to the physician), have discovered that the gift has been denied unto us, and we have meditated long within ourselves how we might remedy our ill-starred attempts at chastity. And turning the matter over on all sides, we found nothing encouraging or propitious until we began to chew the cuds, it were, like the cattle, over those words of Christ just quoted. For then a sort of loathing of ourselves began to creep over us from the odour of it until we began to be disgusted that through careless thinking we had made a law unto ourselves of that which Christ had left free, as if the maintenance of chastity depended upon our own strength. Then presently a blush of shame overspread our faces, just as Adam, when he was going to be like the gods, found first nothing but his own nakedness, then an angry God, and shortly after a whole cart-load of ills. For who would not repent when he had looked upon the pitiable result of his own carelessness? For what else is it, by the everlasting God, than absolute folly, nay even shamelessness, to arrogate to one's self what belongs to God alone? To think one's self able to do that than which there is nothing one is less able to do? But after that loathing of ourselves, through which we recognized at once our rashness and our weakness, the hope of a remedy began to show itself, though from afar. For weighing more carefully Christ's words and the custom of our predecessors in this matter, we found that the whole question was far easier than we had thought. For when he says, " All men cannot receive this saying," and again, " He that is able to receive it, let him receive it," he prescribes no punishment for them that cannot receive it. Nay, either because of the vastness of the thing which he did not wish enjoined upon each and all, or on account of our weaknes, which he knows better than we ourselves, he did not want this thing laid up against us, and so left it free. Therefore our souls which had been nigh unto despair were mightily refreshed when we learned those who were unable to receive the saying were threatened with no punishment by him who can send both body and soul into hell. But the fathers seemed to have cast an anxions eye in this direction too, when they showed themselves unwilling to enjoin chastity upon all without exception or to require a vow of chastity from others— the priests, at least, and even shielded human weakness with clever words, as was proper, in this way:—When the sponsor who was accustomed to make answer for all who were to be confirmed was asked, "Are they righteous, these whom you present?" he was wont to answer: "They are righteous." "Are they well trained?" "They are well trained," etc. When, however, they came to chastity—"Are they chaste?" he answered, "As far as human frailty allows." Thus it appears that neither our predecessors nor the fathers in our own day wanted that bound hard and fast which Christ had suffered to be free, lest they might smear the sweet yoke of the Lord with bitter wormwood. Having, I say, thus balanced these considerations, to wit, that we are held to the maintenance of chastity by neither divine nor human law, we considered nevertheless that though chastity go free, yet animal passion ought not to roam promiscuously, but to be bounded by rule and constancy, and forced into reasonable limits, like the rest of the course of our life, which though free becomes wildness and confusion, unless it be restrained by moderation, that we sink not to the level of swine. And this we see the Maker of all things willed from the beginning of creation, when he fashioned for Adam from his rib one woman only as a helpmeet and not a group or crowd of women, and joined her presently by so firm a bond that a man leaves father and mother sooner than his wife, for the two unite to form one flesh. Furthermore, if we run through the whole of the New Testament we find nowhere anything that favours free concubinage, but everything in approval of marriage. Therefore it appears to us most true and most right that for a Christian no third possibility besides chastity or marriage is left, and that he should live chastely if that is given unto him from above, or marry a wife if he be on fire with passion, and this we shall show more clearly in a little while from the truly sacred writings. Hence we beseech your mercy, wisdom and learning, illustrious Leader, to show yourself the first to lay hold upon the glory of taking the lead over all the bishops of Germany in right thinking upon Christianity, since you see Christ bestowing especial favour upon this age of ours and revealing himself more clearly than for several ages since, while from the whole great body of bishops scarcely one or two thus far have shown themselves fairly on the side of the revivified Christianity, and while others continue to thrust ill-feigned chastity upon the unfortunate general body of our fellow bishops, do you suffer those who are consumed with passion to marry wives, since this, as has been shown, will be lawful according to Christ and according to the laws of men. From the whole vast crowd we are the first to venture to come forward, relying upon your gentleness, and to implore that you grant us this thing, not, as we think, without due consideration. For when on one side we were being crushed by human ordinances, struggling in vain against the weakness of the flesh (for the law stimulates to sin rather than restrains it), and on the other, Scripture was smiling upon us with approval, we thought it no wrong to bring forward the passages on which we rely, that it might be evident to you whether we treated them intelligently or not, and when it appeared, as we hoped, that we had employed the Scriptures righteously, that you would grant what we ask for in all humility.

The first passage of all that makes us free and that we trust to as to a sacred anchor is Matthew xix. For we reason thus from it: If Christ willed that chastity be free to us, good-by to the man who tries to make a law of it. The demonstration of the second is: If at the voice of God Peter feared to call that common which God had purified, we may boldly declare that it is not right for any man to declare that that is not lawful which God has suffered to be lawful. For if in that which is of little account God was unwilling to accept the judgment of Peter, how much less in a matter of much greater moment will he accept the judgment of one inferior to Peter? Our feeling on this point is clear enough from what has gone before, when we add that the words of Christ on the subject we are speaking of are the words of him who is the way and the truth and the life. For he says in another place, " The words which I have spoken are spirit and life." How then were it not lawful and safe to trust to them? Nay, we shall believe accursed rather than merely wicked anything that shall have been sought out to contradict the words of God. They are spirit and life, the things that he has said. Therefore what we say is flesh and death. The second passage is Paul to the Corinthians I., ch. vii. 1 and 2 : " It is good for a man not to touch a woman. Nevertheless, to avoid fornication, let every man have his own wife, and let every woman have her own husband." Here first we concluded that he would be blest to whom it had been given of God to be able to do without a wife. And while we willingly yield this glory to those who live chastely, we are grieved that it has been denied unto us, though we bear it patiently with God's help. Next as to the point that to avoid fornication, every man should have his own wife. He who said " every man " made exceptions of none, neither priest nor monk nor layman. Hence it is clear, as we hinted above, that for a Christian there is nothing between chastity and marriage. He must either live chastely or marry a wife. The third passage is in the same chapter, verse 9 : " If they cannot contain, let them marry : for it is better to marry than to burn." Therefore if one cannot contain one's self, if one burns, let him marry. We have been so on fire from passion —with shame be it said !—that we have done many things unseemly, yet whether this should not be laid upon those to some extent who have forbidden marriage we refrain from saying now, thinking it enough that the fire of passion alone (and that so frequent and violent as to threaten the mind) is pronounced sufficient reason for marriage. The fourth passage is verse 25 in the same chapter: " Now concerning virgins I have no commandment of the Lord: yet I give my judgment," etc. Paul, the teacher of the nations, the chosen instrument of God, with whom Christ had spoken intimately from heaven more than once, says that he has no commandment of the Lord in regard to virginity, and has an unpurified man such commandment? Then too Paul had said much of the value of virginity and its advantages, and much of the trials and unhappiness of marriage, and he added, verse 35, " And this I speak for your own profit; not that I may cast a snare upon you," wishing, though he had greatly praised the state of virginity, not to seem of opinion that it ought to be commanded. The fifth passage is 1 Timothy iii. 1, foll. : " This is a true saying, If a man desire the office of a bishop, he desireth a good work. A bishop then must be blameless, the husband of one wife," etc. And a little later he adds " having his children in subjection with all gravity." Here we noted that though it is a thing of high repute to be a bishop, yet he bids a bishop have a wife, whether one only or one at a time we will not now discuss. We noted also that the name bishop is the name of an office, not one of arrogant pride, and therefore we had no fear to call ourselves also bishops, that is, watchers, because the other terms which are in common use to-day either seem over-ambitious or are foreign words. With the name of watcher, however, how can any one be puffed up? Can he think it a state of high dignity and not a position of duty when the only function of a watcher is to watch? The sixth passage is from the same Paul to Titus 1, 5 and 6 : " For this cause left I thee in Crete, that thou shouldest set in order the things that are wanting, and ordain elders in every city; if any be blameless, the husband of one wife, having faithful children," etc.

And this passage is as like unto the passage above as one pea is like another. The seventh is likewise from 1 Timothy, ch. iv 1–3: " Now the Spirit speaketh expressly, that in the latter times some shall depart from the faith, giving heed to seducing spirits and doctrines of devils, speaking lies in hypocrisy, having their conscience seared with a hot iron, forbidding to marry," etc. Here we would have those prick up their ears who make a fine show of chastity and keep it ill; for what they do secretly is wicked even to think of. The Spirit speaking in Paul says that in the latter days, in which we are no doubt also included, it shall come to pass that some will turn away from the faith unto their own works which are not of God. Also that this shall happen at the instigation of evil spirits who shall speak things good in appearance only, and shall commend them especially by the mouths of those who go about in sheep's clothing raging like wolves, and therefore they have ever been singed in their own eyes and condemned by their own judgment. And they shall forbid marriage. Behold, Most Reverend Father, the origin of their feigned chastity! The eighth passage is ch. xiii. 4 to the Hebrews: " Marriage is honourable in all, and the bed undefiled; but whoremongers and adulterers God will judge." This passage seems so clearly to confirm our contention that we think it the duty of bishops (granted that they be watchers) to drive into marriage those whom they have detected in fornication. For fornication must be met, because besides exposing one to judgment it also offends one's neighbor.

Influenced then by these passages we are at length persuaded that it is far more desirable if we marry wives, that Christ's little ones may not be offended, than if with bold brow we continue rioting in fornication. To this your Highness will no doubt agree when you reflect that the sin of him who offends one of the little ones of Christ can scarcely be atoned for, even though a millstone be hung about his neck and he be cast into the depths of the sea. And what, pray, is a stumbling block of offence, if the shameless fornication of priests is not a stumbling block of offence? And let your Highness not deign to listen to those who snap out like this: "Behold, Most Reverend Fathers, the religion of these men! What else are they after than turning the freedom of Christ into the lust of the flesh, according to the judgmenr of Paul to the Galatians 5 and of Peter 1, ch. ii?" For to make no mention now of how the cohabitation of marriage is regarded by God, although we do not deny that the act proceeds distinctly from the flesh, yet we know that it is far from harmful, since Paul says (1 Corinthians vii. 28): "And if a virgin marry she hath not sinned," because God no doubt looks without anger upon this thing on account of our weakness, or rather the sin dwelling in us. And the same Paul (Galatians v. 19) reckons it not among the works of the flesh. Yet this answer is not necessary, since it is clearly evident that if we had wished to indulge in this thing for pleasure's sake, we should never have allowed ourselves to be tied up with the halter of wives when thus, besides suffering countless arrogances, we are cut off from the opportunity of making good the unpleasantness and other drawbacks of a long married life. But since most of us fill the office of bishops, in which above all things there should be no room for grounds of offence (for a bishop ought to be blameless, as has been made clear above), we have all tried to see how we could cease from the offence, while in other respects (if we may speak freely without boasting) we are not of such untutored morals as to be in ill repute among the flock entrusted to us for any other failing save this one alone. For the sake of Christ the Lord of all of us, therefore, by the liberty won by his blood, by the fatherly affection which you owe to us, by your pity of our feeble souls, by the wounds of our consciences, by all that is divine and all that is human, we beseech you mercifully to regard our petition and to grant that which was thoughtlessly built up be thoughtfully torn down, lest the pile constructed not in accordance with the will of our Heavenly Father fall some time with a far more destructive crash. You see what the world threatens.

Therefore your Fatherhood ought to regard it as wise foresight and not unreasonableness that we come to petition you. For unless wise aid be applied in many places it will be all up with the whole body of ecclesiastics. And please do not refer us to the decrees of the predecessors of your Fatherhood. For you see how they fail to meet the case, and delay in the hope that though we have been first beaten with rods we can then presently endure the sting of scorpions. Our weakness must be indulged, nay, something must be ventured in this matter. O happy the invincible race of Hohenlandenberg, if you shall be the first of all the bishops in Germany to apply healing to our wounds and restore us to health! For what historian will ever pass over the achievement unmentioned? What scholar will not trumpet it abroad? What poet will not sing it to coming generations? What embalming will not protect it from decay and destruction? The door of well doing is surely open before you. You have only to take care lest you do not hold your hands firmly clasped, and so let the offered opportunity slip through them. For we presage that things are going to put on a new face whether we will or no, and when this happens we shall lament in vain having neglected the opportunity of winning glory. We have on the side of our request that Creator who made the first human beings male and female; we have the practice of the Old Testament, which is much more strict than the New, under which, however, even the highest priests took upon their necks the gentle yoke of matrimony; we have Christ, who makes chastity free, nay, bids us marry, that his little children may not be offended, and our petition meets with loud approval on all sides. Nay, even Paul, speaking with the spirit of God, enjoins marriage. All the company of the pious and judicious are with us. If you disregard all this we know not how you can embrace your race with affection, for you will surpass their brave deeds, and win more than their laurels and statues, if you only grant us this favour. If, however, you cannot possibly be persuaded to grant it, we beseech you at least not to forbid it, according to the suggestion of another than ourselves. For we think you are brave enough to do right without fear of those who can even slay the body. And in fact you will have to refrain at least from interfering. For there is a report that most of the ecclesiastics have already chosen wives, not only among our Swiss, but among all peoples everywhere, and to put this down will certainly be not only beyond your strength but beyond that of one far more mighty, if you will pardon our saying so. Accordingly, scorn us not as of little account; even a rustic often speaks very much to the point. And though we be but little children, we are yet Christ's, and far from scorning us, you may confidently trust that salvation will be yours if you receive us. As to ourselves, we shall never cease to sing your praises if you but show yourself a father to us, and shall render you willing and glad obedience. Grant a gift to your children, who are so obedient that they come to you before all things, and so trusting that in this matter, however difficult it is thought to be, they have ventured to appeal to you only. The Most High God long preserve your Excellency in prosperity and in the knowledge of God! We pray with all humility that you will take all we have said in a spirit of justice and kindness.

Einsiedeln, Switzerland, July 2d, 1522.

Your Most Reverend Fatherhood's most obedient servants,

> BALTHASER FRACHSEL,
> GEORGE STAHL,
> VERNER STEINER,
> LEO JUD,
> ERASMUS FABRICIUS,
> SIMON STUMPF,
> JODOC KILCHMEYER,
> HULDREICH MÜLLER,
> CASPAR MEGANDER,
> JOHN FABER,
> HULDREICH ZWINGLI.

III. ACTS OF THE CONVENTION HELD IN THE PRAISE-WORTHY CITY OF ZURICH ON THE 29TH DAY OF JANUARY, ON ACCOUNT OF THE HOLY GOSPEL—BEING A DISPUTATION BETWEEN THE DIGNIFIED AND HONORABLE REPRESENTATIVE FROM CONSTANCE AND HULDRYCH ZWINGLI, PREACHER OF THE GOSPEL OF CHRIST, TOGETHER WITH THE COMMON CLERGY OF THE WHOLE TERRITORY OF THE AFORESAID CITY OF ZURICH, HELD BEFORE THE ASSEMBLED COUNCIL IN THE YEAR 1523.*

* *Works*, i. 114-168. Translated from the Zurich German by Lawrence A. McLouth, Professor of German, New York University. The matter between brackets is that given in the *Works*, i. 158 sqq., as addenda, but here inserted in proper place.

The Protestant Reformation in German Switzerland, as for the most part in Germany and England, was largely dependent upon the good will of princes and other rulers, who joined it for political ends. No one can gainsay the great advantage of their support. So in Zurich Zwingli endeavored to win over to his side the members of the City Council, rightly arguing that if successful he would be able to preach the Reformation through the canton, no matter what might be the opposition. He made his appeal to the magistracy to be allowed to hold a public debate, at which they should sit as judges, and give the victory to that side which presented the stronger arguments. He looked forward with great confidence to such a public debate, for which he had prepared the way by his preaching and writing and talking ever since he came to Zurich in December, 1518. The City Council took up the idea, and were perhaps flattered by the position they would take in this debate. They issued the invitations to the people of the canton and city of Zurich and to the bishops of Constance and of the adjoining dioceses. Zwingli prepared and had printed 67 Articles as a programme for the debate, and looked forward with great eagerness to the time set, which was the 23d of January, 1523.

On that eventful day six hundred persons—priests and laymen of the canton of Zurich, along with a few delegates from the bishop of Constance and some others—met in the Town Hall and held the debate, which is preserved to us by Erhart Hegenwald, a schoolmaster in Zurich, who informs us that he wrote it from memory immediately after hearing it. His account was edited by Zwingli and published in Zurich. John Faber (or Fabri), Vicar General of the diocese of Constance, one of the ablest disputants on the Roman Church,

THE FIRST ZURICH DISPUTATION. 41

To the worthy ecclesiastical Lord and Father Sir John Jacob Russinger,* Abbot at Pfäbers, to His gracious Lord Chamberlain Master Erhart Hegenwald † offers his willing service and wishes peace in Christ.

Worthy ecclesiastical Lord and Father: I understand how your dignity and grace is inclined to read and further the Gospel doctrine and truth of God from Christian feeling, which fact I conclude among other things from the following: That Your

side, bore the brunt of the attacks upon that church. Zwingli was the principal speaker on the other side. Fabri also published his account of the debate. "Ein warlich underrichtung wie es zie Zürich bey de Zwinglin uff den einen und zwentzigsten tag des monats Januarii rest verschine ergangen sey." (Leipzig? 1523.) In it, naturally, he appeared to greater advantage than in Zwingli's account, but it seems to have given offence to an enthusiastic portion of the audience, and some of these young men thought they had a good opportunity to bring out a satire in the interests of the new faith, and so they concocted a book which was called "The Vulture Plucked." "Das gyren rupffen. Nalt inn wie Johann Schmidt Vicarge ze Costentz mit dem büchle darinn er verheiszt ein ware bericht wie es uff den 29 tag Jenner M.D.xxiij. ze Zürich gangen sye sich übersehe hat. Ist voll schimpff unud ernestes." This was a gross attack upon Fabri, and he was very indignant and appealed to the city authorities of Zurich to bring the offenders to book, but the city authorities regarded the whole affair as a kind of joke and took no action in the matter. The three accounts of this important debate supplemented one another; the one which may be said to be authentic is here translated, the second is somewhat colored in favor of the Roman Church, and the third, which contains a good deal of truth, along with more or less deliberate falsehood, have been properly drawn upon by the editors of Zwingli's works, and the corrections and additions they have made from the last two accounts are here incorporated.

The result of the debate was the enthusiastic approval of Zwingli's teachings, and an order from the authorities not only to continue their presentation, but enjoining such teaching upon all the priests of the canton. Thus this debate, which is known as the First Disputation, is of great historical interest as marking the official beginning of the Reformation in German Switzerland.

* He was one of Zwingli's friends and correspondents, and active in the cause of the Reformation, but returned to the Roman Church after Zwingli's death.

† He was a school teacher in Zurich.

Grace undertook to come to the meeting upon the day appointed by the burgomaster and the Council of the city of Zurich concerning the dissension and trouble which had arisen in the city on account of doctrines or sermons, but from business reasons and other accidental causes you were detained and hindered from attending. And although in addition to all the clergymen, preachers and priests that have livings in the city of Zurich and its territories there were invited and summoned to this praiseworthy meeting also many other foreign nobility and common people, prelates, doctors, masters, both secular and ecclesiastical lords, likewise the praiseworthy representative from Constance, when these had appeared at Zurich before the Council in session certain enemies of the Gospel truth (as I hear) ridiculed the matter, announcing and saying that a tinker's day was being held at Zurich, and that nothing but tinkers were attending. These things have influenced and caused me to describe all the actions, speeches either for or against, which took place in such praiseworthy assembly of learned, honest and pious men, both ecclesiastical and secular, so that every one might see and know whether such action taken and speeches made were by tinkers and pan-menders, also whether the opposing party (which has asserted that the matter is known abroad) tells the truth or lies. For I was there myself and sat with them, heard and understood and remembered all that was said there, and after that I wrote it down in my home, questioned and examined others who had been present at the meeting as to the cases in which I thought I might not have understood correctly. With the true knowledge and witness of all those who were there and took part, about six hundred or more, I may assert that I have written down not more nor less nor different words (as far as the content is concerned) than were spoken in the assembly. I write and send this to Your Grace, and beg Your Grace to accept it with good will and favor as a service. I also urge as a fellow brother in Christ Your Grace to remain in the future as in the past steadfastly by the Gospel truth, to practice and read industriously in the Gospel and St. Paul and other Holy Scriptures as Your Grace has the reputation of doing, also to live in Christian conformity with the same according to your full power; to send such reports of action at Zurich to the others who are related to Your Grace in friendship or otherwise in Christian society, as for instance, the worthy and ecclesiastical Lord, etc., Abbot at Disentis,* to be read, so that the truth may be known, the Gospel advanced, Christian love increased, men fed with the word of God, our will and spirit may remain united with Christ through His word in peace, joy and harmony here for the time being and there forever. Amen.

Given in the praiseworthy city of Zurich the 3d day of the month of March, in the year 1523.

In order that every one may understand the matter better I have prefixed and written down the mandate of those of Zurich, which mandate was sent out into all the territory and dependencies of the city beforehand as an argument as to the causes for the above-mentioned meeting:

We, the burgomaster, the Council and the Great Council, which they call the two hundred of the city of Zurich, announce to each and every priest, preacher, minister and clergyman who has a living and residence in our cities, counties, principalities, high and low courts and territories, our greeting, favorable and affectionate will, and would have you know that now for considerable time much dissension and trouble have arisen between those who preach from the pulpit the word of God to the common people, some believing that they have preached the Gospel faithfully and wholly, whereas others blame them as though they had not acted skillfully or properly. On the other hand the others call them sources of evil, deceivers and sometimes heretics; but to each one desiring it these offer to give account and reckoning about this everywhere with the aid of God's Scriptures to the

* Andreas von Valara, who had been abbot since 1512.

best of their ability for the sake of the honor of God, peace and Christian unity. So this is our command, will and desire, that you preachers, priests, clergymen, all together and each one separately, if any especial priests desire to speak about this, having livings in our city of Zurich or outside in our territories, or if any desire to blame the opposing party or to instruct them otherwise, shall appear on the day after Emperor Charles' Day, the 29th day of the month of January, at the early time of the Council, in our city of Zurich, before us in our town hall, and shall announce in German, by the help of true divine Scripture, the matters which you oppose. When we, with the careful assistance of certain scholars, have paid careful attention to the matters, as seems best to us, and after investigations are made with the help of the Holy Scriptures and the truth, we will send each one home with a command either to continue or to desist. After this no one shall continue to preach from the pulpit whatever seems good to him without foundation in the divine Scriptures. We shall also report such matters to our gracious Lord of Constance, so that His Grace or His representative, if He so desire, may also be present. But if any one in the future opposes this, and does not base his opposition upon the true Holy Scriptures, with him we shall proceed further according to our knowledge in a way from which we would gladly be relieved. We also sincerely hope that God Almighty will give gracious light to those who earnestly seek the light of truth, and that we may in the future walk in that light as sons of the light.

Given and preserved under the imprinted seal of the city on Saturday after the Circumcision of Christ and after his birth in the twenty-third year of the lesser reckoning. [Jan. 3, 1522.]

Now when all of the priests, ministers and clergymen in the territories of Zurich obediently appeared at the hour and time announced there were in the Great Council room at Zurich more than six hundred assembled, counting the local and foreign representatives, together with the praiseworthy representation from Constance, to which an invitation to the same had been sent from Zurich, and when everybody had found a seat at the early time of the Council the burgomaster of Zurich began to speak as follows:

Very learned, noble, steadfast, honorable, wise, ecclesiastical Lords and Friends: For some time in my Lords' city of Zurich and her territories dissensions and quarrels have arisen on account of certain sermons and teachings delivered to the people from the pulpit by Master Ulrich Zwingli, our preacher here at Zurich, wherefore he has been attacked and blamed as a deceiver by some and by others as a heretic. Wherefore it has come about that not only in our city of Zurich, but also everywhere else in the land in my Lords' territories such dissensions have increased among the clergy, and also the laity, that daily complaints of the same come before my Lords, and the angry words and quarreling do not seem likely to come to an end. And so Master Ulrich Zwingli has frequently offered to give the causes and reasons for his sermons and doctrines preached here in the public pulpit so often in Zurich in case a public discussion before all the clergy and the laity were granted him. At this offer of Master Ulrich the honorable Council at Zurich, desiring to stop the disturbance and dissension, has granted him permission to hold a public discussion in the German language before the Great Council at Zurich, which they call the two hundred, to which the honorable and wise Council has summoned all of you priests and ministers from her territories. It also requested the worthy Lord and Prince, etc., Bishop of Constance, to send his representative to this meeting, for which favor the honorable Council of Zurich expresses especial thanks to him. Therefore if there is any one here who may feel any displeasure or doubt in Master Ulrich's sermons or doctrines preached here at Zurich in the pulpit, or if any one desires to say anything or knows anything to say in the matter to the effect that such sermons and teachings are not true, but misleading or heretical, he can prove the truth of the same before my Lords, the often mentioned Master Ulrich, and show him at once his error by means of the Scriptures, and he shall be free and safe and with perfect immunity, so that my Lords may in the future be relieved of the daily complaints which arise from such dissension and quarrels. For my Lords have become weary of such complaints, which have been increasing gradually from both clergy and laity.

At these remarks and invitation Sir Fritz von Anwyl,* knight, and Chamberlain of the Bishop of Constance, made answer, and spoke as follows:

Very learned, worthy, noble, provident, wise, etc. The worthy Lord and Prince, Sir Hugo,† by grace of God Bishop of Constance, my gracious Lord, well knows and is for the most part well informed that now everywhere in his Grace's bishopric many quarrels and dissensions of many kinds with regard to doctrines or sermons have arisen in almost every place. And although his Grace has ever been of the desire and feeling, and always will be if God will, to show himself always gracious, kind and willing in all those things which can further peace and harmony, still his Grace at the especial request and petition of the wise and honorable Council of Zurich has ordered your accredited representatives here present, the worthy Lords, Sir Doctor Vergenhans, canon, his Grace's Vicar,‡ Sir Doctor Martin,§ of Tübingen, together with myself, his Grace's servant, to listen to and to hear such causes of dissension. He has recommended us to act in such matters not otherwise than kindly, to say the best that we can in the matter, so that it result in the honor, peace and har-

* He later went over to the Reformed Church.

† Von Hohenlandenberg, d. 1532.

‡ Johannes Heigerlin, commonly called Faber or Fabri, because his father was a smith. He became successively pastor at Lindau, vicar-general of Constance (1516) and bishop of Vienna (1530). Born at Lentkirch, near Lake Constance, in 1478, he died at Baden, near Vienna, May 21, 1541.

§ Blansch. He wrote later at Constance against the Reformed preachers.

mony for the honorable Council of Zurich, likewise the worthy clergy. Wherefore, learned, worthy, honorable, wise Lords and good friends, I say: If there is any one here present who desires to make any remonstrance or accusation on account of the doctrines or sermons that have been delivered here, we shall, according to the commands of my gracious Lord of Constance, as his Grace's representatives, listen gladly and willingly, and for the sake of peace and harmony, as far as in us lies, shall help to judge the dissension, if such has arisen or shall arise, in order that a worthy clergy may remain in peace and friendship until my gracious Lord and Prince, together with his Grace's scholars and prelates, shall further discuss and consider these matters. That was the sum of his whole discourse.

Then Master Ulrich Zwingli spoke in answer, and his remarks in the beginning were as follows:

Pious brothers in Christ, Almighty God has always shown His divine grace, will and favor to man from the beginning of the world, has been as kind as a true and almighty father, as we read and know from all the Sriptures, so that everlasting, merciful God has communicated His divine word and His will to man as a consolation. And although at some times He has kept away this same word, the light of truth, from the sinful and godless struggling against the truth, and although He has allowed to fall into error those men who followed their own will and the leadings of their wicked nature, as we are truly informed in all Bible histories, still He has always in turn consoled His own people with the light of His everlasting word, so that, whereas they had fallen into sin and error, they may again be lifted by His divine mercy, and He has never entirely forsaken them or let them depart from His divine recognition. This I say to you, dear brethren, for this purpose. You know that now in our time, as also many years heretofore, the pure, clear and bright light, the word of God, has been so dimmed and confused and paled with human ambitions and teachings that the majority who by word of mouth call themselves Christians know nothing less than the divine will. But by their own invented service of God, holiness, external spiritual exhibition, founded upon human customs and laws, they have gone astray, and have thus been persuaded by those whom people consider learned and leaders of others to the extent that the simple think that such invented external worship is spiritual, and that the worship of God, which they have put upon themselves, necessariy conduces to happiness, although all our true happiness, consolation and good consists, not in our merits, nor in such external works, rather alone in Jesus Christ our Saviour, to whom the heavenly Father Himself gave witness that we should hear Him as His beloved Son. His will and true service we can learn and discover only from His true word in the Holy Scriptures and in the trustworthy writings of His twelve apostles, otherwise from no human laws and statutes. Since now certain pious hearts have ventured to preach this by the grace and inspiration of God's holy spirit, and to bring it before the people, they call these preachers not Christians, but persecutors of the Christian Church, and even heretics. I am considered one of these by many of the clergy and the laity everywhere in the Confederation. And although I know that for the past five years I have preached in this city of Zurich nothing but the true, pure and clear word of God, the holy Gospel, the joyous message of Christ, the Holy Scripture, not by the aid of man, but by the aid of the Holy Ghost, still all this did not help me. But I am maligned by many as a heretic, a liar, a deceiver, and one disobedient to the Christian Church, which facts are well known to my Lords of Zurich. I made complaint of these things before them as my Lords; I have often entreated and begged of them in the public pulpit to grant me permission to give an account of my sermons and preachings (delivered in their city) before all men, learned or not, spiritual or secular, also before our gracious Lord, the Bishop of Constance, or his representative. This I also offered to do in the city of Constance, providing a safe permit was assured me, as has ever been done in the case of those from Constance. At such request of mine, my Lords, perhaps by divine will, you have granted me permission to hold a discussion in German before the assembled Council, for which privilege I thank you especially as my Lords. I have also brought together in outline the contents and import of all my speeches and sermons delivered at Zurich, have issued the same in German through the press, so that every one might see and know what my doctrine and sermons at Zurich have been, and shall be in the future, unless I am convinced of something else.* I hope and am confident, indeed I know, that my sermons and doctrine are nothing else than the holy, true, pure Gospel, which God desired me to speak by the intuition and inspiration of His spirit. But from what intent or desire God has wished such things to take place through me, His unworthy servant, I cannot know, for He alone knows and understands the secret of His counsels. Wherefore I offer here to any one who thinks that my sermons or teachings are unchristian or heretical to give the reasons and to answer kindly and without anger. Now let them speak in the name of God. Here I am.

At such remarks of Master Ulrich the Vicar † from Constance arose, and answered as follows:

Learned, worthy, noble, steadfast, favorable, wise, etc. My good fellow-brother and Lord, Master Ulrich, begins and complains that he has always preached the holy Gospel here publicly in Zurich, of which I have no doubt, for who would not truly and faithfully preach the holy Gospel and St. Paul, providing God had ordained him as a preacher? For I am also a preacher, or priest, perhaps unworthy, but I have taught those entrusted to me for instruction in the word of God in nothing but the true Gospel, which I can also prove with true witness. And I shall for the future not in any way cease to preach this, providing God

* This refers to the 67 Articles he issued preparatory to the Disputation.

† That is the vicar-general.

does not require me for other labors in the service of my gracious Lord of Constance. For the holy Gospel is a power of God, as St. Paul writes to the Romans (i. 16), to each one who believes therein.

But now that Master Ulrich begins and complains that certain people blame him as not having spoken and preached the truth, but offers and has offered to answer for his speeches and sermons to any one, also (even) in Constance, I say, dear Lords, that if Master Ulrich, my good Lord and friend, should come to me in Constance I would show him as my good friend and Lord all friendship and honor as far as lay in my power, and if he so desires would also entertain him in my house, not only as a good friend, but also as a brother. Of this he is assured at my hands. Further, I say that I did not come here to oppose evangelical or apostolical doctrines, but to hear those who are said to speak or to have spoken against the doctrine of the holy Gospel, and if any dissension should arise or should have arisen to help to judge and to decide the matter in kindness, as far as may be, to the end of peace and harmony rather than disturbance (discord). For the Gospel and the divine Paul teach only what serves to grace and peace, not to disturbance and strife.* But if there is a desire to dispute and oppose good old customs, the ways and usages of the past, then in such case I say that I shall not

---

* ["You well understood how Zwingli spoke about peace and strife; and the words he spoke you refer to yourself. Zwingli spoke not about the strife of weapons or the discord of the faithful. For you know well that he said: 'God be thanked that the pious city of Zürich is so inclined to peace, and knows well that this comes from the word of God alone, which they hear and accept so faithfully.' But I say that the Gospel commands strife between the faithful and the Godless. Do you not know how Christ says in the Gospel of Matt. x. 34, 'I am not come,' etc.? How can it be preached in peace? Indeed, if the whole world were believers it might be; otherwise not. For Christ is the stumbling-block, at which many will be offended; these are of the world, and the devil is their Lord, who will undertake to maintain his empire without ceasing with his own?" (Hans Hager in "Gyrenrupfen.")]

undertake to dispute anything here at Zurich. For, as I think, such matters are to be settled by a general Christian assembly of all nations, or by a council of bishops and other scholars as are found at universities, just as occurred in times past among the holy apostles in Jerusalem, as we read in Acts xv. For if such matters touching the common customs and the praiseworthy usages of the past were discussed, and some decision reached against them, such changes would perhaps not please other Christians dwelling in other places, who would doubtless assert that they had not consented to our views. For what would those in Spain, in Italy, in France and in the North say about it? Such things must surely, as I said, be ratified and maintained as formerly, by a general council, in order to be valid elsewhere. Therefore, dear lords, I speak now for myself. As a Christian member and brother in Christ I beg and urge you to consider these things well, lest hereafter further and greater strife and harm may result. Accordingly it would be my sincere advice to drop any difference or dissension that may have arisen concerning papal or other ecclesiastical ordinances (*constitutions*) of long standing, and without further disputing to lay aside and postpone them, to see if they could not be arranged meantime more peacefully and advantageously. For my gracious Lord of Constance is informed that it is decided at Nuremberg by the estates (*Ständen*) of the empire to hold a general council of the German nation within a year, in which I hear half the judges selected are secular and the other half ecclesiastical, and they are to judge and decide about the things which are now disturbing nearly all the world. If such takes place these matters should be referred to them as having the authority and power. And so it is the earnest desire of my Lord, as far as possible, to have such differences about the clergy settled without dispute for the good of yourselves and all (other) Christians. For though these old ordinances, laws and customs should be discussed *pro* and *con* upon scriptural basis, who would be judge of these matters? According to my opinion whatever such things one would discuss should be brought before the universities, as at Paris, Cologne or Louvain. (Here all laughed, for Zwingli interrupted by asking: " How about Erfurt? Would not Wittenberg do?" Then the legate said: "No; Luther was too near." He also said: "All bad things come from the North.") There one can find many taught in the Scriptures, who have ability to handle so great subjects. In this remark I do not wish to be taken as speaking to the discredit of any one's honor or knowledge, but as a Christian member, and with entire good nature I announce this. But as far as my office and commission are concerned, I have been sent here, as I said before, for no other purpose than to listen, and not to dispute.*

* ["You have left out the right sense, namely, that everything should be written down. Now speak and give answer if we did not dispute fore and afternoon about a judge, when Master Ulrich Zwingli declared that he would not suffer any one as judge except all Christian believers. Have you not ears and heard that I have often referred to this opinion; always at times when heretics arose a council was held, and by its means the heretics had been thus subdued? Hereupon I named Arius, Sabellius, Nestorius, Manichee and many others; and what was thus recognized thereby it should remain. For if this were not done and held (have you not heard that I said?), there would be as many beliefs as there are many countries, yea as many as there are cities, villages, estates, houses and people, if one does come with matters pertaining to the interpretation of the Scriptures before the councils. I have further shown that in recent years in such matters as have arisen thus between scholars, and always in times of misunderstanding in regard to the Scripture, the universities have been chosen as judges. But when one of you spoke, his words were considered as flowing from the spirit of God, as if into you alone the spirit of God enters (as St. Paul writes), and you alone were the wine-rooms of Jove, and all secrets of the empire of God were made known in them; but what the holy Fathers spoke, wrote and ordained, and also the speeches of us, the ambassadors, were to be considered as human nonsense, as I have related at length. St. Paul himself awaited and received from the apostles a letter (Acts xv.), in which they wrote: 'For it seemed good to the Holy Ghost and us,' etc., and yet he was ordained by God as magister, as 'magister gentium.' Hence the worthy Master Ulrich Zwingli should justly also await and accept decision and judgment. This was said by me more than

Then Master Ulrich Zwingli spoke as follows: Pious brothers in Christ, the worthy Lord Vicar seeks so many evasions and subterfuges for the purpose of turning your simplicity from your understanding with artful, rhetorical, evasive words.* For he claims and says that he does not desire to discuss the good old

once before noon, but never before noon answered by the worthy Master Ulrich. To be sure, after noon he did say a little, but did not better the matter, but as far as he was concerned (as I understood it) made it worse. (Faber.)

"Hereupon Hans Hab, according to 'Gyrenrupfen,' answered: 'It may be that Zwingli forgot to answer in the forenoon; what does that matter? Who would have cared to answer your lengthy nonsense? But didn't he answer it after dinner? Hence let us sit in judgment upon the XV. chapter of the Acts, then we shall find it is against you, and not for you. You have spoken in this manner, we will now let it be, and as often as one wished to consider the books you have gotten out of it in another fashion.' Faber continues: 'In his little book about the choice of food Zwingli has permitted all food, and still it is found in the letter which Paul received at Jerusalem from the twelve apostles that the sacrifice of calves and other meat which was offered to the idols was forbidden. He thinks that this ordinance has expired if there is no more heathenism or idolatry, which I did not answer for good reason. But see whether there be not in Africa still idolatry, and Christians still live among them in the newly-discovered islands,' etc. Hereupon Hab (ib.) again: 'Do you not remember that Zwingli said Paul himself did not keep it? Why don't you look at the Scriptures with him?' Faber continues: 'Not I, but Mr. Fritz v. Anwyl, reported concerning this at the council of Nürnberg. For that I refer to him and your lords of Zürich. But if nevertheless I have said it, then see whether Master Ulrich or I had better information from Nürnberg—look at the decree of Nürnberg. But the new teachers and evangelists from the North do not wish any weight to be given to past or future decrees or councils unless they favor them. But they do rightly; they know that their doctrine would be condemned before even half of the fathers had gathered—they cannot endure the councils. Their song must not only be the song of the angels, but of God, and whatever the pious fathers say only human foolishness.' (Faber, correction.) How often have you heard from Zwingli that he did not wish to have only two judges, but to have all believers judge whether you or he is corrupting the Scriptures. But you were unable to come to this." ("Gyrenrupfen.")]

*["Have you not heard that Zwingli said there was too much of my talk, and I thereupon offered to prove my statements if all things were noted down, for I do not care to speak into the air?" (Faber.)]

customs or venerable usages concerning ecclesiastical ordinances, but I say that we do not want to ask here how long this or that custom or habit has been in use. But we desire to speak of the truth (to find out), whether a man is bound by divine ordinance to keep that which on account of long usage has been set up as law by men. For we of course think (as also the pope's own decree says) that custom should yield to truth. As to claiming that such matters should be settled by a Christian assembly of all nations, or by a council of bishops, etc., I say that here in this room is without doubt a Christian assembly.* For I hope that the majority of us here desire from divine will and love to hear, to further and to know the truth, which wish Almighty God will not deny us if we desire it to His honor with right belief and right hearts. For the Lord says: Where two or three are gathered together in my name, I am there among them. Also in times past did not bishops assemble in councils as secular princes? How then are we to claim and say that the pious fathers of past times assembled for Christian business? Were there not doubtless such powerful prelates and bishops as now, as they say there must be? This is truthfully proved by the testimony of trustworthy writings of old. And this is proved also by the word "Episcopus," which when properly turned into German means no more than a watchman or overseer who has the care and attention of his people, and who is also charged with instructing them in the divine belief and will; in good German this is a clergyman (Pfarrer). Since now here in this assembly there are so many honest, pious, Christian men, not alone living within the territories of my Lords of Zurich, but also coming from elsewhere, and also many learned, Godfearing bishops and clergymen, who sit here without doubt to further the truth of God and to hear and to know the divine truth, there is then, in spite of what the Vicar says, no reason why they should

* ["In which there are many Godfearing curates; also many doctors and real friends of God." (Bullinger.)]

not discuss these matters, speak and decide the truth. To the remark that the other nations would not consent, I answer that this is just the complaint which is made every day concerning the " big moguls " (*grossen Hansen*, literally " big Jacks), bishops and priests, that they undertake to keep the pure and clear Gospel, the Holy Scriptures, from the common people. For they say that it is not proper for any but themselves to expound the Scriptures, just as though other pious men were not Christians and had nothing to do with the spirit of God, and must be without knowledge of God's word. And there are also some of them who might say that it is improper to publish the secrets of the divine Scriptures.* For there is no doubt in my mind that if the pure truth of Christ alone, not adulterated with human ordinances, were preached to the above-mentioned peoples or nations, and not covered up with papal and imperial mandates and those of bishops, they would as pious Christian hearts accept the truth and let the customs or ordinances (*constitutions*) of men go, and enlightened by God's word, would be in harmony and agreement with the others. However, as to the council which is said to be announced at Nuremberg, it seems to me that the thing is proposed only to put off the common people desirous of God's word. For I tell you, dear Lords, that letters came to me about three days ago from Nuremberg,† which I could show if necessary, in which there was, to be sure, some mention made of a council, but I do not understand that anything has really been decided. For pope, bishops, prelates and the 'big moguls' will allow no council in which the divine Scriptures were set forth in their clearness and purity. It is also plain that nothing will come of it this year, however much the common Christian earnestly did toward it, because sufficient supplies could not be

* [" I did not write a book ' de non revelandis mysteriis,' but against the rash, against those who in an impious manner handle holy things or Scriptures.' (Faber.)]

† These letters are no longer extant.

collected in so short a time for so large an assembly. I concede also that a council will be announced in time. But meanwhile how are we to treat those whose consciences have gone astray so far as to desire eagerly to know the truth? Would you rob these thirsty souls of the truth, let them hang in doubt, frighten them by human ordinances, and let them live or die in uncertainty as to the truth? Really, my pious brethren, this is no small thing. God will not demand of us what pope, bishop and council establish and command, nor how long this or that has been in praiseworthy and ancient usage, but He will find out how His divine will, word and commandments have been kept.*

Now finally, since reference is made to the judges which my Lord Vicar thinks cannot be found outside the universities, I say that we have here infallible and unprejudiced judges, that is the Holy Writ, which can neither lie nor deceive. These we have

* [Hager in "Gyrenrupfen" presents the dispute about the council thus: "After this Mr. Fritz, the majordomo, very cleverly presented the command of his master, saying that his master had been surely informed, that in a year there would be a council. Concerning this Zwingli did not wish to speak. Thereupon you immediately began to speak, and rose and said the same as Mr. Fritz had just said, and in a nice way referred to the future council and showed yourself a little more, just as if the matter had not also been commended to you. Thereupon Zwingli arose, and said we should not be led astray by the council; he also had had a letter in which he was informed how the German princes had demanded from the pope that he have a council within a year, but that the pope had formally assented had not yet happened, nor is it possible (he said) that within the space of a year a general council could be gathered together; furthermore the three mightiest lords, King of France, Emperor, and King of England, were at war with each other, who could not easily be conciliated; also that the fixing of the council would be left to the Germans. Hence one could see that the promise of a council was only a postponement, not a definite resolve; but it mattered little whether they had a council or not, for he believed that no man would live to see a council in which the word of God would be allowed to rule. Therefore, even if a council should be held at once, one would not care either, for we would depend upon and preach the word of God; may the councils determine herein what they please." After this he from Neftenbach arose and spoke.]

present in Hebrew, Greek and Latin tongues; these let us take on both sides as fair and just judges.*

Also we have here in our city, God be praised, many learned colleagues who are as sufficiently taught in these three languages as none at the universities just named and mentioned by the Lord Vicar. But I am speaking of those who conduct the above-mentioned universities as superiors and heads; I do not mean Erasmus of Rotterdam and others, who stay at times at the universities as strangers and guests. Here in this room are sitting also doctors of the Holy Writ, doctors of canonical law, many scholars from the universities. They should hear the Scriptures which are referred to, have them read, to see if that is so which they try and pretend to support by divine Scriptures. And as if all that was not sufficient there are in this assembly many Christian hearts, taught doubtless by the Holy Spirit, and possessing such upright understanding, that in accordance with God's spirit they can judge and decide which party produces Scripture on its side, right or wrong, or otherwise does violence to Scripture contrary to proper understanding. There is therefore no reason why excuse should here be made. Hence, dear friends, do not let the speeches here made frighten you. And especially you of Zurich should consider it a great blessing and power of God that such an undertaking should be made here in your city to the praise and honor of God, in order that the pious subjects of your territories and lands should no longer, as heretofore, be suspended in doubt and dissension. With humble hearts call upon God. He will not refuse you His divine recognition, as the epistle of James promises, if you ask in true faith, and do not let yourselves

* ["On the contrary I told how Paul did not boast of the languages when he went to the Corinthians, not 'in sublimitate sermonis' or high wisdom. Thus one finds in the life of Hilary that the evil spirit often spoke in Greek and other tongues. And therefore I did not boast, rightly, about the languages, although I brought with me to you from Constance the Hebrew and Greek Bible; also had them both with you at the city hall. Do you think I have never heard or read Hebrew or Greek?" (Faber.)]

be dissuaded and deceived in any way by smooth and pleasant (well-appearing) words.

At these words of Zwingli's every one remained silent for a time, and no one wanted to say anything upon the matter, till the burgomaster of Zurich arose and urged any there present who wished to say anything about the matter, or knew anything to say about the affair, to step forward. But no one spoke.

Since thus every one was silent, and no one was anxious to speak against Master Ulrich, who had before been called a heretic behind his back, Master Ulrich himself arose and spoke: For the sake of Christian love and truth I urge and beg all who have spoken earnestly to me on account of my sermons to step forward and to instruct me, for the sake of God, in the truth in the presence of so many pious and learned men. In case they do not do this I assure them that I shall summon publicly by name each of them, of whom I know many to be present. But on account of brotherly love I wish to inform them beforehand, so that they may arise of themselves unsummoned by me and prove me a heretic.*. But no one desired to come forward or say anything against him.

Meantime Gutschenkel [a buffoon from Bern], standing in front by the door, cut a ridiculous caper, and cried out: "Where are now the 'big moguls' that boast so loudly and bravely on the streets? Now step forward! Here is the man. You can all boast over your wine, but here no one stirs." All laughed at that.

Then Master Ulrich arose again, urged and begged a second time all who had accused and attacked him about his sermons to step forth and prove him a heretic. In case they did not do that, and did not step forward unsummoned by name, he would

* ["Am I not right? If you do not do that I shall name those who call me heretic, but I warn you in advance that it is more honest to step forward uncalled." (Bullinger.) The word of the abbot of Cappel: "Where are they now who wish to burn us?" Bullinger places here.]

THE FIRST ZURICH DISPUTATION.   59

for a third time publicly summon them, etc., as above. When every one remained silent as to the invitation and challenge of Master Ulrich a priest by the name of James Wagner arose, a clergyman at Neftenbach,* and spoke as follows: Learned, wise, honorable, specially favorable, lords (gentlemen?) and princes: Since there is no one who wishes to speak of these matters after the repeated summons of Master Ulrich, I must, as the least skillful, say something. It is well known to you all, gentlemen, that our gracious Lord of Constance this year issued a mandate † ordering people to retain and keep the *traditiones humanas* until they were rescinded and changed by a general council. Now since no one will say anything against Master Ulrich's articles, which oppose the *constitutiones humanas*, I say for my part, and hope and think, that we ought not to be bound to keep that mandate, but should preach the word of God, pure and unadulterated by human additions. You know also, dear Lords, how the clergyman of Fislisbach ‡ was arrested according to the mandate, taken to Baden before the Diet, which afterwards gave him into the keeping of the bishop of Constance, who finally put him in prison. If we are to teach and preach according to the contents of the mandate, then Master Ulrich's words have no force. But since there is no one here present who dare (darf) say anything against them, to show them untrue, it is plain that proceedings with the gentleman from Fislisbach were too short. For this reason Ispeak, this good gentleman and clergyman said

* A village 12 miles northeast of Zurich.

† In Füssli's *Beiträgen*, IV., 125-129.

‡ On the border of Switzerland, but in Baden. His name was Urban Weiss. He had announced from his pulpit on his return from the Zurich meeting of August 15, 1522, that he would no longer call upon the Virgin Mary or the saints. He also married. The bishop of Constance complained against him at the Diet of Baden, which wished him arrested, but some friends went surety for him. However, the Diet in November, 1522, ordered his arrest. He was examined in Constance, and apparently as the result of the use of torture recanted and then was liberated.

further, and I would like to have judgment as to how I should act in the future as to such mandate of the bishop.*

* [Faber accuses Hegenwald of error in the order of his speeches.

"You note me down as if I had made the fourth speech, and bring forth a speech of which truly I would be ashamed, provided I could not erase it by means of the Scriptures better by the grace of God. You have noted me down as if I had immediately broken forth after the speech of Zwingli, which you know is not true. For I learnt long ago from Roman histories that an ambassador should not exceed his authority. This I have not forgotten, that one should not preach unless he be sent. Therefore since I have not been sent by my gracious lord as a combatant, but as a spectator, yea as a peaceful umpire, I did not wish to answer the many speeches and demands; also partly exhortation of Zwingli. And where there had been a long silence, you know that Mr. Ulrich having dared to name several, requested us from Constance urgently, still I maintained silence until the priest (whom you call), v. Mittenbach (Neftenbach), referred to my gracious lord and myself so much and so clearly that I thought, and I also said it to the mighty lord Fritz Jacob v. Anwyl, that I could not leave that unanswered. For although you closed the speech according to your wont, still you omit that the priest says among other things that the bishop of Constance had forbidden to preach the Gospel—write what the Vicar there said—then you will find that I said before, I am not here to suppress the Gospel and St. Paul, for who would do that in view of the tale how the angel had brought and proclaimed to the shepherds upon the pasture when Christ was born the consoling message that in the Gospel was the salvation, yea the way and the truth, in comparing the New and Old Testament; also the four evangelists are the four rivers of Paradise, which make fruitful the whole world with the water of divine grace; it has been arranged with better order, as St. Paul says, and I also have helped in it, since my 'scholastici doctores' have been diligently read and underscored by me, so that they also have become dirty from my hands. Thus I have also seen that it would be better and more wholesome to leave sophistry and to bring forward the Gospel and the prophets and also other divine writings. Therefore I held to the first proposition, how this might happen and the Gospel be brought forth, which then is true even if Master Ulrich Zwingli had never come to Zürich. But I was not thus minded, and did not help to arrange the proposition so that the Gospel should be preached in a revolutionary manner, but according to the essential Christian and peaceful understanding. And furthermore I declared the Gospel does not consist in reading, but in the strength of God, yea in the correct interpretation and understanding, and I have proved by two places in the Gospel of Matthew, Matt. iv. 6, where the tempter cites the saying Ps. xc. From this I have shown

At such complaint the Vicar from Constance again arose, and spoke as follows: These remarks are meant to refer partly to my gracious Lord of Constance and partly to me as his Grace's Vicar, therefore it is proper that I answer them. The good gentleman —I really do not know who he is—spoke first as follows, saying that this year our gracious Lord of Constance issued a mandate ordering people to keep the *constitutiones humanas*, that is the human ordinances and praiseworthy customs. To this I say, dear lords and gentlemen, there are truly many unfair, ungodly, unchristian opinions and errors at hand, which very often are preached and put before the people, not only here in the Confederation, but also elsewhere in my gracious Lord's (of Constance) bishopric by unskillful preachers, which opinions and errors, my dear lords and gentlemen, serve more to disobedience, disturbance and discord than the furthering of Christian unity. For they desire to estrange us from the good old inherited customs and usages descended upon us from our old pious Christian fathers many hundred years ago. Perhaps it was with this in mind that my gracious Lord issued the mandate for the sake of peace and unity in his Grace's bishopric. Of what the real contents of the mandate were I have no accurate knowledge, for at that time, as is known to many, I was absent from home.

that also the evil spirit might, as an old scholar, use and know the Scriptures— and Matt. ii. 6, where the scribes cite the saying of Micah of Bethlehem, but omitted the following correct point—thus by means of these two quotations I have well proven that it is not always sufficient to cite the Gospel or the Scriptures (although they have the first seat and the greatest honor), and that the Scriptures do not consist in the reading, but in the correct interpretation; thus and not otherwise it was done. Why didn't you note that down also for me? Why do you conceal that from me? And in still more unfair and wrongful fashion did you note down this and other of my speeches, how I so often cited the pope and the pope's affairs." (Faber, correction.) "When you cited how also the devil had made use of the Scriptures, Zwingli had answered that is what he was there for, to give answer that he had used them correctly. But you do not wish to take hold of the Scriptures." (Hans Hager in "Gyrenrupfen.")]

Therefore as far as concerns this mandate I do not desire to speak further. But since the good, pious gentleman (I don't know where he sits, because I cannot see him,) has referred to the priest imprisoned at Constance my office requires me to make answer. You all know, dear sirs, how this priest was turned over to my gracious Lord of Constance by the common peers [lit. confederates: citizens of the Confederacy] in the diet at Baden as a guilty man. Accordingly my gracious Lord had the prisoner examined and questioned by appointees of his Grace, and the prisoner was found to be an ignorant and erring man in the divine Scriptures, and I myself have often pitied his unskillful remarks. For by my faith I can say that I questioned him myself, went to him in Christian love, set forth to him some of the Scriptures from St. Paul, and he made—what shall I say?— very inaccurate answers. Ah, my dear sirs, what shall I say about this good, simple fellow? He is really untutored, and is not even a grammarian.* For in Christian brotherly love, kindly and without any anger, I mentioned to him some Scriptures, as for instance, that the noble Paul exhorted Timothy, saying: Pietas ad omnia utilis (kindness and greatness are good in all things), and his answer was so childish and unchristian as to be improper to mention and report in the Confederation. But that you may really know, my dear sirs, I spoke with him about praying to the dear saints and to the mother of God, also about their intercession, and I found him so ignorant and unchristian on these points that I pity his error. He insists on making living out of the dead, although the Scriptures show that also before the birth of Christ the dear saints were prayed to and called upon for others, as I finally convinced and persuaded him by means of Scriptures, that is, by Genesis, Exodus, Ezechiel and Baruch. I also brought matters so far that he recanted his error, and desires to recant all his errors about the mother of God and the dear saints. I also hope that he will be grateful to me and soon be released.

* That is not a Latinist.

Therefore, my dear sirs, with regard to the impirsoned priest there is truly no reason why my gracious Lord of Constance, or his representative, should be blamed for this affair. For nothing has been done other than what was proper, fair and becoming.

To this Master Ulrich answered as folows: Dear brethren in Christ, it doubtlessly happened, not without especial destiny and will of God, that my Lord Vicar has just spoken about the praying to and the intercession of the saints and the mother of God. For that is not the least of the Articles issued by me, upon which I have preached somewhat, and at which so many simple folk are troubled as though they were frightened by a heretical [lit. un-christian] sermon. For I know, and truly find in the divine Scriptures, that Jesus Christ alone can bless us, who, as Paul says, alone is the justice of all men, who has expiated our sins, and He alone, our salvation and Saviour, is the means of intercession between His heavenly Father and us humans who believe, as Saint Paul clearly says to the Hebrews, and as you of Zürich have often heard from me when I preached to you from your favorite, the epistle to the Hebrews. Now since my Lord Vicar announces and publicly boasts of how he convinced the imprisoned priest at Constance, the clergyman of Fislisbach, by means of the divine Scriptures, of the fact that one should pray to the dear saints and the mother of God, therefore that they are our mediators with God, I beg of him for the sake of God and of Christian love to show me the place and location, also the words of the Scriptures, where it is written that one should pray to the saints as mediators, so that if I have erred, and err now, I may be better instructed, since there are here present Bibles in the Hebrew, Greek and Latin languages. These we will have examined by those present who are sufficiently well taught in the above-mentioned tongues, so I desire no more to be shown than the chapters in which such is written, as my Lord Vicar states, then we will have it found and read, so that we may see whether it is the meaning of Scripture that the saints are to be prayed to as mediators. In case that is so, and is really found to be in Scripture (as the Vicar also asserts to have convinced the imprisoned priest), I also will gladly, as an ignorant man, submit to instruction where I have erred.

ANSWER OF THE VICAR TO THE WORDS OF MASTER ULRICH.

DEAR SIRS : I see very well that the game is going beyond me. I said before that I was present not to dispute, but as the representative of my gracious Lord to speak kindly if any dissension arose on account of the disputation. Thus I very well see things are going with me as the wise man said, the foolish are easily caught in their words, but it is perhaps the fault of my folly that I undertook to speak not as a wise man. Since I have been summoned to answer by Master Ulrich, I will say that some hundreds of years ago it happened, my dear sirs, that heresy and dissension arose in the Church, the causes and beginners of which were Novatians, Montanists, Sabellians, Ebionites, Marcionites and others, under whose false teachings and error many articles like these of our times were planted in men, and by their teachings many believing folk went astray. Among these some asserted that praying to the dear saints and their intercession, as also of the mother of God, and that purgatory, too, did not exist, but were man's invention, and the like. In order to close up such misleading roads and ways of error many pious bishops and fathers met in many places, at one time in Asia, then in Africa, then somewhere in Greece, that they might hold synods and councils, and to avoid and stop heresy and such things. And afterward *constitutiones* (that is, ordinances and decisions,) were made, prescribed and commanded about those matters by the holy fathers and the popes that such (heretical views) should not be held, having been rejected by the Christian Church. And although this was firmly and irrevocably ratified a long time ago by decrees of the popes and bishops, and considered wrong in Christian churches, still later schisms, dissenting parties and sects have sprung up in

Europe, as, to mention their names, the Bohemians, Picards, who were led astray by such heretics as Wyclif and Hus, living contrary to the decrees and ordinances of the holy popes, acting contrary to the regulations of the Christian Church and not putting any faith in the intercession of the saints, or still less in purgatory. And although such heresy and error were later rejected by all men of Christian belief, and although those who live and remain in such error were considered, recognized and proclaimed by the holy councils as sundered members of the mother of Christian churches, still one now finds those who stir up these things anew, and undertake to bring into doubt that which many years ago was recognized and decided upon as untrue and erroneous by pope and bishop. They undertake to drive us from old customs, which have endured and stood in honor these seven hundred years, planning to overturn and upset all things. For first they went at the pope, cardinals and bishops, then they turned all cloisters topsy-turvy, after that they fell upon purgatory. And when they had left the earth they at last ascended to heaven and went at the saints and great servants of God. Saint Peter with his keys, indeed our dear Lady, the mother of God, could not escape their disgraceful attacks. And I know some places where they had gone so far as even to Christ Himself.

Shall it now go so far that not only the authorities and ecclesiastics on earth, but also God and the chosen in heaven, must be punished? If so, it is a pity. Shall not all that be nothing and count as nothing which the pious, holy fathers assembled in the holy spirit of God have made and unanimously decided? It cannot but have grown up to the great injury and disgrace of all Christendom. For the holy fathers and all our ancestors must have erred, and for now fourteen hundred years Christianity must have been misled and ruled in error, which it were unchristian to believe, I do not need to say. Now if the intercession of the dear saints has ever been ratified as necessary and useful by popes, bishops, fathers and councils, and if since the time of the holy pope Gregory (II.) it has continued in use among all Christianity, it seems strange to me that now for the first time people desire to consider this wrong and erroneous, contrary to Christian ordinance, although there are few men who do not feel the aid of the mother of God and the dear saints, not alone among us Christians, but also among some unbelieving heathen. If we here at Zürich are now to speak and fight against such customs common to all the world, and especially those preserved so long by Christians, let each one think for himself how that would please those in the Orient, the Occident, from sunrise to sunset, also those in Hibernia, Mauritania, Syria, Cappadocia or in the Cyclades. I do not need to mention countries nearer our lands. Truly, dear sirs, it would be well to consider beforehand what dangers and dissensions might arise for Christianity if one were not in harmony and agreement with the whole community in these matters. For you see, as also a heathen called Sallust in "Jugurtha" testifies, that small things arise from unity, but from dissension great things decrease and fall away. Therefore my advice would be, not to consider anything of these affairs which pertain to the whole Church, but to save them for a general council. And although Master Ulrich refers to Bibles in Hebrew, Latin and Greek, and thereby consoles himself, which Scripture also those here present being taught sufficiently well in the three languages should examine, and such Scripture as is pertinent to the case they should judge and consider, still I say, in the first place, that is not a small gift of God to (be able to) expound the above-mentioned languages, and I do not boast that I possess it. For these are especial gifts of God, as also Paul says to the Corinthians (xii. 7–10) : Unique datur manifestatio spiritus ad utilitatem, to each is given the manifestation of the spirit for use, to the one faith, to the other eloquence, to this one the interpretation of languages, etc. Of these graces or gifts I cannot boast of possessing any, as I know nothing of Hebrew, am not well taught in Greek, and understand Latin only tolerably.

For I am no orator or poet, and do not pretend to be. Finally I say, the evangelical and apostolical Scripture is not found in the wise, brilliant or flowery, smooth words, but in the power of God, as Paul says, 1 Cor. ii. 4. Thus, as before, it seems to me not to be sufficient that one apply or bring forward Scripture, but it is also important that one understand Scripture correctly. With that in view perhaps one should attend to such matters at the universities (as at Paris, Cologne or Lyons, or elsewhere), as I said before.

ANSWER OF MASTER ULRICH.

SIR VICAR: There is no further need of such smooth and round-about words. I desire that you tell me only with what portion of Scripture you convinced the priest imprisoned at Constance, clergyman of Fislisbach, that he was not a Christian, and brought him to a revocation of his error. This is the point upon which we desire to hear in kindness your answer. Show us simply where in the books heretofore cited by you in the matter of praying to the saints and of their intercession it is stated that they are our mediators. This we desire to know from you. Therefore I beg you for the sake of Christian love, do this with plain, unadulterated, divine Scripture, as you boast to have done in the case of the priest imprisoned at Constance. Indicate the chapter and answer the question as asked in simple words, saying here or there it is written. Then we will see if it is so, and in case we are persuaded and convinced of it we will gladly submit to instruction. There is no need of long speeches.* For your long quoting and citing of many writings of the ancients looks more like seeking the praise and favor of the audience than the furthering of the truth. Probably I also could bring in many narratives and essays of the ancients, but it is not to the point. We well know that many things were decided upon in times

* ["Upon Fathers and councils one no longer depends, unless they prove their case by the Scriptures." (Bullinger.)]

past by the fathers in council assembled which were afterward repealed and revoked by others who thought they assembled in the spirit of God, as is plainly found in the Nicene Council and that of Gangra,* in the first of which the clergy was allowed to marry, and all those who spoke against it were cursed, while the second decided upon the opposite.† It is also a fact that many times ordinances (*constitutiones*) have been issued

* [Held in the 4th century. Gangra was the capital of ten Asia Minor provinces of Paphlagonia.]

† [" 'Not a word is written concerning this in the canons of the council of Nicæa.' To be sure Zwingli said that Paphnutius in the council of Nicæa had been, by which Zwingli means that marriage at that time (although he partly errs) was permitted. Now in the council of Gangra you say in your report Zwingli had said it had been forbidden. How could you lose your memory in such fashion that you could write such? On the contrary he said that it had been permitted in the council of Gangra, and doubtlessly he based this upon another pamphlet, which he called 'Apologeticum,' and written in Latin quatering (see Latin version). Rogo nunc ut concilio parendum, etc. You do him wrong, now I must take his part. Furthermore beware, my pamphlet here will be read the sooner by those who are at Zürich and accepted as good. Zwingli also has referred to the Carthaginian council. In the first place I showed how there are two kinds of councils, namely, those of the general Christianity, which are called 'oecumenica' or 'universalia' in Greek and Latin; then the 'particularia.' Now it is never found that in the matter of faith the 'universalia' were ever opposed to each other. The Carthaginian council was only a special one. And to every bishop was left his free will and opinion; and only later the council of Nicæa was held by 318 Fathers, (thus) they may have had an honest excuse. Why have you omitted this report?" (Faber.) Heinrich Wolf answered thereupon: "Zwingli simply said that in a council Paphnutius with difficulty had secured permission for the marriage of the priests, also spoke well against such statutes. Now you come forward and say that he placed Paphnutius in the Nicæan council, although he said to-day (as I asked him about it) that he had never read about a council which had forbidden marriage, but about popes 500 years after the birth of Christ. But since the papists speak so consistently about the Nicæan council he made his point, how he really had never read carefully the history of this council, and thus had believed you papists. And you have brought forth the Nicæan council, and not Zwingli; then you opposed the Gangrensian council by saying that it was not a general one." ("Gyrenrupfen.")]

THE FIRST ZURICH DISPUTATION. 69

and ordered by the fathers in council to which their successors paid no heed. For example, that the mother of God conceived without sin was decided in public council at Basel, and yet no preaching monk is so foolish as to speak against it. Also many ordinances or rules of the fathers are found which were changed afterwards, especially in our times, and otherwise not kept or given up by the influence of money, so that such things are allowed which were formerly forbidden by the fathers. From this we can see that councils have not always acted in the spirit of the Holy Ghost, but sometimes according to human will and judgment, which is of course forbidden by divine Scripture. For the Holy Ghost does not say this to-day and to-morrow that, but its ordinances and regulations must remain everlasting and changeless. The pious fathers whom we call holy are not for that reason to be dishonored and attacked as to their piety or holiness. For nothing is easier or from native weakness more natural than to err, especially when out of conceit or over-hasty judgment depended upon their own opinion instead of upon the rule of God's Word. This all shows us that the pillars and supports of many of the fathers, as Augustine and Jerome, are not in harmony in their writings; that often the one thinks not only something else, but by Scripture proves the contrary. But as to the fact that they say it would be too bad if we Christians, and especially our forefathers, had lived so long in error, since from the time of Gregory the intercession of the saints has been accepted and kept, I say that it is not a question of *when* a thing begun in the Church. We know well that the litany was established in the time of Gregory and kept down to the present. But all we desire is to hear the Scripture upon which my Lord Vicar bases his recommendation that we should pray to the saints. For if such a custom began at the time of Gregory then it did not exist before,* and if before that time men were Christians

* ["I said even more about the time further back, especially in the time of Cyprian, 1300 years ago, there was intercession of the saints; yes, I shall try it still further back." (Faber.)]

and were saved, though they did not hold to the intercession of the saints, and perhaps knew little of it, then it follows that they did not sin who believed in Christ alone and did not consider the intercession of the saints.

For we know really from the Scriptures that Jesus Christ alone is the mediator between us and God, his heavenly Father, as has been stated before. Furthermore, I say that many learned men have spoken and fought against the ordinances, and especially against the so-called holy ones, useless and superfluous customs, also against great power and tyrannical show; but the great moguls, popes, bishops, monks and prelates, do not wish to be touched on their sore spots, and tell the unlearned crowd that their rule has been erected by God, and that He has ordered them to govern thus, hence all those opposing, or only having such thoughts, are not alone heretics and shut out from the rest of Christianity, but as cursed and the property of the devil they have been exiled, outlawed, condemned, and some have been sentenced to the stake and burnt. Therefore, dear brethren, although one says to you—perhaps in order to frighten you the more—how our pious parents and ancestors have erred, and on account of such heresy have been deprived of salvation: I tell you (on the contrary) that the decisions and judgment of God are hidden from mankind and incomprehensible to us, and no one should impiously concern himself therewith. God knows that we all have faults and are sinners, yet through His mercy He makes up our deficiencies and enables us to accomplish something, yea even such deeds for which perhaps our strength alone is not sufficient. Consequently it is in no wise befitting that we desire to judge and pronounce upon the secrecy of God in such matters. He knows full well where He may overlook and pardon, and we must not interfere with His decision and compassion, in which manner He has treated and dealt with each one. We trust in Him as our eternally good Father, who can, as 2 Peter ii. 9 says, well protect His own, and deliver the godless over to eternal suffering. Nor does it do any good to say that there are few people who will not feel comfort through the intercession of the saints. I say, where such help comes from God, we will not judge why God acts thus and helps man in such fashion as He desires. But where this occurs from infatuation by the devil as a judgment of God upon the unbelieving man, what shall we say then? Ye know well what work the devil has sometimes done in many places, which if it had not been obstructed would have resulted in great deception and injury of all Christendom. Furthermore, that is an evil teaching which proclaims that other nations will not consider us Chritsians if we do not obey the ordinances, *i. e.*, the laws of former times, as this is ordered and demanded by the papal decrees. For indeed there are many ordinances in the canons of the Roman bishops and popes which the aforesaid nations do not obey and still they are none the less Christians. Concerning the above I shall make use of the following short comparison: Ecclesiastical property is (as they say) in the power of the Roman pope, and he may bestow and grant the estates to whomsoever he pleases. Now look ye how this ordinance is obeyed in Spain and France; there the ecclesiastical benefices or estates are not granted to any foreigner, let the pope say what he pleases. But we foolish Germans must permit the sending of stablemen and mule-drivers from the papal court to take possession of our benefices and curacies and be our spiritual guides, although they are ignorant of and know naught concerning the Scriptures, and if we do not tolerate this we are disobedient to the Christian Church. But the above-mentioned nations do not obey the ordinance and still are without question pious Christians. Hence, Sir Vicar, I desire that you do not make use of bombastic speeches, which do not even bear upon my question, but, as I have asked before, tell at once where is written in the Scriptures concerning the holy invocation and intercession of the Virgin Mary, as you pretended you could show in Exodus, Baruch, etc. That is what we desire to hear. Hence answer in regard to this obscure point. We do not ask what has been accomplished or decided in this or that council. This all does not bear upon the matters which we ask you, otherwise we will be speaking for a month concerning these matters.

VICAR.

Gentlemen: I am accused of speaking very evasively and not to the point. I have excused myself before for not being able to speak eloquently, and I have also listened to you (Master Ulrich). [Here Master Ulrich interrupted: There is no need of so much teasing.] That you accuse me of seeking to add to my own fame rather than the advancement of truth I cannot prevent. I wished to assist in making peace and doing the best. But when Master Ulrich claims that I say much concerning things settled by councils of yore, and then changed by later ones, I say that there are two kinds of councils referred to. Some are known as " concilia universalia " (these are common or general gatherings), where many of the bishops and Christian leaders meet, as in the four foremost councils, Nicæa, Constantinople, Ephesus and Chalcedon, and some others. Whatever was accomplished and done in these has never been entirely changed by the others, but has been preserved like the Gospel. Some are known as " concilia particularia," of which there have been many, not consisting of all the fathers of the common parishes about, but of special ones, as was the council of Gangra, and many others. In these probably something has at times been settled which later, perhaps not without cause, has been decided otherwise. But it never has been that the priests were permitted to have wives. And although the Eastern Church, especially in Greece, wished to have this considered just, the pious fathers of other nations would not permit this and forbade it, considering from weighty reasons * that the marriage of priests is detrimental to the

* ["Although I said that I wanted to defend it well against the destroyers of divine gifts and services. But I did not say it. You thought I would say it. Although I did not think of the pope, the ceremonies and many other things, it is no proof that such are useless." (Faber.)]

churches and not for the good of the service of God, as also Saint Paul says, 1 Cor. vii. 32 : " Qui sine uxore," etc. " He that is unmarried careth for the things that belong to the Lord." vii. 27 : "Solutus es ab," etc. "Art thou loosed from a wife? seek not a wife !" There he speaks of those who serve the Gospel as priests. Id. vii. 20 : " Let every man abide in the same calling wherein he was called." Such and many other causes have induced the holy fathers not to allow and permit marriage to priests. Indeed it could not happen without partition of the property of the churches.

ZWINGLI.

Marriage forbidden to priests is not found everywhere, as one pretends, but imposed by man contrary to a divine and just law. This is evident, first of all, in St. Paul, 1 Cor. vii. 2 : " Nevertheless, to avoid fornication, let every man have his own wife, and let every woman have her own husband." Since he says " every " undoubtedly he does not wish the priests to be excluded. For he confirms and refers to the marriage of priests, especially in writing to 1 Timothy iii. 2 [4] : "A bishop (*i. e.*, priest) then must be blameess, the husband of one wife, vigilant, sober, of good behavior, given to hospitality, apt to teach, etc. One that ruleth well his own house, having his children in subjection in all gravity." In the same fashion he speaks, iii. 8, concerning the deacon, whom we call evangelist. And Paul also writes to Titus i. 5, 6 : " For this cause left I thee in Crete, that thou shouldest set in order the things that are wanting, and ordain elders (whom we call priests or deacons) in every city, as I had appointed thee : If any be blameless, the husband of one wife, having faithful children," etc. Undoubtedly the holy Paul, inspired by the Holy Ghost, recognized our inability and incapacity to remain chaste by our own will except through the grace of God. Hence he says in the afore-mentioned place, 1 Cor. vii. 7 : " For I would that all men were even as I myself," and i. 1. : " It would be good for man to be thus," but Paul adds, vii. 7, and says: "But every man hath his proper gift of God, one after this manner and another after that." Therefore Paul places no restriction upon the marriage of priests, and indeed writes expressly: "A bishop (*i. e.*, priest) and a deacon shall have a sober wife and well-bred children;" and furthermore he permits marriage to all people, and says, 1 Cor. vii. 28, 7 : "But and if thou marry thou hast not sinned. But every man hath his proper gift of God," etc. It is evident from this that marriage is not forbidden to priests by divine law, and that chastity is to be maintained, not by means of our resolutions, but with the help of the grace of God. This real truth and wisdom of God Christ also proves to us, Matt. xix. 10, 12 : " His disciples say unto him, if the case of the man be so with his wife it is not good to marry. But he said unto them, all men cannot receive this saying save they to whom it is given. And there be eunuchs which have made themselves eunuchs for the kingdom of heaven's sake (that is, due to the evangelical doctrine). He that is able to receive it let him receive it!" Do you hear that Christ says here that it is not possible for all people to keep chastity except such as have received it from God? Hence He does not forbid the twelve apostles to marry. Nor did God in vain give Adam a woman as helpmate; He could have given him a man as helpmate if He had wished to keep him chaste. But He said: "Crescite et multiplicamini!" And although this is known to every one, still the pope is able, by means of his ordinance, to demand from each priest or other ecclesiastic chastity and that he be unmarried contrary to divine law, and he can weigh down the poor consciences corrupted by sin and shame; and he permits public offense and sin contrary to the sunny and pure ordinance of God. I say that I know of no greater scandal in Christendom than that marriage is forbidden to priests (I am speaking about the pastors ; the others let them lie, whatever they do), yet they are allowed to commit fornication publicly as long as they give money.

They pretend that if the priests had wives the property of the churches would be divided and disappear. My God, what sort of a reason is this? Do we then never spend the property of the churches uselessly? We will our real and movable property to the illegitimate wives and children, if we have any, contrary to God's will. What would that harm the benefice if a priest had a dear wife and well-bred children brought up for the service of God out of the benefice? The benefice could retain its property and income, which it has, although the priests may at times have mismanaged. Priests have not always been forbidden to marry. This is proved by Pelagius,* in which is found a decree of the pope (Diss. XXXI., cap. ante trienn.) that the subdeacons of Sicily shall forsake their wives, which they had taken in accordance with the divine ordinance, and shall not have intercourse with them; which statute Gregory I. later on rescinded. Consequently if it was ordered in former times by Pelagius that priests shall have no wives, and this was rescinded by Gregory, then it could not always have been as at present, but the law must have been made by man, which God never required to be kept.

VICARIUS.

It has never happened since the time of Tertullian and the council of Nicæa, 1200 years ago, that priests had wives or were allowed to have them

Thereupon one of the council at Zurich said: But they are allowed to have mistresses.

The vicar was astonished for a while, but resumed: It is true that the subdeacons in Sicily who had taken wives previously contrary to the custom of the Roman churches were permitted by the aforesaid Gregory to keep them. But only on the condi-

---

* Alvarus Pelagius, bishop of Silves, Portugal, d. at Seville, 1352, whose *Summa de planctu Ecclesiæ* ("The Chief Points of the Church's Complaint"), written in 1332, published, Ulm 1474, Venice 1560, is a frank statement of the disorders of his time and a plea for the exaltation of the Papal See.

tion that in future no one would be consecrated who would not pledge himself to remain unmarried and chaste. Thus also it was resolved in the council at Carthage that no bishop, priest or deacon should have intercourse with women, but remain chaste without wife. Hence I say that it will be no easy matter to show that marriage was ever permitted to priests.*

ZWINGLI.

And even if you say since the time of the apostles, still marriage is not forbidden to priests by divine ordinance, but allowed

---

* ["Don't you recollect that I said I do not like to speak concerning the marriage of priests? On account of this I have kept quiet and have omitted to state a better reason. But where have you hidden the fact that I said that from the time of the apostles one does not read that one who was consecrated as subdeacon, deacon, priest or bishop could marry again after his wife had died? Did I not say further that it is thus understood, not alone in the Western, but also in the Eastern Church—in Crete, Corcyra, etc., also in India, in the case of the Presbyter John, and among the Russians? so that any one who took a virgin as wife may be consecrated as priest, but that if she die that he can take no more; in the same manner if he has no wife before he is consecrated he can take none after the consecration; this I have shown. Why do you omit this? It was indeed necessary for you to include the subtile, honorable interruption of one who spoke about the prostitutes; and you also placed Gutschenkel † as a character in the comedy. Since the good Master Ulrich consoles himself much in his speeches and writings with a text which he found in XXVII. dist. c., 'Si quis discernit,' which is claimed to have been made in Gangrensian council, know then that there were not more than 16 bishops in that council; these made 19 canons against the majority that even desired to abolish holy marriage. But therein they did not reject the state of virginity and widowhood, hence also the marriage of priests was not, as you think, admitted by the pious Fathers. They spoke about the priests who had wives before the consecration—and bethink yourself what councils over 18 bishops would prefer, even although they should prefer it were so, as it is not, as Zwingli says. Now see how the supplication issued by your and our common gracious lord of Constance shall be answered. About the marriage of priests I do not like to speak (several times repeated). Accusations of two wrong quotations were made." (Faber.)]

† The half-witted fellow mentioned above.

and permitted, as I have proved before. And that priests formerly had wives is sufficiently evident, since formerly many sons of priests have become popes and bishops, which could not have happened if they had not been born in wedlock. How is it that one always prefers human laws and human meddling, and always sets human traditions above the will of God? Although one finds that also the fathers have protested against many ordinances, and you know how vehemently the pious man Paphnutius * opposed such a statute and would not agree to marriage being forbidden to priests. Furthermore, Eusebius writes that some of the apostles had their wives with them, which facts are sufficient indications that the present custom was begun by people of later times, but that marriage was not forbidden by divine ordinance either to layman or priest. And although in the council of Nicæa, as you say, it was forbidden to priests to have wives, still what about that? In former times baptism by heretics was considered by many fathers as just and valid, as Cyprianus tells us, but later in the council at Carthage this was declared to be worthless and was set aside.

To such varied arguments of Master Ulrich the vicar had nothing more to oppose and say, except in regard to the baptism by heretics, and that on account of the following reasons: Master Ulrich has said that the baptism of heretics was considered valid

* Bishop of a city in Upper Thebais; had his right eye gouged out and his left knee-cap injured in the Maximian persecution (305), and was banished to the mines. He appeared in the Nicene Council 325, and was honored as a confessor. When it was proposed to enact a law which forbade the married clergy to continue to live with their wives, Paphnutius declared very earnestly that so heavy a yoke ought not to be laid upon the clergy; that marriage itself is honorable and the bed undefiled; that the Church ought not to be injured by an undue severity. "For all men," said he, "cannot bear the practice of rigid continence; neither perhaps would the chastity of the wife be preserved." He favored dissuading clergymen from marrying after ordination, but allowing those who had married prior to ordination to retain their wives. His own known virginity and his sufferings for the cause gave so great weight to his words that he was unanimously sustained by the Council.

by several, and thus referring to Cyprianus. But the vicar demanded that one should record the words of Master Ulrich, because he believes he may catch him in small matters, for Master Ulrich may not have been very careful in the use of his words. Therefore he also demands that a copy of Cyprianus should be brought, so that the dispute may be decided. But the vicar said: Supposing the words of Cyprianus are as I think, and not as you? And thereupon a quarrel arose, which had naught to do with the questions which the vicar had been called upon so often to answer. Therefore I have not taken pains to remember and note this. But if I understood the matter both were right. For Zwingli referred to those who had been baptized by heretics, who should, according to Cyprianus, be baptized again in the churches, which several thought was needless. But the vicar was speaking of those who once baptized by Christians had gone over to heresy and later on wished to reënter the Christian Church; these did not need another baptism, but merely absolution by the imposition of hands, etc. Several were, however, also opposed to this, as Cyprianus writes in his letters to Pompeius and to Quintinus.

After there had been considerable talk concerning this matter, Dr. Sebastian Hofmann,[*] of Schaffhausen, a member of the order of the Barefoot Monks, spoke thus: Learned, spiritual, honor-

[*] He was properly called Sebastian Hofmeister, or in the scholastic form Oikonomos. Because his father was a "wagner," *i. e.*, wheelwright, he was himself erroneously called Wagner, or in Latinized form Carpentarius. He was born at Schaffhausen in 1476; entered the Barefoot (Franciscan) monks there; studied in Paris the classical tongues and Hebrew, and came home in 1520 as a Doctor of the Sacred Scriptures, and the same year he taught in the Franciscan monastery in Zurich and so came in contact with Zwingli. He embraced the Reformation, and introduced it into Lucerne and into Schaffhausen (both 1523), whither persecution drove him. It is indeed as the Reformer of Schaffhausen that he is best remembered, yet his career there was brief, for in 1525 he had to leave that city. He preached in Zurich (1526) and taught Hebrew in Bern (1528), but died September 26, 1533, as preacher at Zofingen, thirty miles sontheast of Basel. Two of his writings were commonly attributed to Zwingli.

able, wise, favorable, gracious, dear gentlemen, it is necessary that I also speak in this matter. Last year I was lector at Lucerne, where, according to my best knowledge and belief, I preached, as I hope and know, nothing else except the word of God from the Scriptures, and in these sermons at Lucerne I have mentioned, like many others, the many useless customs of intercession and invoking of the saints and the mother of God, and I taught in accordance with the contents and teachings of the holy Scriptures. On account of such sermons, made, as stated above, at Lucerne, various accusations against me were sent to Constance, among which was the sermon about the invocation of the saints. I was accused of being a heretic, condemned, and therefore driven out of Lucerne. And now as my lord, the vicar, has pretended before and stated that the appeal and invocation of saints is founded upon the Scriptures and mentioned in the Old Testament, I pray for God's sake that the vicar, as he was wont to boast to have overcome the priest imprisoned at Constance, show the place, as formerly often had been asked of him, especially since on account of this I have been accused by my gracious lord at Constance of being a heretic, and I will accept it with many thanks and willingly allow myself to be taught in case I have perchance erred in my sermons, have not told the truth, or have misread or misunderstood the Scriptures.

ZWINGLI.

We know from the Old and New Testaments of God that our only comforter, redeemer, savior and mediator with God is Jesus Christ, in whom and through whom alone we can obtain grace, help and salvation, and besides from no other being in heaven or on earth.

THE VICAR, LAUGHING.

I well know that Jesus Christ alone is the comfort, redemption and salvation of all, and an intercessor and mediator between us and God, his heavenly Father, the highest round by which alone is an approach to the throne of divine grace and charity, according to Heb. iv. 16. Nevertheless one may perhaps attain the highest round by means of the lower.* It seems to me the dear saints and the Virgin Mary are not to be despised, since there are few who have not felt the intercession of the Virgin and the saints. I do not care what every one says or believes. I have placed a ladder against heaven; I believe firmly in the intercession of the much-praised queen of heaven, the mother of God, and another may believe or hold what he pleases.

ZWINGLI.

That would indeed be a foolish piece of business if one could arrive at the highest round without the lower or without work, or if he were on it to begin at the lowest. Sir Vicar, we do not dispute here concerning how one should appeal to the saints or what your belief is. We desire only that you show us it in the Gospel, as has been formerly often demanded and begged of you.

Thereupon Master Leo Jud † arose and spoke thus: Gracious, careful, honorable, wise, favorable, dear gentlemen, I have been made by you, gentlemen, here at Zurich, a people's priest and

---

* ["I said, one may do that. 'Must' and 'can,' are they not two different things? The debate was not about 'must,' but about 'can.' Did you not hear from me about the ladder of Jacob fastened to heaven on which are many rounds? Did you not hear how quickly and speedily Zwingli wished to swing himself up to the cross of Christ? Do you not think if he wished to go to the Lord on the cross that then rightly he would also have found Mary, John and the other people of the Gospel?" (Faber.)]

† Born at Gemar, near Rappoltsweilen (or Ribeauville), Elsass, thirty miles southwest of Strassburg, the child of a clerical marriage, 1482; studied at Basel; inclined first to pharmacy, but took up theology, and had Zwingli as his fellow-student under Thomas Wyttenbach; M. A., 1506; became deacon of St. Theodore's church, Basel; pastor of St. Pilt, four miles east of his birthplace; people's priest at Einsiedeln in succession to Zwingli, and at his suggestion, 1518; the same, and by the same influence, at St. Peter's, Zurich, 1522; coadjutor of Zwingli and Bullinger, particularly remembered as principal translator of the Zurich Bible; died in Zurich, June 19, 1542.

pastor, perhaps unwisely, in order to proclaim to you the word of God, the Gospel of Christ, which I shall try to do according to my best capabilities, in as far as the grace of God will assist me and the Holy Ghost aid me. But surely now many ordinances of man have been retained from long habit in the churches, and have intermingled with the Gospel, so that the clergy frequently have preached and commanded their keeping equally with the Gospel: yet I now declare that I shall not obey such human ordinances, but shall present and teach from love the joyful and pure Gospel, and whatever I can really prove from the Scriptures, regardless of human ordinance or old traditions, since such human ordinances, decreed by pope or bishop, have been here recognized and proved to be by the Articles * emanating from Master Ulrich to be entirely opposed to the Gospel and truth, and still there is no one here who desires or is able to say anything truthful or fundamental against him. And so although my Sir Vicar has pretended to prove and show by means of the Gospel the invocation and intercession of the saints, such has not yet been done, although frequently requested. Therefore I also pray to hear and to know from him where it is written in the afore-mentioned biblical books concerning the invocation and intercession of the saints. For perhaps also in my sermons, if God lends me grace, it will be declared and proclaimed that one should invoke to Jesus Christ alone, and only look to him for all compassion, all help, mercy and salvation, which shall be sought and demanded from no other being. Therefore, Sir Vicar, I desire that you teach me if I have erred, and report from the Gospel, showing place and location where it is written that the saints are to be invoked by us or that they are intercessors. Such I shall receive with many thanks, and will gladly allow myself to be taught by you.

* Referring to the Sixty-seven Articles issued by Zwingli for the basis of argument in the Disputation.

VICAR.

Ne Hercules quidem contra duos. Shall I strive with two? That was considered even too difficult for the strong Hercules (according to a proverb of the ancients). Dear Sir, I have nothing to do with you.

Leo: But I have something to do with you.

Vicar: I do not know who you are.

Leo: I shall gladly be your good friend in so far as you desire.

Vicar: That I shall not refuse, for I am not here to become an enemy of any one. If you are then my good friend, as you say, it will happen to us as to Socrates and Solon,* who also through argumentation became good friends.

Leo: Then you have one friend more than formerly.

To prevent such and other gibes Master Ulrich began to speak: Would to God that the saying, Ne Hercules quidem, etc., would be understood and followed as readily by some as it ordinarily is the custom to quote it. Sir Vicar, we desire to hear the quotation concerning the invocation and intercession of the saints, not such useless talk and nonsense.

VICAR.

It is the custom and usage of Christian churches, and is kept thus by all Christian folk confirmed by the litany and the canons missal,

* ["Look, how can you say that to excuse myself I quoted in the beginning the saying of Solon, how then it was written by the wise man Solon that when once he was sitting with scholars, who were debating, and Periander asked him whether he was silent from lack of words or because he was a fool, he answered no fool can keep quiet? Therefore I did not refer to Socrates (as you say), but to the saying of Xenocrates when he was one time asked why he alone kept still and allowed all the others to speak, he had answered that what I sometimes said I regretted, but that which I have not said that I have never regretted. Thus it happened, and not otherwise, and as a witness of the truth I cited the proverb: Audiens sapiens sapientior erit. And as another witness Zwingli interrupted the speech by saying that there was no need of fawning and hypocritical style. Now look how you have hit it?" (Faber.)]

that we appeal to the Virgin to intercede for us; this the mother of God herself says in the gospel of St. Luke. Ex hoc beatam me dicent: "All generations shall call me blessed," and her cousin Elizabeth addressed her in a friendly manner, saying: Unde mihi hoc, etc." And whence is this to me, that the mother of my Lord should come to me?" Likewise, "blessed art thou among women," etc. This also the maiden in the Gospel proves to us, who cries: "Blessed is the body which has borne thee, and blessed the breasts which thou hast sucked." [Interruption by Zwingli: We are not asking concerning the holiness and dignity of Mary, but concerning invocation and intercession.] We also sing daily: Sentiunt omnes tuum levamen. "All feel thy aid who honor thy memory."* But since my talk is held to be useless and foolish I will rather keep still.

Thus the vicar kept still and sat down, and then Doctor Martin from Tübingen arose, and spoke thus concerning these matters:

Dear Sirs: Much has been said here against the usage and ordinance of the Christian churches which has been decreed and ordered by holy councils and fathers assembled in the name of the Holy Ghost, which, moreover, long has been held without fault as a praised custom and long usage. To oppose and to object to it is a sacrilegious deed, for what has been decreed and resolved by the holy councils and fathers, namely, by the four councils, should be obeyed in Christian churches like the Gospel, as we have written in Diss. XV. For the Church assembled in council in the name of the Holy Ghost cannot err. Therefore it behooves no one to speak against their decrees and ordinances, as Christ bears witness in the holy Gospel when he says: Qui vos audit, me audit. "He that heareth you heareth me, and he that despiseth you despiseth me." Thus Christ speaks to his disciples and those who in place of the twelve apostles (as bishop and pope) govern the Christian churches; as then the Roman

* ["Show us that in the Scriptures; the rest is human nonsense." (Bullinger.)]

Church is now since many centuries the mother of all others, which is confirmed by words of Christ, Matt. xvi. 18, 19, as this is explained in Diss. X. and XII., cap. in nova et cap. quamvis. Concerning this there is here talked and quarreled against the invocation of the dear saints, just as if such honest and divine usage followed in Christendom many centuries were not founded upon the Scriptures, although St. Jerome in "Ad Jovianum" writes much concerning the intercession of the saints, and that this is advantageous to us he proves from the hopeful Scriptures. That we also receive true report concerning this from the canon of the holy mass, introduced by the old popes and bishops, and composed by Gregory and sung in all Christendom, proves that the intercession and invocation of the dear saints and the Virgin Mary is not considered useless. We also see this in our daily experience of miracles which occur everywhere. Consequently it seems wrong to me to consider and value such as useless and contrary to the Scriptures, etc.

ZWINGLI.

The good gentleman also intervenes and urges much in favor of the ordinances and usage of the Church, the fathers and councils gathered together and inspired by the Holy Ghost, and thinks one should not speak against them, etc. I say he will by no means prove that the councils have all been gathered in the name of the Holy Ghost for the purpose of all the ordinances which they made, since it has been proved before that they often have decreed contrarily, and have resolved upon, done and rescinded one thing to-day, to-morrow another, although the Holy Ghost is at all times alike, and does not oppose his decision once rendered. But when he says what has been decreed by councils and fathers is to be obeyed like the Gospels, I say what is as true as the Gospels and in accordance with the divine Spirit one is bound to obey, but not what is decreed in accordance with human reason. But as to what further than this is to be considered by pope or council as a mortal sin we do not think that we are in duty bound to treat that the same as the Gospels; we wish to be free, not to burden our consciences with that. E. g., if pope or council commands us, at risk of mortal sin, to fast, or to eat no egg, no butter, no meat, which God has not ordered us to do, Luc. x. 7; Col. ii. 16, 21, but is permitted and made voluntary, therefore we will not believe that such and other ordinances decreed by the councils are decreed by the Holy Ghost, and to be respected equally with the Gospel. How does it happen that they wish to order us to eat no cheese, no eggs, no milk, but stinking oil, with which they scarcely oil their shoes at Rome, and otherwise eat chickens and capons? But if one says it is thus written in the canons and decreed by the fathers, I say it is written otherwise in Paul, and Christ has given another and easier law. Now do we owe more obedience to God or the Holy Ghost, or to human beings? Acts v. 32. But when he declares the Church has decreed such, she cannot err, I ask what is meant by "Church?" Does one mean the pope at Rome, with his tyrannical power and the pomp of cardinals and bishops greater than that of all emperors and princes? then I say that this Church has often gone wrong and erred, as every one knows, since it has destroyed the land and its inhabitants, burnt cities and ravaged the Christian people, butchering them for the sake of its earthly pomp, without doubt not on account of a command of Christ and his apostles. But there is another Church which the popes do not wish to recognize; this one is no other than all right Christians, collected in the name of the Holy Ghost and by the will of God, which have placed a firm belief and an unhesitating hope in God, her spouse. That Church does not reign according to the flesh powerfully upon earth, nor does it reign arbitrarily, but depends and rests only upon the word and will of God, does not seek temporal honor and to bring under its control much territory and many people and to rule other Christians. That Church cannot err. Cause:

she does nothing according to her own will or what she thinks fit, but seeks only what the spirit of God demands, calls for and decrees. That is the right Church, the spotless bride of Jesus Christ governed and refreshed by the Spirit of God. But the Church which is praised so highly by the Papists errs so much and severely that even the heathens, Turks and Tartars know it well. But when he refers here to the words of Christ, Luke x. 16, "He that heareth you heareth me, and he that despiseth you despiseth me," and then refers this to pope, bishop, regents of the Roman churches, I say that such is not the meaning of Jesus Christ, that we should obey them in all things as they order. For Christ the Lord knew well that such great braggarts would sit upon the chair of Moses who would burden the necks of the poor with unbearable and heavy loads, which they themselves would not touch with a finger. Hence the saying, "He that heareth you heareth me," etc., will not serve for that for which the papists and sophists interpret it, but the right meaning is, as is also shown by what precedes and follows. When Christ sent his disciples to preach the Gospel in country and city he spake: "Go ye and preach," saying the kingdom of God is approaching, etc.. And later Christ said: "He that receiveth you receiveth me," as Matt. x. 40 says. This means they should preach His word and bring it to the people, but not human foolishness and law. For one serves the Lord in vain if one prefers human doctrine and decree. And may the good gentleman furthermore remember what Jerome writes in ad Jovinian concerning the invocation or intercession of the saints that he has not read correctly. For it is written ad Vigilantium; but how Jerome twists the Gospel in regard to invocation or intercession of the saints, as he does often in other places, that all know who read Jerome with good judgment.* Finally, in regard to the canon

* ["Zwingli said that if he were only half a man, stood on one leg and closed one eye, he would nevertheless yield not to Jerome." (Faber.) "Thereupon Heinrich Wolf said 'such words were never heard from his lips,

which is read in the mass, and in which invocation and intercession of the saints are referred to, I say one sees readily that the canon has not been made by one alone, but composed by several. For there are many useless words therein, as haec dona, haec munera, etc., from which may be inferred that it has not been made by one scholar. The apostles never celebrated mass thus; one also finds that in several instances the custom of the canon is different from ours, which I shall point out and shortly prove, if God wills it. Concerning the miracles which are done by the saints we have spoken before. Who knows through whom or why God decrees this? * We should not attribute this so readily on account of our unbelief to the saints when we hesitate concerning Christ and run to those creatures for help. This all is proof of a weak faith and small hope in Jesus Christ, whom we do not rightly and entirely trust. Why do we flee from Him and

yea never thought of during his lifetime.' To be sure, when you referred to Jerome in regard to the intercession of the saints, he said the argument which Jerome uses there has no basis in the Scriptures." ("Gyrenrupfen.")]

* ["You have omitted that Zwingli even spoke against the public Gospel: 'when one says that the saints accomplished miracles then the devil has done it.'" (Faber.) "About the intercession of the saints he promises a separate book: 'the whole heavenly host will be with me, without suppressing Christ, but rather let him be mediator.' Luchsinger answers: He (Faber) thinks because Zwingli said something about the wrong craze for miracles, therefore no one should remember that any more, and each one think perhaps something has been said about it; it doubtlessly was as Hans Heyerli (Faber) said. The matter is this: Hans Heyerli and D. Martin Blansch, of Tübingen, wished to prove the intercession of the saints by means of the miracles (which has all occurred now in a roundabout manner, for as every one knows they have attacked no article). Yes, the saints have done miracles. Zwingli answered: Miracles are not a sign of divinity, as Christ himself declares, Matt. vii. 22, but where real miracles do occur through the saints God does them himself, never the saints, as St. Peter speaks in the Acts iii. But there occur many miracles by the aid of the devil, so Matt. xxiv. 24: He also accomplishes miracles, and changes himself into the shape of an angel of light. Thus Zwingli spoke, and that fool distorts it thus." ("Gyrenrupfen.")]

seek aid from the saints, especially as we do not recognize certainly from the Scriptures that they are our intercessors?

After this Dr. Sebastian,* from Schaffhausen, a member of the order of the Barefoot Monks, arose and began to admonish the assembled council that they should manage and protect the evangelical doctrine as until now, since there was no one there who could bring forward, upon frequent requests, anything more definite from the Scriptures. But he could not finish; the vicar interrupted and said :

Dr. Sebastian, you should keep still and not speak thus. You know well what you promised my gracious master; it does not behoove a man to be so vacillating, to be moved like a reed by the wind ; you had not promised that before.

Answered the aforesaid Dr. Sebastian : Dear gentlemen, what I have promised the bishop that I have faithfully and honorably kept, but his people have not fulfilled and carried out what they promised to me; that you may testify what I have said here in public.

After this speech there arose another doctor, lector and preacher from Bern, of the order of the Barefoot Monks,† and admonished the wise council of Zurich, speaking as follows :

Honorable, careful, wise, gracious, favorable gentlemen of Zurich, your intention and opinion, published in all places by means of open letter for the aid of the Gospel, pleases me well, and praised be God that you are the people to further and not to obstruct the word of God, and pray God that He will not turn away and cause your wisdom to desert from such a godly under-

* Dr. Sebastian Hofmeister.

† Sebastian Meyer, born at Neuenburg on the Rhine, in Elsass, twenty miles north of Basel, 1465; studied at Basel and in Germany; became D. D.; entered the Franciscan order; taught in monasteries in Strassburg and Bern; was a rather violent friend of the Reformation. He accepted Lutheran views on the Eucharist, and died in Strassburg, 1545, after preaching in Bern and Augsburg as well as there.

taking, and that He will give and lend you power and might, strength and comfort, that you will be frightened by no temporal power, whether of pope, bishop or emperor, but so act in these matters that it will redound to God in the future and your eternal praise. And do not mind that you are a small body and few. I do not say this to scorn you, but I mean it thus, that you are not equal to a whole kingdom and are considered too few to struggle against so many nations. Remember that God has always by means of the smallest and weakest caused His divine word and will to appear in the world, keeping the same hidden from the great sages of this world. Therefore fear not those who can injure the body; they cannot harm the soul. Do not mind that there are now opposed to the truth of the Gospel bishop, pope and sophists. Thus is it considered by God to make the wise of this world ignorant, and cause the truth to be made clear by the simple. Therefore I beg your wisdom to remain steadfast in the word of God, which I shall also faithfully report to my lords of Bern, whose preacher I am, not in the cathedral, but a lector of the order of Barefoot Monks, and I shall sing your honor and praise. Then he sat down again.

After this the mayor of Zurich again exhorts if any one wishes to say more in regard to these matters he should do it. My lords, he says, are tired of sitting. It will also soon be time to dine.

Then arose a canon of Zurich, by name Master Jacob Edlibach, and spoke thus:

Now listen, dear sirs: My good friend and brother, Master Ulrich, has before exhorted, in the name of Christian love, all those who have anything against him to speak. Now I have had a dispute with him concerning several matters and sayings, but the same was finally brought by both of us before the chapter, where it was settled, so that I thought it was over and should be referred to by no one any more. But now, since Master Ulrich has exhorted those who have spoken against him so frequently to step forth in the name of God, I have thought he may mean me also. Hence I say if Master Ulrich desires that that which was treated of between me and him remain in the knowledge of my lords of the chapter I am satisfied, and shall refer to it no more. For the matter is bad and worthless; also I know naught concerning Master Ulrich, except as a good friend and brother of the chapter. But in so far as he does not wish this, and urges me on, then I shall bring it before you gentlemen. For there are some behind there inciting and saying in scorn one dare not speak.

ZWINGLI.

Dear sirs: I had earnestly resolved to call all those here three times by name who have accused me of being a heretic and the like, but I had really forgotten it now, and furthermore I would never have thought of the good gentleman, Master Jacob Edlibach. It is simply this, I did treat with him concerning a matter before the prior and chapter, which I did not think necessary to bring, indeed would never have thought of bringing forward here. But since he himself, uncalled for, arises and desires to refer to and settle the matter here, I am well satisfied.

MASTER JACOB.

It is of no consequence. I came to Master Ulrich's house and he satisfied me, and although not entirely, still I am satisfied. I know nothing concerning him, except all good. I consider him a good gentleman and brother, hence if he wishes to leave matters as they have been settled before the prior and chapter, I am entirely content.

ZWINGLI.

You may well refer to it here; I am well satisfied, and I had rather have it before these gentlemen, since you yourself reported it.

But there were several there, perhaps relatives of the aforesaid Master Jacob, who said and thought that Master Ulrich ought to act more politely, since one had scarcely incited Master Jacob to speak.

To this Master Ulrich answered that he had never thought of the said Master Jacob, nor would it have occurred to him that he should speak concerning this, etc.

Thus there arose a dispute; some of the councilors wanted the matter to be settled before the chapter, since it had been commenced there; the others thought that it should be tried in the presence of the scholars and gentlemen; but finally the matter was no more thought of and thus quieted, perhaps left to the chapter and thus remained unreferred to. This I report (although not serving much to the purpose) that I may not be accused of not understanding and refuting all speeches and opposition which occurred at that time.*

* ["How could you say truthfully that you have reported and understood all speeches and rebuttals, when I show to you that you have wronged not only me, but others, also Zwingli. You have omitted from my statements two quotations, with their additions, Matt. xxviii. 20: 'I am with you,' etc., and John xiv. 16: 'I will pray the Father, and he shall give you another Comforter,' etc. Do you know now what I said thereupon? Since the appealing to the saints has gone on, also the mass has been held as a sacrifice throughout the whole of Christendom, not only now for a thousand, but for thirteen and fourteen hundred years, and if it were not true or righteous, then Christ would have wickedly forgotten us and the eternal truth; yes, he would have badly kept his word. But he has said: Behold this is a mystery; nor has he also said: Only after 1000 or 1200 years shall I first come again to my bride the churches. He said: Every day unto the end of the world. And although we did not heed these words of Christ, regardless of the fact that his words are everlasting, according to Isaiah, and he alone is the truth, and furthermore cannot lie, according to St. Paul, and he is the one whom St. John calls the faithful and true, and sooner will heaven and earth perish rather than his words, still we would have the other promise of the Holy Ghost, who, it has been promised, will remain with us unto eternity. Hence I do not in great affairs carelessly leave or desert from the Church, but I entrust that rather to Christ. Now what I report has been kept by the Church for so many centuries, hence I would be very careful, since the two things in regard to the saints and the mass are not contrary to the Gospel, and

After this the mayor of Zurich permitted every one who did not belong to the council to go to his lodging and dine, until further request, for it was now approaching noon. But the councilors the aforesaid mayor ordered to remain, perhaps to consult further concerning this.* Thus they arose, and many of the strangers went to their lodging. This much was done in the forenoon.

After all had eaten they were told to appear again in the city hall to hear the decision made by the wise council of Zurich.†

After all had gathered, there was publicly read before the council as is written hereafter:

When in the name of the Lord and upon the request of the mayor, council and great council of the city of Zurich, and for the reasons contained in the letters sent to you, you had obediently appeared, etc., and when again a year having passed since the honorable embassy of our gracious Lord of Constance, on account of such matters as you have heard to-day, was here in the city of Zurich before the mayor, small and great councils, and when these matters having been discussed in various fashions

I also can prove it with the Scriptures, and thus I feel like the honest old peasants: when one wishes to abolish their old traditions and praiseworthy usages, which are not contrary to God, they do not like to obey and allow it. And thus I feel in regard to the said sayings, I trust to Christ and God and the Holy Ghost that thus far they have not deserted us, and I say also agree with St. Jerome, that in regard to these matters I shall rightly hold to the faith which I have received from the maternal breast. Although the doctrine of yourself and your brethren would be very acceptable to me, for I would not be allowed to pray, fast or do other good works, but if I did them I should commit a sin, therefore I would probably go to heaven. But since perchance I cannot ask much, therefore I do not wish to lose the intercession of the saints, and especially of the Virgin Mary." (Faber.)]

* ["Bullinger puts here the word of the mayor: And the sword with which he from Fislisbach was murdered does not wish to appear to fight."]

† ["Which has been decided upon in accordance with the debate held." (Bullinger.)]

THE FIRST ZURICH DISPUTATION. 93

it was reported that our gracious Lord of Constance was about to call together the scholars in his bishopric, also the preachers of the neighboring bishoprics and parishes, to advise, help and treat with them, so that a unanimous decision might be reached and each one would know what to rely on, but since until now by our gracious Lord of Constance, perhaps from good reasons, not much has been done in this matter, and since more and more disputes are arising among ecclesiasts and laymen, therefore once more the mayor, council and great council of the city of Zurich, in the name of God, for the sake of peace and Christian unanimity, have fixed this day, and for the advantage of the praiseworthy embassy of our gracious Lord of Constance (for which they gave their gracious, high and careful thanks) have also for this purpose by means of open letter, as stated above, written, called and sent for all secular clergy, preachers and spiritual guides, together and individually, from all their counties into their city, in order that in the examination they might confront with each other those mutually accusing each other of being heretics. But since Master Ulrich Zwingli, canon and preacher of the Great Minster in the city of Zurich, has been formerly much talked against and blamed for his teachings, yet no one, upon his declaring and explaining his Articles, has arisen against him or attempted to overcome him by means of the Scriptures, and when he has several times also called upon those who have accused him of being a heretic to step forward, and no one showed in the least heresy in his doctrines, thereupon the aforesaid mayor, council and great council of this city of Zurich, in order to quell disturbance and dispute, upon due deliberation and consultation have decided, resolved, and it is their earnest opinion, that Master Ulrich Zwingli continue and keep on as before to proclaim the holy Gospel and the correct divine Scriptures with the spirit of God in accordance with his capabilities so long and so frequently until something better is made known to him. Furthermore, all your secular clergy, spiritual guides and preachers in your cities and counties and estates shall undertake and preach nothing except what they can defend by the Gospels and other right divine Scriptures; furthermore, they shall in no wise in the future slander, call each other heretic or insult in such manner. Those which seem contrary and do not obey will be restrained in such manner that they must see and discover that they have committed wrong. Done the Thursday after Carolus, in the city of Zurich, on the 29th day of January, in the year 1523.

Thereupon Master Ulrich Zwingli arose and spoke thus: * God be praised and thanked whose divine word will reign in heaven and upon earth. And you, my lords of Zurich, the eternal God doubtlessly will also in other affairs lend strength and might, so that you may in future advance and preach the truth of God, the divine Gospel, in your country. Do not doubt that Almighty God will make it good and reward you in other matters. Amen.

Whether this decision having been read pleased the vicar of Constance or not I really don't know, for he spoke thus:† Dear gentlemen, much has been spoken to-day against the praiseworthy old traditions, usage and ordinance of the holy popes and fathers, whose ordinances and decrees have until now been held in all Christendom true, just and sinless.‡ To pro-

* ["Zwingli spoke with great joy after the aforesaid decision had been read." (Bullinger.)]

† ["And first here the vicar became angry, saying: My dear gentlemen, I read to-day Master Ulrich's Articles for the first time, which before I had had no time to glance over." (Bullinger.)]

‡ ["'You know that it is true that before I or all priests had come to Zürich no one knew your word, whereon the dispute was based, and I tell you that I would have thought sooner of death than that there should be a debate at Zürich concerning the intercession of the saints. Hence you probably marked well that I said I thought I had come to Zürich, but I see I am in Picardy, and this saying I explained to be from the here-

tect and maintain this I have offered myself to the high councils. But now when for the first time to-day I have looked and glanced through the Articles of Master Ulrich (for I have not read them before), it seems to me truly that these are wholly and entirely at variance with and opposing the ritual (*i. e.*, opposed to the praiseworthy splendor and glory of the churches done and decreed for the praise and honor of God), to the loss of the divine teaching of Christ. This I shall prove.

ZWINGLI.

Sir Vicar, do it. We would like to hear that very much.

VICAR.

It is written, Luke ix. 50: Qui non est adversum vos, etc. " He that is not against us is for us." Now these praiseworthy services or splendor of the churches (like fasting, confession, having festival days, singing, reading, consecrating,* reading mass and other similar things) have always been decreed and ordered by the holy fathers, not against God, but only for the praise and

---

tic Picard.† Hence although I was not prepared nor thought about the matter, still I desired to argue concerning it, and show wherewith I had proved the imprisoned priest to be in error whom you wished to make a bishop, so that you also might fall into the Arian heresy.' (Faber.) And before he said: 'Master Ulrich had published the 67 articles only a day before this session, and before any one at Constance or any other city knew a word of it, and Master Ulrich also admitted it may perchance have been issued too late.' Werner Steiner remarks in writing: 'These (the Articles) were handed to him by the pastor of Frauenfeld ‡ on the journey hither, about 2 or 3 days ago.' "]

* [From the saying of Luke ix. not six words have been quoted. ("Gymrupfen.")]

† Picard, the founder of an heretical sect of the Manichean order, the Picardists, in the 15th century. The customary charge of immorality was brought against them. It spread from its home in Picardy to France and Germany, finally to Bohemia, where it was ruthlessly suppressed by the great Hussite leader, Ziska, in 1421.

‡ Twenty-one miles northeast of Zurich.

honor of God Almighty, and it seems very strange and unjust to me to consider and refute them as though wrong.

ZWINGLI.

When my Sir Vicar speaks and quotes from the Gospel, "He that is not against us is for us," I say that is true. "Now the customs and ordinances of the Church are ordered and decreed by men, not against God," etc. Sir Vicar, prove that. For Christ always despises human ordinance and decree, as we have in Matt. xv. 1–9. When the Jews and Pharisees blamed and attacked the Lord because his disciples did not obey the doctrine and ordinance of the ancients Christ said to them: "Why do ye also transgress the commandment of God by your tradition?" etc. And the Lord spoke further: "Ye hypocrites, well did Esaias prophesy of you, saying, This people draweth nigh unto me with their mouth and knoweth me with their lips, but their heart is far from me. But in vain do they worship me, teaching for doctrines the commandments of men." One sees here that God does not desire our decree and doctrine when they do not originate with Him, despises them, and says we serve Him in vain, which also St. Paul shows to us when he writes thus: Dear brethren, let no man beguile you by human wisdom and deceit, in accordance with the doctrine or decree of men, in accordance with the doctrines of this world, and not those of Christ. "Let no man therefore judge you in meat, or in drink, or in respect of a holiday, or of a new moon, or of the Sabbath days. Which are a shadow of things to come," etc. Col. ii. 16 ff. God wants from us His decree, His will alone, not our opinion. God the Lord cares more for obedience to His word (although they use the word "obedience" for human obedience) than for all our sacrifices and self-created church usages, as we have it in all the divine writings of the prophets, twelve apostles and saints. The greatest and correct honor to show to God is to obey His word, to live according to His will, not according to our ordinances and best opinion.

VICAR.

Christ said, according to John xvi. 12 : " I have yet many things to say unto you, but ye cannot bear them now. Howbeit when he, the Spirit of truth, is come, he will guide you into all truth." Much has been inaugurated by the holy fathers inspired by the Holy Ghost, and especially the fasts and the Saturday by the twelve apostles, which also is not described in the Gospel, in which doubtlessly the Holy Ghost taught and instructed them.*

ZWINGLI.

Sir Vicar, prove from the Scriptures that the twelve apostles have inaugurated Saturday and fasts. Christ said in the aforesaid place the Spirit of God will teach them all truth, without doubt not human weaknesses. For he spoke according to John xiv. 26 : " The Holy Ghost, whom the Father will send in my name, he shall teach you (the twelve apostles are meant) all things, and bring all things to your remembrance (advise and recall) whatsoever I have said unto you." As if he said undoubtedly, not what you think fit, but what the Holy Ghost teaches you in my name in accordance with the truth, not with human thoughts. Now then the holy apostles have never taught, inaugurated, ordered and decreed otherwise than as Christ had told them in the Gospel. For Christ said to them, ye are my friends if ye do that which I have decreed and commanded. This the dear disciples diligently did, and did not teach otherwise than as the right Master had sent them to teach and instruct, which is proven by the epistles of St. Paul and St. Peter. Hence your arguments cannot avail anything. For that I can say truly that I could name more than sixty in this room from among my

* ["Also the saying John xvi. 12 I did not refer to, for I knew the verse did not belong here; just as little did I say about fasting Saturdays." (Faber.) Hereupon Heinrich Wolf maintains he referred to the quotation from John xvi.: Christ still had many things to say to the disciples, but they could not bear it now, and Zwingli answered him, and showed how he had distorted the word of Christ. (" Gyrenrupfen.")]

lords, laymen not learned in the Scriptures, who all could refute your argument as presented until now, and by means of the Gospel overcome and refute.

VICAR.

Very well, Master Ulrich, do you admit that, that one should only keep what is writ in the Gospel, and nothing besides? Do you admit that?

ZWINGLI.

Sir Vicar, I pity you that you present such sophistical, hair-splitting or useless arguments. Perhaps I could also indulge in such devices, perchance I have also read it formerly in the sophists, hence I do not wish to be entrapped by such subterfuges and tricks. I shall answer and argue with the pure Scriptures, saying there it is written. That is befitting a scholar, to defend his cause by the Scriptures.

VICAR.

You have read in St. Paul that he accepted and taught traditions which formerly were not written in the Gospel.* [Zwingli

* ["That I said and say still, that we are bound to hold many things that are not openly written, but which the Church holds and we believe, and furthermore have been reported by the teachers of the first churches as having come to us by order of the 12 apostles; thus I wished to prove that the forty days' fast, also the Sunday which in the Apocalypse St. John calls 'diem dominicam,' was decreed by the 12 disciples; if we do not wish to despise, depose or suppress them, then it is fitting that what so many centuries by Christendom generally, also by the heretics, has been held we should also keep, even if it be not openly printed in the Scriptures." Furthermore he remarks: "It is a harmful error not to admit anything unless it be expressly described in the Scriptures. The Sadduceans also denied the resurrection because it was not expressed in the Scriptures. I praise you all that you preach the Gospel and St. Paul, for that is the right rock. But what we have also from the time of the 12 apostles you should not cast so carelessly aside. If your speech were true we would be obliged to leave the 'symbolo apostolorum,' the 'homoousio,' yes from the persons in the Godhead, from free will; we no more could believe that Anna was the mother of Mary," etc. (Faber.)]

interrupts: That we wish to hear.] For when he inaugurated among the Corinthians the custom of the sacrament as he had received it from the Lord he said among other things: Cetera, cum venero, disponam. 1 Cor. xi. 34. "And the rest will I set in order when I come." There St. Paul announces that he will further teach them to honor and to use the sacrament. But that such was true, and that the twelve apostles gave instructions, presenting them as traditions which were not decreed by the Gospel, I shall prove from St. Paul to the Thessalonians. Master Ulrich interrupts, asking: Where is it written? The vicar answers: You will find it in the second chapter. Zwingli says: We will look at it. But it is not there; we will look for it in the last epistle. But very well, continue. The vicar answers: Thus says St. Paul: Nos autem debemus gratias agere, etc. 2 Thess. ii. 13–15. "But we are bound to give thanks always to God of you, brethren beloved, etc., because God hath chosen you to salvation, etc., through belief of the truth, whereunto he called you by our gospel, etc. Therefore, brethren, stand fast and hold the traditions (*i. e.*, teachings) which ye have been taught, whether by our word or our epistle." [Here Master Ulrich said: He is misusing the Scriptures; I shall prove it.] Saint Paul says here that one should stand fast and hold the traditions, whether emanating from his words or his epistle. This is proof that he taught and instructed that which formerly had not been written, but clearly and openly invented.

ZWINGLI.

In the first place, when he says St. Paul gave traditions to the people of Corinth which before had not been decreed, I say no, for he says in the same place: "For I have received of the Lord that which also I delivered unto you." But when he says: "And the rest will I set in order when I come," it does not mean what the vicar says; on the contrary he is punishing the Corinthians on account of misuse and mistake in the taking and use of the divine sacrament. For of the wealthy, who assembled in the churches for the sacrament, some overate themselves and became satiated, while the other poor people, at times hungry, had nothing to eat. This is what St. Paul complains of when he writes: What! have ye not houses to eat and to drink in? as if he were saying the sacrament is not for the necessity of the body, but as a food for the souls. Therefore St. Paul concludes: "And the rest will I set in order when I come." Not that he wishes to teach otherwise than as Christ has ordered him, but in order to stop and better their misuse does he say this, which the Word shows: Tradidi vobis, etc.

Secondly, since Sir Vicar pretends that human ordinance and teaching are to be held, this also is not written in the Gospel; he refers to St. Paul to the Thessalonians, where he writes: "Therefore, brethren, stand fast and hold the traditions which ye have been taught, whether by word or our epistle." I say Paul did not speak, teach, write or instruct in anything except what the Lord had ordered him. For he testifies everywhere, and also proves it to be true, to have written or preached naught except the Gospel of Christ, which God had promised before in the Scriptures of His Son through the prophets.*

VICAR.

Master Ulrich, you said in your Articles that the mass is no offering. Now I shall prove that for 1400 years "missal" has been considered a sacrifice and called an offering. For "missa" is a Hebrew word, known by us as sacrifice, and also the apostles were known as "missam sacrificium."

Zwingli: Sir Vicar, prove that. Vicar: To-day I spoke as a Vicar; now I speak as a John. Zwingli: Yes indeed; had you long before to-day taken off your vicar's hat it would have suited you well at times to-day; then one could have spoken

* ["And the traditions do not disagree with the Scriptures, so that when the apostles wrote one thing another was opposed to it." (Bullinger.)]

with you as with a John.* I say that you should prove from the Scriptures that the mass is a sacrifice, for, as St. Paul says, Heb. ix. 12, 25, 26, Christ not more than once was sacrificed, not by other blood, but " by his own blood he entered once into the holy place," etc., nor yet that he should offer himself often, as the high priests in the Old Testament had to do for the sin of the people, for then must Christ often have suffered. Likewise, St. Paul writes, Heb. x. 12, 14, " But this man after he had offered one sacrifice forever sat down on the right hand of God." Likewise, " For by one offering he hath perfected forever them that are sanctified." Likewise, By so much does this sacrifice surpass the sacrifices in the Old Testament fulfilled by the high priest, by so much more powerful is this declared to be that it was sufficient once for the sins of all people. Heb. vii. 22–27. Who is so unreasonable as not to note that Christ must never be sacrificed in the mass as a sacrifice for us when he hears that the

* [Hans Hab remarks: "Faber attacked the Articles severely, but could not prove that they are unchristian. It happened thus, when after dinner the decision was read: Just like the peasant boys, you first began in earnest after the matter was closed, and even then you did not wish to attack any Article, to make it unchristian by means of the Scriptures, as you attacked them, but you raised the Articles in your own hand and said: Now I do not wish to speak as a vicar, but as a John, and I say, Master Ulrich, that your Articles are not like unto the truth, and are not based upon the Gospel and the writings of the apostles." Zwingli answered: " Sir Vicar, if you had taken off your hat long ago one could have treated about something. But in answer to your speech I spoke thus: You shall prove your wicked speech with the deed, and do well and attack only one Article, so that we may not let this day pass by uselessly, for so well are these Articles founded that heaven and earth must break sooner than one of these Articles. Upon this you answered, as always before, this was not the place to debate, but you wished to debate in writing and have judges. Thereupon Zwingli answered he was indifferent whether one noted down everything that was spoken, but he wanted no judge over the word of God, for the word of God should judge the people, and not the people the word of God. About that you teased Zwingli, whether he would not take those of Zürich as judges? Zwingli replied, no—so much at this time, although much was still added thereto." ("Gyrenrupfen.")]

Holy Ghost speaks from the Scriptures, For not more than once (semel) by one offering he entered into the holy place; otherwise he must die often? Now matters have come to such a state that the papists have made out of the mass a sacrifice for the living and dead, contrary to the joyful Scriptures of God; they wish to protect this also, so that they may defend their name of scholar or their avarice. We also know well that "missa" does not come from Hebrew or Greek; but you present nothing from the Scriptures.

VICAR.

I will do that and prove it before the universities, where learned judges sit. And choose a place, be it Paris, Cologne or Freiburg, whichever you please; then I shall overthrow the Articles presented by you and prove them to be wrong.

ZWINGLI.

I am ready, wherever you wish, as also to-day I offered to give answer at Constance, if a safe conduct (as to you here) is promised to me and respected. But no judge I want, except the Scriptures, as they have been said and spoken by the Spirit of God; no human being, whichsoever it be; and before you overthrow one Article the earth must be overthrown, for they are the Word of God.

VICAR.

This is a queer affair. When, e. g., two are quarreling about an acre or about a meadow, they are sent before a judge. Him they also accept, and you refuse to allow these matters to come before a judge. How would this be if I should propose that you take my lords of Zurich as judges? Would you not accept these and allow them to judge?

ZWINGLI.

In worldly affairs and in quarrels I know well that one should go before the judges with the disputes, and I also would choose and have as judges my lords of Zurich, since they possess justice.

But in these matters, which pertain to divine wisdom and truth, I will accept no one as judge and witness except the Scriptures, the Spirit of God speaking from the Scriptures.

VICAR.

How would it be if you chose a judge and I also one, both impartial, be it here or somewhere else, would you not be satisfied what these two recognized and pronounced as true sentence?

Hereupon Sir Fritz von Anwyl, major-domo of the bishop of Constance, spoke:

Must we then all believe as those two, and not hold otherwise?

Hereupon there was a laugh, so that the vicar became silent and answered nothing. But when it had again become quiet the vicar spoke thus:

Christ in the Gospel * says, Matt. xxviii. 20, He will remain with us even unto the end of the world. In another place [Matt.], xxvi. 11, he says: "For ye have the poor always with you; but me ye have not always." Now if there were no one who decided concerning these sayings, who could know how one should grasp these two sayings thus opposed to each other? One must then have a judge.

ZWINGLI.

The Spirit of God decided itself from the Scriptures that the Lord is speaking of two kinds of presences, of the corporal and the spiritual. The Scripture speaks evidently of the corporal presence or bodily attendance of Christ, and declares that Christ died, was buried, arose on the third day, and having ascended to the heavens sits on the right of his Father. Hence one notices readily from the Scriptures how one shall understand that when the Lord says: "Me ye have not always." In the same fashion, when He says He will remain with us even unto the end of the world, the Scriptures teach that Christ is the word of God, the wisdom, the will of his heavenly Father, the truth, the way, the

* ["I shall not be with you always, and then." (Bullinger.)]

light, the life of all believers. Therefore one evidently sees that spiritually he remains with us unto the end of the world. Hence one needs no other judge besides the divine Scriptures; the only trouble is that we do not search and read them with entire earnestness.*

Thereupon Dr. Martin of Tübingen speaks, saying:

You interpret the Scriptures thus according to your judgment, another interprets them another way; hence there must always be people who decide these things and declare the correct meaning of the Scriptures, as this is symbolized by the wheels of Ezekiel.

ZWINGLI.

I do not understand the Scriptures differently than it is interpreted by means of the Spirit of God; there is no need of human judgment.† We know that the ordinance of God is spiritual, Rom. vii. 14, and is not to be explained by the reasoning of man in the flesh. For the corporal man in the flesh does not understand the things which are of the Spirit of God. 1 Cor. ii. 14. Therefore I do not wish to have or accept a man as judge of the Scriptures.

VICAR.

Arius and Sabelius would still walk on earth or rule if the matters had not been brought before judges.

ZWINGLI.

I shall do as the fathers, who also conquered by means of the

---

* ["In regard to the quotation from Matt. xxviii. 20, Zwingli gave you (Faber) the following answer: It is true that Christ has promised to remain with us to the end of the world. That he also keeps his promise faithfully, ye pious brethren in Jesus Christ, you should have no doubt. God is with us probably as with no council. For we keep His word, and seek the truth from his word alone. Those who do that, God is with them." (Luchsinger in "Gyrenrupfen.")].

† ["The Scriptures decide themselves in the presence of men." (Bullinger.)]

Scriptures, not by means of human understanding.* For when they were disputing with Arius they did not accept men, but the Scriptures, as judges, as one finds. When Arius said it is also proven by the Scriptures, as he thought, that the Son of God is less than the Father, John xiv. 28, the dear fathers sought the Scriptures, allowing them to judge, and showed that it was written, John x. 30, " I and my Father are one." Also, xiv. 9, 10, " He that hath seen me hath seen the Father. Believest thou not that I am in the Father and the Father in me?" Also, " The Father that dwelleth in me, he doeth the works." Such declarations of the Scriptures the dear fathers considered, and showed that Christ had two natures, human and divine, and proved by the Scriptures, not by the judgment of men, that the saying which Arius quoted, The Father is more than I, referred to the humanity of Christ and the later sayings spoke of the Godhead, as was shown by the Scriptures themselves, and the Scriptures interpreted the Scriptures, not the fathers the Scriptures. Thus St. Augustine overcame the Arians, Manicheans, etc.; Jerome the Jovians, Pelagians; Cyprian his opponents and heretics, at the

* [" Did you not also hear that thereupon Zwingli answered: A council never overcame a heretic except with the Scriptures, for it would have been useless if one had tried to overcome Arius in another fashion except by the Scripture. Hence he also stood there, demanding that one listen to the Scriptures in regard to all the Articles; these should be judges over him, and according to that he would allow all Christians to recognize not only several, but all, whether he had used the Scriptures rightly or not; and he asked who was judge between Hilary and Arians, between Jerome and Jovian, between Augustine and the Manicheans; with nothing besides the Scriptures they proved their cause, and thus allowed it to come before all people without a single judge. And what you attacked afterwards, just as if he had boasted of great abilities, that you invented. For Zwingli spoke of the rest who were there thus: There are in the hall probably men as learned in Hebrew, Greek and Latin as at Tübingen, Basel, Freiburg and elsewhere." (Hans Hab in "Gyrenrupfen.") He adds thereto: "Zurich has probably as many people learned in the three languages as he and his papists in a heap, and who understand the Scriptures better than those at Lyon and Paris."]

same time with books referred to and Scriptures quoted, so that the Scriptures, and not they, were the judges. The Scriptures are so much the same everywhere, the Spirit of God flows so abundantly, walks in them so joyfully, that every diligent reader, in so far as he approaches with humble heart, will decide by means of the Scriptures, taught by the Spirit of God, until he attains the truth. For Christ whenever he argued with the learned Jews and Pharisees referred to the Scriptures, saying: "Search the Scriptures." John v. 39. Also, "What is written in the law." Luke x. 26, etc. Therefore I say the matter needs no human judge. But that at various times such matters generally have been brought before human judges and universities is the reason that the priests no longer desired to study, and paid greater attention to wantonness, at times to chess, than reading the Bible. Hence it came about that one considered those scholars and chose them as judges who had attracted unto themselves only the appearance or diploma of wisdom, who knew naught concerning the right Spirit of God or the Scriptures. But now through the grace of God the divine Gospel and Scriptures have been born and brought to light by means of print (especially at Basel), so that they are in Latin and German, wherefrom every pious Christian who can read or knows Latin can easily inform himself and learn the will of God. This has been attained, God be praised, that now a priest who is diligent may learn and know as much in two or three years concerning the Scriptures as formerly many in ten or fifteen years. Therefore I wish all the priests who have benefices under my lords of Zurich or in their counties, and have them exhorted that each one is diligent and labors to read the Scriptures, and especially those who are preachers and caretakers of the soul, let each one buy a New Testament in Latin, or in German, if he does not understand the Latin or is unable to interpret it. For I also am not ashamed to read German at times, on account of easier presentation. Let one begin to read first the gospel of St. Matthew, especially the v., vi. and vii. chapters. After that let him read the other gospels, so that he may know what they write and say. After that he should take the Acts. After this the epistles of Paul, but first the one to the Galatians. Then the epistle of St. Peter and other divine texts; thus he can readily form within himself a right Christian life, and become more skillful to teach this better to others also. After that let him work in the Old Testament, in the prophets and other books of the Bible, which, I understand, are soon to appear in print in Latin and German. Let one buy such books, and never mind the sophistical and other empty writings, also the decree and work of the papists, tell and preach to the people the holy Gospel, written by the four evangelists and apostles, then the people will become more willing and skillful in leading a peaceful Christian life. For matters have reached such a state that also the laymen and women know more of the Scriptures than some priests and clergymen.

Thereupon spoke a priest, decan of Glattfelden:

Shall one then not read Gregory or Ambrose, or cite their writings in the pulpit, but only the Gospel?

ZWINGLI.

Yes, you may read them. And when you find something written therein which is like the Gospel or quoted from the Gospel, there is no need of using Gregory or Ambrose, but one first of all honors Christ and says, this the Gospel or Scriptures tell us. And this is not only my opinion, but Gregory or Ambrose is also of this opinion. For the dear fathers themselves confirm their writings with the Gospel and Scriptures, and where they depeud upon their own thoughts they err readily an generally.

Another priest, by name Hans v. Schlieren, asks:

But what shall he do who has a small benefice and not sufficient wherewith he could buy such books, the Testament? I have a poor little benefice; it is also necessary for me to speak.

ZWINGLI.

There is, if God wills, no priest so poor but he cannot buy a Testament, if he likes to learn. Somewhere he will find a pious citizen and other people who will buy him a Bible, or otherwise advance the money so that he can pay for one.

After this the vicar began to speak roughly, saying:

Very well, Master Ulrich. I say that your Articles, as these are noted down, are opposed to the Gospel and St. Paul, also not in harmony unto the truth. That I offer to prove in writing or orally, wherever you please. Choose for yourself judges for these matters, to render a decision therein, in whichever place suits you, then I shall prove to you in writing or orally that your Articles, which appeared in print, are untruthful and opposed to the Gospel.

ZWINGLI.

Do that, when and wherever you please, and the quicker and sooner the more agreeable and satisfactory it is to me. Write against my Articles or opinions whenever you wish, or argue against them wherever you please. Why don't you do it here, right now? Attack one of my opinions, since you say they are opposed to the Gospel and St. Paul; try to prove them wrong and false. I say, Vicar, if you can do that, and prove one of my Articles false by means of the Gospel, I will give you a rabbit cheese. Now let's hear it. I shall await it.

VICAR.

A rabbit cheese, what is that?* I need no cheese. All is also not written in the Gospel that is unrighteous and opposed to Christ; † where do you find in the Gospel that one shall not have his daughter or his sister's daughter to wife?

---

* "A rabbit cheese" is Swiss for a remarkably fine cheese. Glarus, where Zwingli was settled for ten years (1506–1516), was then and is still noted for its cheeses.

† ["Where did I speak an unfit, immodest or worthless word, as Zwingli

ZWINGLI.

It is also not written that a cardinal shall have thirty benefices. Master Erasmus v. Stein, canon at Zurich, said: It is written in Leviticus, and is forbidden. Answers the vicar, saying: Erasmus, you will not find it, although you search long for it. One could still live a friendly, peaceful and virtuous life even if there were no Gospel.*

always did with his ridiculing and other things, which for the sake of peace I shall not repeat?" (Faber.) Conrad Aescher answers: "Zwingli has treated the matter with such earnestness that he could not have been more in earnest; to be sure he had to laugh with the rest when you came with your old tales, which we tailors and shoemakers had also learned long ago. But you act like all bad women, blame other people for what they do themselves. Nobody began his speeches with more ridiculing than you; why you smiled so friendly that we were afraid that the stove of the room would become so attached to you that it would run after you. Zwingli has said nothing shameful or immodest, but you have, when you said, where is it forbidden in the Bible that a father may not marry his daughter? and when you said one could live righteously even without the Gospel," etc. ("Gyrenrupfen.")]

* ["At the end of your account you made the false statement that I said one might still live in a friendly, peaceful and virtuous way even if there were no Gospel. Do you think I am mad, and speak only in unchristian fashion thus? especially as before that I made such a speech in praise of the Gospel, and in my book against Martin Luther I praised so highly and emphasized the Gospel, etc.? And you dare to accuse me of these words which in my life I never thought of? Where were you sitting that you could hear what I said? While several were then speaking every one arose and went away, and no one sitting could have heard me. Do you wish to to know what in the hum of voices, as the people were getting up and leaving, I said? Thus I spoke: One may preach the Gospel and still keep the peace. Zwingli thought it could not be, so I declared it could be. Thus you misquote me. Did not the Gospel come with the peace and the peace with the Gospel? But you say only: God has not sent peace upon earth." (Faber.) Hans Hager answered him: "Why, how can you deny what one can witness and prove with so many true men, so that I offer to prove it before my lords of Zurich at whatever hour and moment you will? I do not say that it occurred at the end, because it did not occur at the end. It may also have happened to Erhard [Hegenwald] that he forgot it until the end. What does that matter? You said it, no matter when you said it. What does that matter, as long as you had to lie?" (Gyrenrupfen.)]

ZWINGLI.

You will find in Leviticus xviii. that relationship of marriage with collateral lines, and even further than the sisters, is forbidden. And if the distant and further removed member of the house or blood relationship is forbidden, then much more is the nearest forbidden and not allowed, as you may read in Lev. xviii. 17. I pity you that you come with such foolish or useless and thoughtless remarks, and thus cause offense among the people. That is to give real scandal and vexation to your neighbor. You could have kept that silent and opposed me with other writings; it would have been more worthy of you.

Now every one arose, and nothing more was said at that time; every one went to where he had something to attend to.*

It was also said by the mayor of Zurich, as is afterwards written: The sword, with which the pastor of Fislisbach, captured at Constance, was stabbed, does not wish to appear. The aforesaid mayor remarks that the vicar had not yet shown any Scripture with which he boasted to have overcome the aforesaid lord of Fislisbach.

There also spoke the worthy Mr. R., abbot of Cappel,† saying: Where are they now who wish to burn us at the stake and bring wood; why do they not step forward now?

That is the sum and substance of all actions and speeches at the assembly of Zurich, etc., before the assembled council, where also other doctors and gentlemen were present on account of the praiseworthy message of the bishop of Constance and

---

* ["And were very tired of the irrelevant quotations and speeches of the Vicar." (Bullinger.)]

† Wolfgang Roupli (or Joner), son of the mayor of Frauenfeld; became abbot 1521; accepted the Reformation and reformed his monastery. He called there Bullinger, who was Zwingl's successor, as teacher of the cloister school, 1522.

Master Ulrich Zwingli, canon and preacher at the great cathedral of Zurich, which (assembly) occurred at the time and on the day, as stated above, in the year 1523, on the 29th day of January.

THE SIXTY-SEVEN ARTICLES OF ZWINGLI.

The articles and opinions below, I, Ulrich Zwingli, confess to have preached in the worthy city of Zurich as based upon the Scriptures which are called inspired by God, and I offer to protect and conquer with the said articles, and where I have not now correctly understood said Scriptures I shall allow myself to be taught better, but only from said Scriptures.

I. All who say that the Gospel is invalid without the confirmation of the Church err and slander God.

II. The sum and substance of the Gospel is that our Lord Jesus Christ, the true Son of God, has made known to us the will of his heavenly Father, and has with his innocence released us from death and reconciled God.

III. Hence Christ is the only way to salvation for all who ever were, are and shall be.

IV. Who seeks or points out another door errs, yea, he is a murderer of souls and a thief.

V. Hence all who consider other teachings equal to or higher than the Gospel err, and do not know what the Gospel is.

VI. For Jesus Christ is the guide and leader, promised by God to all human beings, which promise was fulfilled.

VII. That he is an eternal salvation and head of all believers, who are his body, but which is dead and can do nothing without him.

VIII. From this follows first that all who dwell in the head are members and children of God, and that is the church or communion of the saints, the bride of Christ, Ecclesia catholica.

IX. Furthermore, that as the members of the body can do nothing without the control of the head, so no one in the body of Christ can do the least without his head, Christ.

X. As that man is mad whose limbs (try to) do something without his head, tearing, wounding, injuring himself; thus when the members of Christ undertake something without their head, Christ, they are mad, and injure and burden themselves with unwise ordinances.

XI. Hence we see in the clerical (so-called) ordinances, concerning their splendor, riches, classes, titles, laws, a cause of all foolishness, for they do not also agree with the head.

XII. Thus they still rage, not on account of the head (for that one is eager to bring forth in these times from the grace of God,) but because one will not let them rage, but tries to compel them to listen to the head.

XIII. Where this (the head) is hearkened to one learns clearly and plainly the will of God, and man is attracted by his spirit to him and changed into him.

XIV. Therefore all Christian people shall use their best diligence that the Gospel of Christ be preached alike everywhere.

XV. For in the faith rests our salvation, and in unbelief our damnation; for all truth is clear in him.

XVI. In the Gospel one learns that human doctrines and decrees do not aid in salvation.

ABOUT THE POPE.

XVII. That Christ is the only eternal high priest, wherefrom it follows that those who have called themselves high priests have opposed the honor and power of Christ, yea, cast it out.

ABOUT THE MASS.

XVIII. That Christ, having sacrificed himself once, is to eternity a certain and valid sacrifice for the sins of all faithful, wherefrom it follows that the mass is not a sacrifice, but is a remembrance of the sacrifice and assurance of the salvation which Christ has given us.

XIX. That Christ is the only mediator between God and us.

ABOUT THE INTERCESSION OF THE SAINTS.

XX. That God desires to give us all things in his name, whence it follows that outside of this life we need no mediator except himself.

XXI. That when we pray for each other on earth, we do so in such fashion that we believe that all things are given to us through Christ alone.

ABOUT GOOD WORKS.

XXII. That Christ is our justice, from which follows that our works in so far as they are good, so far they are of Christ, but in so far as they are ours, they are neither right nor good.

CONCERNING CLERICAL PROPERTY.

XXIII. That Christ scorns the property and pomp of this world, whence from it follows that those who attract wealth to themselves in his name slander him terribly when they make him a pretext for their avarice and wilfullness.

CONCERNING THE FORBIDDING OF FOOD.

XXIV. That no Christian is bound to do those things which God has not decreed, therefore one may eat at all times all food, wherefrom one learns that the decree about cheese and butter is a Roman swindle.

ABOUT HOLIDAY AND PILGRIMAGE.

XXV. That time and place is under the jurisdiction of Christian people, and man with them, wherefrom is learnt that those who fix time and place deprive the Christians of their liberty.

ABOUT HOODS, DRESS, INSIGNIA.

XXVI. That God is displeased with nothing so much as with hypocrisy; whence is learnt that all is gross hypocrisy and profligacy which is mere show before men. Under this condemnation fall hoods, insignia, plates, etc.

ABOUT ORDER AND SECTS.

XXVII. That all Christian men are brethren of Christ and brethren of one another, and shall create no father (for themselves) on earth. Under this condemnation fall orders, sects, brotherhoods, etc.

ABOUT THE MARRIAGE OF ECCLESIASTS.

XXVIII. That all which God has allowed or not forbidden is righteous, hence marriage is permitted to all human beings.

XXIX. That all who are called clericals sin when they do not protect themselves by marriage after they have become conscious that God has not enabled them to remain chaste.

ABOUT THE VOW OF CHASTITY.

XXX. That those who promise chastity [outside of matrimony] take foolishly or childishly too much upon themselves, whence is learnt that those who make such vows do wrong to the pious being.

ABOUT THE BAN.

XXXI. That no special person can impose the ban upon any one, but the Church, that is the congregation of those among whom the one to be banned dwells, together with their watchman, *i. e.*, the pastor.

XXXII. That one may ban only him who gives public offence.

ABOUT ILLEGAL PROPERTY.

XXXIII. That property unrighteously acquired shall not be given to temples, monasteries, cathedrals, clergy or nuns, but to the needy, if it cannot be returned to the legal owner.

ABOUT MAGISTRY.

XXXIV. The spiritual (so-called) power has no justification for its pomp in the teaching of Christ.

XXXV. But the lay has power and confirmation from the deed and doctrine of Christ.

XXXVI. All that the spiritual so-called state claims to have of power and protection belongs to the lay, if they wish to be Christians.

XXXVII. To them, furthermore, all Christians owe obedience without exception.

XXXVIII. In so far as they do not command that which is contrary to God.

XXXIX. Therefore all their laws shall be in harmony with the divine will, so that they protect the oppressed, even if he does not complain.

XL. They alone may put to death justly, also, only those who give public offence (if God is not offended let another thing be commanded).

XLI. If they give good advice and help to those for whom they must account to God, then these owe to them bodily assistance.

XLII. But if they are unfaithful and transgress the laws of Christ they may be deposed in the name of God.

XLIII. In short, the realm of him is best and most stable who rules in the name of God alone, and his is worst and most unstable who rules in accordance with his own will.

ABOUT PRAYER.

XLIV. Real petitioners call to God in spirit and truly, without great ado before men.

XLV. Hypocrites do their work so that they may be seen by men, also receive their reward in this life.

XLVI. Hence it must always follow that church-song and outcry without devoutness, and only for reward, is seeking either fame before the men or gain.

ABOUT OFFENCE.

XLVII. Bodily death a man should suffer before he offend or scandalize a Christian.

XLVIII. Who through stupidness or ignorance is offended without cause, he should not be left sick or weak, but he should be made strong, that he may not consider as a sin which is not a sin.

XLIX. Greater offence I know not than that one does not allow priests to have wives, but permits them to hire prostitutes. Out upon the shame!

ABOUT REMITTANCE OF SIN.

L. God alone remits sin through Jesus Christ, his Son, and alone our Lord.

LI. Who assigns this to creatures detracts from the honor of God and gives it to him who is not God; this is real idolatry.

LII. Hence the confession which is made to the priest or neighbor shall not be declared to be a remittance of sin, but only a seeking for advice.

LIII. Works of penance coming from the counsel of human beings (except the ban) do not cancel sin; they are imposed as a menace to others.

LIV. Christ has borne all our pains and labor. Hence whoever assigns to works of penance what belongs to Christ errs and slanders God.

LV. Whoever pretends to remit to a penitent being any sin would not be a vicar of God or St. Peter, but of the devil.

LVI. Whoever remits any sin only for the sake of money is the companion of Simon and Balaam, and the real messenger of the devil personified.

ABOUT PURGATORY.

LVII. The true divine Scriptures know naught about purgatory after this life.

LVIII. The sentence of the dead is known to God only.

LIX. And the less God has let us know concerning it, the less we should undertake to know about it.

LX. That man earnestly calls to God to show mercy to the dead I do not condemn, but to determine a period of time there-for (seven years for a mortal sin), and to lie for the sake of gain, is not human, but devilish.

ABOUT THE PRIESTHOOD.

LXI. About the consecration which the priests have received in late times the Scriptures know nothing.

LXII. Furthermore, they know no priests except those who proclaim the word of God.

LXIII. They command honor should be shown, *i. e.*, to furnish them with food for the body.

ABOUT THE CESSATION OF MISUSAGES.

LXIV. All those who recognize their errors shall not be allowed to suffer, but to die in peace, and thereafter arrange in a Christian manner their bequests to the Church.

LXV. Those who do not wish to confess, God will probably take care of. Hence no force shall be used against their body, unless it be that they behave so criminally that one cannot do without that.

LXVI. All the clerical superiors shall at once settle down, and with unanimity set up the cross of Christ, not the money-chests, or they will perish, for I tell thee the ax is raised against the tree.

LXVII. If any one wishes conversation with me concerning interest, tithes, unbaptized children or confirmation, I am willing to answer.

Let no one undertake here to argue with sophistry or human foolishness, but come to the Scriptures to accept them as the judge (foras cares! the Scriptures breathe the Spirit of God), so that the truth either may be found, or if found, as I hope, retained. Amen.

Thus may God rule.

The basis and commentary of these articles will soon appear in print.

IV. ORDINANCE AND NOTICE. HOW MATTERS CONCERNING MARRIAGE SHALL BE CONDUCTED IN THE CITY OF ZURICH.*

We, the Burgomaster, Council and the Great Council, which they call the Two Hundred, of the city of Zurich, offer to each and all people's priests, pastors, those who have the care of souls, and preachers, also to all over-governors, under-governors, officials and any others who have livings, homes or seats in our cities, counties, principalities, high and low courts and territories, our greeting, favorable and affectionate good wishes. I call your attention to what each one of you has noticed and seen up to the present time, that many kinds of complaints and errors have arisen in matrimonial affairs. Since the parties have been summoned before the court at Constance or other foreign courts again and again, and have been judged at considerable cost; since they, at that place, and in cases where the people were well off in temporal goods, have been detained without judgment, and, as far as we know, to their own danger, etc., and in order that such great cost, trouble and labor among you men and women having business with each other with regard to matrimony, and who live and are at home in our territories, high and low courts, may be put aside, done away with and avoided, and also in order that each may be properly judged with promptness, thus we have ordained the following common ordinances concerning marriage, and have given notice of them, and have undertaken to practice them for a time, with the understanding that they are to be decreased, or increased, or entirely done away with. And if any parties come from our true and beloved confederates, from whatsoever place, who desire to seek and make use of law with regard to matrimony on account of the small cost among us, bringing each from his local authorities letters and seals testify-

---

* Printed at Zurich by John Hager. Zwingli's *Works*, *II.*, 2, 356-359. Translated from the original German by Prof. Lawrence A. McLouth. Bullinger expressly remarks that Zwingli was the author of the order of the canonical court.

ing that such right may be extended to them, then they shall be accepted for the sake of especial friendship, and they shall be treated with regard to this law in every way as our own, but we shall not otherwise burden ourselves with any one dwelling outside of the territories of the city of Zurich.

And in order that such legal business may be attended to promptly, as necessity demands, we have chosen as judges six men, two from the people's priests in our city, who are taught in the Word of God, also two from the small, and two from the large council. Among these, each one shall serve two months as magistrate or judge, shall summon, order, collect, examine, practice and execute such court business as necessity demands.

Whatever they pronounce and judge, according to the contents of the following articles and ordinances, shall stand. If, however, any of our people, or others, wish to appeal, it shall be made to no other body than the Honorable Council in our city of Zurich.

The court days are, and shall be, on Monday and Thursday. The seat or place of the court the judge shall choose and announce. Accordingly, when it has struck one o'clock in the afternoon, then the judges, secretary, the court beadle, and whoever serves the court, shall be there, on pain of breaking their oath, and shall assist in the action, as is proper. But if any one cannot be there on account of business of the city, or other lawful cause, then the burgomaster shall, by means of the beadle, appoint another, and let him sit. And whoever is judge at a time shall have possession of the seal of the court, and shall, through the beadle, announce orally or by other notice the sessions and orders, always in good time. The cases which come before him, and which need consideration or deliberation, he shall not postpone or hold up more than a week, so that the people may be joined or separated promptly.

And here follow the articles and ordinances concerning marriage.

First, a general ordinance: That no one shall enter into matrimony in our city and country without the testimony and presence of at leat two pious, honorable citizens in good standing.

EXPLANATION OF THIS ORDINANCE.

No one shall marry, engage or give to another his son or daughter without the favor, knowledge and will of the father, mother, guardians or others, who are responsible for the young people. Whoever transgresses this shall be punished according to the manner of the case, and the marriage shall be invalid.

Now in order that marriage requirements may not be made lower than before, no marriage shall hold which a minor shall enter into without the knowledge of the above-mentioned, his father, mother, guardian, or other people responsible, as have been named, before the minor is fully nineteen years old. But if it happens before this, then the ones mentioned, the father, etc., can hinder it and nullify it. But in case these are careless, and have not provided for their children in the nineteen years, then the children may marry and care for themselves, with God's help, unhindered by any one and without any payment. Neither father, mother, legal representative or any one shall force or compel their children to a marriage against their will at any time. But where that has happened, and is legally reported, it shall not be valid and the trespasser shall be punished.

Marriages that have been arranged for or already consummated shall not be hindered or disturbed, as is right and proper, in any degree, by anything, cause or reason, except the clearly expressed causes as are in the holy Scriptures, Leviticus xviii.

And what has heretofore been achieved by dispensations and money shall be done away with entirely, and cause no more trouble.

EXCEPTIONS TO THE LAW.

When two take each other who are free, and who had no one to whom they were under obligation or who took an interest in them, or two are engaged to each other, they shall stand by each other. But the girl shall be over fourteen and the boy over sixteen.

But where they are engaged, and have no references, according to the above ordinance, a marriage shall not be valid. Accordingly, let each one take care and avoid such disgrace and injury.

But if one seduces, disgraces or ruins a daughter, maid or young woman, who was not yet married, he shall give her a morning gift, and shall marry her. But if her father and mother, or the guardian, or other person responsible, refuse her to him, then the perpetrator shall give a dowry to the girl, according to the judgment of the authorities.

And if any one boasts to the danger and injury of another [matrimonially], and is convicted of such a thing, he shall be severely punished.

Likewise, in order to avoid suspicion, calumny and deceit, we desire that each marriage that is properly performed shall be publicly witnessed in a church, and provided with a license of the parish. Each preacher shall enroll and keep record of all such persons, and no one shall give those under him to another without his favor and will, publicly expressed.

WHAT CAN NULLIFY AND BREAK UP A MARRIAGE.

It is proper for a pious married person, who has given no cause for such act, to put away from himself or herself the other who is caught in open adultery, indeed to leave him or her, and to provide himself or herself with another spouse.

This we call and consider open adultery, which is discovered and proved, with sufficient public notice, before the matrimonial court, as is proper, or is so plain and suspicious in fact that the deed cannot be denied with any kind of truth.

But in order that adultery may not be condoned, and that no one may seek a cause to secure a new marriage by means of adultery, it will be necessary that a severe punishment be placed upon adultery, for it was forbidden in the Old Testament on pain of stoning to death.

The preachers to whom the Word of God and superintendence (of morals) are commended shall ban and exclude such sinners from the Christian parish, but the corporal punishment and the matter of the property shall be referred to the civil authorities.

But that no one for this reason may fear marriage, and resort to prostitution, these sinners, too, as is now announced, shall be excluded.

Since, now, marriage was instituted by God to avoid unchastity, and since it often occurs that some, by nature or other shortcomings, are not fitted for the partners they have chosen, they shall nevertheless live together as friends for a year, to see if matters may not better themselves by the prayers of themselves and of other honest people. If it does not grow better in that time, they shall be separated and allowed to marry elsewhere.

Likewise, greater reasons than adultery, as destroying life, endangering life, being mad or crazy, offending by whorishness, or leaving one's spouse without permission, remaining abroad a long time, having leprosy, or other such reasons, of which no rule can be mdae on account of their dissimilarity—these cases the judges can investigate, and proceed as God and the character of the cases shall demand.

The ordinances shall be carefully and repeatedly announced by all clergymen, and their parishes warned against trespassing them.

Given at Zurich on Wednesday, the 10th of May, in the year 1525.

V. REFUTATION OF THE TRICKS OF THE BAPTISTS BY HULDREICH ZWINGLI.*

HULDREICH ZWINGLI TO ALL THE MINISTERS OF THE GOSPEL OF CHRIST.

Grace and peace from the Lord. It is an old saying, dear brethren, that success is the mother of evils, and this is profoundly true. For since even a little was conceded to the desires of certain ones through our idleness or blindness, these are now

---

* Zwingli's *Works*, *III.*, 357–437. Translated from the Latin by Henry Preble and George W. Gilmore.

On Monday, October 26, 1523, the Second Disputation was held in Zurich, again between Zwingli and the representatives of the Old Faith and other clergy, and in that Disputation for the first time the Baptist party in Zurich made their appearance. The subject of the debate was what position the reform party should take in regard to the use of images in the churches and in regard to the sacraments. The Baptist party in Zurich were the radicals. The origin of this party was in a sort of inquiry meeting—that is, some members of Zwingli's congregation used to meet in a private house and talk over the sermons which they had heard from Zwingli, frequently in his presence. Zwingli may have said in these gatherings a good many things which were not for publication, but he had said enough in his public discourses to show this little group of earnest men that he was on the side of a complete break with the Old Church. Zwingli was a very cautious person, and while he saw plainly that his opinions led logically to very radical reforms, he wished to make haste slowly and come at the changes, which he knew would cause considerable sorrow to many conservative people, by successive steps; but the little group referred to wished to accomplish the same results at once, without tarrying for any, and accordingly they started out without first preparing the people for such action to do the things Zwingli had at heart. Thus they made an attack upon churches and stripped them of their ornaments; they refused to observe the church fasts; and what is of more interest in this connection, they declared that the baptism of infants was unscriptural, and therefore should not be observed. Zwingli was very much distressed at the precipitance of his enthusiastic friends, because such actions were on the side of disorder, and it was very important to guard the growing Reformation from the charge of disorderly conduct. At the same time he could not say that what they did was in itself wrong, as he had himself advocated the removal of all ornaments from the churches, and it is doubtless true that in his earlier addresses from the pulpit he exposed the unbiblical character of the church doctrine upon the general

so incapable of limiting those desires that they prefer to perish themselves and to destroy others rather than give up what they have begun. An example of this is furnished during the life of Christ among men, and this is repeated now in our times when he has relit the torch of his word, doubtless though to our good.

subject of baptism, and probable that he inclined towards ruling out infant baptism, as lacking biblical support.

The followers of a great teacher are frequently guilty of bringing their master into compromising situations, because they make prominent what he thinks of very small account, although it may be in the line of his teaching, and so Zwingli found himself criticised severely in Zurich when his remarks upon infant baptism were repeated. To those who were brought up to regard baptism as necessary to salvation it was a great shock to be told that the ceremony had no validity. To those who believed that the rite of baptism was the Christian obligation in lieu of circumcision, and just as binding, to hear that there was grave doubt whether it should be so considered was to knock the underpinning from their faith. When Zwingli found that opposition to the popular belief and practice upon this point meant that he would be exposed not only to clerical and lay adverse criticism, but probably would lose him his influence with the city magistrates, who were all friends of the Old faith on this doctrine, he devoted a great deal of attention to it, with the result that he convinced himself that as to the subjects of baptism he had been wrong, and henceforth he took the orthodox side. As Zwingli was an honest man and morally courageous, his change of view should be accepted as sincere, and not as time-serving and hypocritical. He soon had a chance to attack his former friends and admirers on other than speculative grounds, because they had been influenced by men like Thomas Muenzer and Balthasar Hubmaier, who were in the stream of the Baptist movement in Germany. Balthasar, indeed, developed into the leading theologian of the Baptists of Switzerland. From Germany the idea came to the little company of Baptists in Zurich to practice the rite of baptism upon believing adults who had already, as the Church claimed, been baptized, upon the theory that only those could be baptized truly who were old enough to have at the time an intelligent comprehension of the doctrines to which they were giving assent, and as this could not have been the case with those "baptized" in infancy, therefore they had never really been baptized. The first of these adult baptisms occurred in a gathering of these Baptists in Zollicon, a little village to the east of Zurich, and was by pouring from a dipper. But these first Baptists in Switzerland cared so little in regard to the mode of baptism that the question does not seem to have been discussed among them, and in the writings of

Then when he had not only endured the betrayer for so long a time, but also openly dissuaded or terrified him, the latter, so far from giving over the malicious design entered upon, of giving up master and parent, did not cease till he had placed the spirit in bonds.* So it is now, when the audacity of the Cata-

Zwingli is not referred to. This is a curious fact, because the modern Baptist church lays great stress upon a certain mode of baptism.

The elaborate attack upon the Baptists here presented derives additional interest from the two documents that it embodies. The first is the attack upon Zwingli written probably by Conrad Grebel, one of the earliest friends of Zwingli, and the second is the Confession of Faith written by the Baptists of Bern. Zwingli replies to both these documents, quoting them verbally and fully, and this enables us to reconstruct them. The Confession of the Bernese Baptists is in very simple language, showing a very honest and God-fearing mind, and is in itself a triumphant refutation of the charges of fanaticism and immorality which Zwingli brings against them. In fact in this paper Zwingli shows himself up in a very bad light.

This is no place in which to describe the outrageous treatment which the Baptist party received in Zurich and elsewhere through Switzerland. The writer feels the freer to use such a term because he is not himself a Baptist, but he comes to the subject merely as a historical student. He considers that the part which Zwingli played in this wretched business is a serious blot upon his reputation, and reveals a defect in his character. The Baptists were pursued relentlessly; drowning, beheading, burning at the stake, confiscation of property, exile, fines and other forms of social obloquy were employed to suppress them and prevent their increase. The fact shows plainly that the persecuting spirit in the times of the Reformation was just as rife among Protestants as among Roman Catholics, and that the devil was abroad in the hearts of those who considered themselves on both sides as the true servants of the Lord Jesus Christ, whose tenderness and love must have been greatly tried by these wicked doings of his friends.

Peace came at last to Switzerland—the peace of the grave-yard and of the sea which gives not up its dead. The orthodox party congratulated themselves upon having got rid of the pestilential heresy of adult baptism, yet the student of history as he looks upon the large, flourishing and world-wide Baptist church of to-day asks himself which side really won the battle for the right of private judgment and liberty of action, the side of the persecutor or the side of the persecuted?

* *I. e.*, died by the halter; allusion to the death of Judas.

baptists has been suffered to proceed so far that they have conceived the hope of confounding all things; who are so untaught that by calling themselves by this name they would increase their estimation; so imprudent (while Christ would have the apostles prudent as serpents) that the confusion which alone they are eager for they suppose they will discover by means of their imprudence rather than find by any skill. This inauspicious race of men has so increased within a few years * that they now cause anxiety to certain cities.† And this in no other way than through unskilled and impious audacity. For while pious learning and discipline has no need of the ministry of hypocrisy (for it is sufficient unto itself through erudition, and by the very unaffected discipline of piety commends itself to others), yet men of this kind are so thoroughly ignorant of that which they boast they alone know (and), so pretend that from which they are farther distant than the hall of Pluto from the palace of Jove, that it is clear that they begin this web endowed with nothing but impious and untaught audacity. For as often as by the use of clear passages of Scripture they are driven to the point of having to say, I yield, straightway they talk about "the spirit" and deny Scripture. As if indeed the heavenly spirit were ignorant of the sense of Scripture which is written under its guidance or were anywhere inconsistent with itself. And if you rightly and modestly call in question their customs and institutions, even if you come as a suppliant and beg them to do nothing rashly, there is no abuse employed by the enemies of the Gospel these do not use, no threats they do not throw at you. What does all this mean, I ask, if it is not the sign of audacity and impious confidence? Since there is so rich a harvest of these—not men (for why must one call those men who have nothing but the

* Since 1523.

† Waldshut, Zurich, St. Gall, Schaffhausen, Basel, Coire, Constance, Strassburg, Worms, Ulm.

human form?), but monsters of deceit—that now the good seed which the heavenly Father so lately sowed in his field must be on its guard, I beg this, that we watch, act, and not let the enemy overthrow us as we sleep. Let us judge soberly, lest we receive a wolf in sheep's clothing. Let us labor, lest that evil that has arisen be attributed to our neglect. For there are, alas, not a few among us who are stricken and moved by every wind and novelty, just like the untaught rabble which embraces a thing the more quickly the more unknown it is. The Catabaptists speak in round tones of God, truth, the Word, light, spirit, holiness, flesh, falsehood, impiety, desire, demon, hell and all that kind of things, not only beautifully, but even grandly and finely, if only hypocrisy were more surely absent. If also you should investigate their life, at the first contact it seems innocent, divine, democratic, popular, nay, supermundane, for it is thought more noble than human even by those who think not illiberally of themselves. But when you have penetrated into the interior you find such a pest as it is shame even to mention. For it is not sufficient for them to abuse the Gospel for gain and to live at the expense of another, and to give themselves up to such base cunning for the sake of their belly, weaving plot out of plot, but they must not only assail, but even destroy, the faith of matrons and girls from whose husbands and parents they obtain hospitality. And not contented with all this, they refuse to pronounce and recognize as wicked the hand made bloody at St. Gall with a cruel parricide, so that you see without difficulty that the same thing is to be expected from their assemblages (which are both nocturnal and solitary), which once at Rome improperly idle matrons when they had gained possession of a certain paltry Greek perpetrated in their subterranean meetings. And although all those deeds are in part so wicked and unworthy of good men, in part so obscene and impure, and in part so monstrous and cruel, that they would hand this age down to posterity as infamous, even though there were no other calamity; nevertheless great as they are, they are insignificant in that they confined the contumely within human bounds, as compared with these which they are guilty of against the piety that regards both Christ and public morals. They deny that Christ himself perfected forever his saints in his one offering of himself. But what is this but drawing from heaven God's Son who sits at the right hand of the Father? And when they have cast him from his kingdom, in whose name, pray, shall they be baptized? Does not the whole New Testament tend to this, that we should learn that Christ is our successful sacrifice and redemption? Out of what books do the Catabaptists draw their doctrine? When therefore they thoroughly deny the sum of the New Testament, do we not see them using catabaptism, not to the glory of God or with the good of their consciences, but as a pretext for seditions, confusion and tumult, which things alone they hatch out? With folly does he boast the baptism of Christ who denies Christ. It is to no purpose that they say after the manner of the Jews (some of whom we know do this) that Christ was a great prophet or a man of God, but not the Son of God, for he can be neither a prophet nor a man of God who brings a lie to wretched mortals —in which (lies) they abound to more than a sufficiency. But Christ asserted that he was the Son of God; on account of this he died; he therefore could not have lied when he said he was God's Son if he was a true prophet or a man of God. How is it that the apostles baptized in Jesus' name when he had given them the formula, "In the name of the Father and the Son and the Holy Spirit?" Jesus must be equal, nay, the same as Father, Son and Holy Spirit. For John, great as he was, and prophet and man of God, did not baptize in his own name. In brief, then, when they clearly deny that Christ is by nature the Son of God, it is through evil design that they rage about baptism, and not for zeal's sake. Morals they corrupted in the following manner: No matter what crime they are caught in committing, even in the very act (for in their church so unstained shameful deeds, adultery, parricide, perjury, theft, evil, guile, and about all crimes there are anywhere, are more common than among those whom they call for contumely " the flesh and the devil." I tell the truth, I lie not; there is none of these that I cannot abundantly prove if the occasion demands)—In whatsoever sin they are taken, I say, they escape in no other way than : I have not sinned, for I am no longer in the flesh, but in the spirit; I am dead to the flesh, and the flesh to me. Do they not betray what they are by this reply? For how can they who are led by the Spirit of God and are sons of God allure to adultery a matron's chastity? With what face offer insult to a simple little maiden ! What an insult to God is this ! What a handle this for those who would already have given themselves from the lust of the flesh to all vice if shame alone had not opposed ! Will not the homicide share with the rake and adulterer, when accused, the formula, " I am now of the Spirit; the wrong done here is not mine, but is of the flesh." What shame, pray, will be left us? What regard for modesty? For they do not reply with the same mind as do we ordinarily who trust in Christ. For we frankly confess : I have sinned, I will correct the error, I will flee through Christ to the mercy of God, from this I will never fall. For they do not refer to Christ ; they have put off all shame, and what will he correct who denies that he has fallen? O, the crime, the audacity, the impudence ! What swine of the school of Epicurus ever thus philosophized? Or what difference is there between right and wrong, O heaven, between holy and crime-laden, man and beast? If you take away shame from humanity, have you not admitted to the theatre all obscenity, have you not eliminated law, corrupted morals? You are not ashamed at slaughter, adultery, harlotry ; you are more a beast than the wolf, lion or horse, which have some shame. Against this class of men we must be on constant watch, all our forces and machines must be brought, my brethren, and the more because they rage so in their hypocrisy and perfidy. They excel in this Empusa, Proteus, the chameleon, or Tarandus,* or whatever is inconstant. By this they assert that the papal party will bring them aid—this openly. They assail far more sharply than do the Romanists all who stand by Christ, by which they evince to what purpose they spare those whom they so anxiously flatter. But all our material cannot and must not be sought elsewhere than from the armory of the Old and the New Testament. Do thou, Father of lights, illumine their darkness, that they may see their error, and as thou wilt sometime do, eliminate this error from the Church quickly, we pray! But thou, whosoever thou art, who boastest in the name or ministry of the Most High God or of the gospel of His Son, consider what and whence these matters are which we allege, and laying passion aside furnish the herb of truth. Farewell!

ZURICH, *July 31, 1527*.

HULDREICH ZWINGLI'S REFUTATION AGAINST THE TRICKS OF THE CATABAPTISTS.

Thus far our preface. Now hear in what order we shall proceed. First, we shall reply to their calumnies, in which they assert they have confuted our fundamental arguments. Secondly, I shall overthrow the basis of their superstition. Then I shall discuss the covenant and the election of God, which abides firm and is above baptism and circumcision; nay, above faith and preaching. I shall add an appendix, in which, with the help of God, I shall refute certain errors recently wrought out by them. But all with a light hand. In the first two parts I shall always

---

* *Empusa* was a spectre of huge size, having one leg of brass and one like that of an ass, sent out by Hecate to frighten travelers. It ate human flesh. It sometimes appeared as a beautiful young woman. *Proteus* was the Old Man of the Sea, who rose at noonday from the flood, came on land and fell asleep among the rocks. If any one could catch him there and hold on to him, notwithstanding his efforts to escape by changing his form, he would be able to learn from him the future with infallible accuracy. *Tarandus* was a horned animal of Northern lands, perhaps the reindeer.

put their words first, faithfuly translated from German into Latin; after that the reply. Thus then they begin:

THE CATABAPTISTS. One of Zwingli's grounds for advocating the baptism of infants is the family of Stephanas. For he says: It is more likely than not that the apostles baptized the children of the faithful, for Paul says, 1 Cor. i. 16, And I baptized also the household of Stephanas; a second is in Acts xvi. 15, when Lydia was baptized and her house; a third in verse 33, a little after, And he was baptized, he and his house, straightway. In these families it is more likely than not that there were infants. Thus far they.

Before I go to the regular reply, I would warn thee of one thing, O reader. This work is called a "Refutation of the Tricks, etc.," because this class of men so abounds and works in tricks that I have never seen anything equally oily or changeable. Yet this is not wonderful. For add to their asseverations of holiness, which they are skilled in working up, their readiness in making fictions and scattering them, and (you see) how they deceive not only the simple, but even the elect, divine providence thus proving its own. The book containing the refutation of our positions * they had for a long time been passing through the hands of their brotherhood, who everywhere boasted that they could so tear up Zwingli's positions that there would be nothing left. I had meanwhile been looking and searching everywhere to see if I

---

*'As appears from the letter of Œcolampadius to Zwingli, dated July 19, 1527 (Zwingli's Works, viii. 80), it is probable that the writing which called out the answers of Œcolampadius and Zwingli had the title: "Ein Gesprech Balthasar Hubemörs von Fridberg. Doctors. auff Mayster Ulrichs Zwinglens ze Zürich Taufbüechlein. von dem Khindertauff. Die warhayt is untödtlich. Erd. erd. erd. höre das wort des herrens. Hiere." Nicholspurg 1526 (quarto). Zwingli's book on Baptism ("Vom Touf, vom widertouf und vom kindertouf"), appeared May 27 1525. It is in his Works, ii. 1, 230–303.

On July 11th in that year Hubmeier issued his "Von dem christlichen Tauf der Gläubigen," to which Zwingli replied by his "Uiber doctor Balthazars toufbüchlin wahrhafte gründte antwurt (1525) Works, ii. 1, 337–369.

could get it, but could find it nowhere, until Œcolampadius, a most upright man, and also most vigilant, found one somewhere and sent it to me. So the first trick was that they sent around their own writings, which through their seared consciences they knew could not endure the light, secretly by the hands of the conspirators, who are as purblind in their ignorance as they are blind in their desire to advance the sect. They did not allow it to come into other hands. But the evil-doer cometh not into the light lest his works be manifest. But how could they submit their works to the church when they have seceded from the church? For you must know, most pious reader, that their sect arose thus. When their leaders, clearly fanatics, had already determined to drag into carnal liberty the liberty we have in the gospel, they addressed us who administer the word at Zurich first,* kindly, indeed, but firmly, so that so far as could be seen from their appearance and action it was clear that they had in mind something inauspicious. They addressed us therefore after the following manner: It does not escape us that there will ever be those who will oppose the gospel, even among those who boast in the name of Christ. We therefore can never hope that all minds will so unite as Christians should find it possible to live. For in the Acts of the Apostles those who had believed seceded from the others, and then it happened that they who came to believe went over to those who were now a new church. So then must we do: they beg that we make a deliverance to this effect —they who wish to follow Christ should stand on our side. They promise also that our forces shall be far superior to the army of the unbelieving. Now the church was about to elect from their own devout its own senate. For it was clear that there were many impious ones both in the senate and in this promiscuous church. To this we replied in the following manner: It is indeed true that there would ever be those who would live unrighteously,

* In 1524. Cf. for these matters Zwingli, Works, ii. 1, 230 sqq., 370 sqq. II., pp. 370 ff and 230 ff.

even though they confessed Christ, and would have all innocence and therefore piety in contempt. Yet when they asserted and contended that they were Christians, and were such by their deeds—as even the church could endure—they were on our side. For who is not against us is on our side.

So Christ himself had taught in just such beginnings of things as were then ours. He had also commanded us to let the tares grow with the grain until the day of harvest, but we hoped boldly more would return daily to a sound mind who now had it not. If this should not be, yet the pious might ever live among the impious. I feared that in that condition of affairs a secession would cause some confusion. The example of the apostles was not applicable here, for those from whom they withdrew did not confess Christ, but now ours did. A great part of those would be unwilling to consent with us to any secession, even though they embraced Christ more ardently than we ourselves. By the continuous action of the word that alone should be promulgated which all ought to know, unless they wished to be wanting to their own salvation. I did not doubt that without disorder the number of the believing would ever grow larger by the unremitting administration of the word, not by the disruption of the body into many parts. That although the senate seemed to them to be of very varying complexion, we were not of that mind. Especially because, while nothing humane seemed alien to them, yet they frankly not only did not oppose the word, but they favored it equally with that Jehoshaphat who strengthened with his cohorts by the law itself the priests and Levites that they might the more freely preach the word through all Judea. Yet one should especially observe that there were ten virgins awaiting the bridegroom, but five of them were wise and prudent and five were slothful and foolish. Replies on this line we made to them as they urged us, and they saw they would not succeed. They brought up other matters. They denounced infant baptism tremendously as the chief abomination, proceeding from an evil demon and the Roman pontiff. We met this attack at once, promised an amicable conference. It was appointed for Tuesday of each week. At the first meeting the battle was sharp but without abuse, as we especially took in good part their insults. Let God be the witness and those who were present, as well from their side as from ours. The second was sharper. Some of them, since they could do nothing with Scripture, carried on the affair with open abuse. When they saw themselves beaten after a considerable conflict, and when we had exhorted them in friendly ways, we broke up in such a way that many of them promised they would make no disturbance, though they did not promise to give up their opinions. Within three, or at most four, days it was announced that the leaders of the sect had baptized fifteen brethren. Then we began to perceive why they had determined to collect a new church and had opposed infant baptism so seriously. We warned the church that it could not be maintained, that this proceeded from good counsel, to say nothing of a good spirit, and for these reasons: They had attempted a division and partition of the church, and this was just as hypocritical as the superstition of the monks. Secondly, though the churches had to preserve their liberty of judging concerning doctrine, they had set up catabaptism without any conference, for during the whole battle about infant baptism they had said nothing about catabaptism. Third, this catabaptism seemed like the watchword of seditious men. Then when they learned this in great swarms they came into the city, unbelted and girded with rope or osiers, and prophesied, as they called it, in the market place and squares. They filled the air with their cries about the old dragon, as they called me, and his heads, as they called the other ministers of the word. They also commended their justice and innocence to all, for they were about to depart. They boasted that already they hold all things in common, and threatened with extremes others unless they do the same. They went through the streets with portentous uproar, crying Woe!

Woe! Woe to Zurich. Some imitated Jonah, and gave a truce of forty days to the city. What need of more? I should be more foolish than they were I even to name all their audacity. But we who by the bounty of God stood firmly by the sound doctrine of Christ, although throughout the city one counseled one way and another the other, we believed we should teach correctly the proof of the Spirit. Something was accomplished in this way, although they changed themselves into all shapes that they might not be caught. When the evil had somewhat subsided, so that the majority seemed likely to judge the matter impassively, joint meetings were appointed. But as often as we met, either publicly or privately, the truth that we had on our side ever came off conqueror. They promised then that they would prove by blood what they could not by Scripture. They did this with so great boldness and boasting that I do not doubt they were a burden to themselves. They practiced catabaptism contrary to the will of the senate and people, the public servants and police were turned back and some of them harshly treated. Finally a meeting was appointed* where each side should be heard to completeness, and when they were brought from the prison to the court or were taken back again one would pity the city and another would make dire threats against it. Here hypocrisy tried its full strength, but accomplished nothing. While some womanish breasts bewailed and turned to pity, yet the truth, publicly vindicated, came off best. For all were allowed to be present during the whole three days' fight. When finally their impudence, though beaten also at that meeting, would not yield, an opportunity was again given them to fight.† In the presence of the church the contest raged for three whole days more, with so great damage to them that there were few who did not see that the wretched people were struggling for the sake of fighting, and not to find the truth. By this battle their forces were so cut up that we

* The first was held Jan. 17, 1525.
† On March 20, 1525.

began to have much more tranquility, especially in the city, but they wandered through the country by night and infested all to the best of their opportunity. After that conference (the tenth, with the others public or private,) the senate decreed that he should be drowned who rebaptized another. Perhaps I obtrude these details upon you to your great disgust, good reader; but it is not heat or bias that has influenced me, only a faithful watchfulness and solicitude for the churches. For many of the brethren who had not discovered the character of these men thought that what had been done to them was too monstrous. But now when these people have begun to devastate their own sheepfolds, they are daily assailing us with letters and shouts, confessing that what they had heard was more than true, that they who have not had experience of this evil may now be rendered the more watchful. I think that the world has never seen a similar kind of hypocrisy. For as knowledge without love puffs up, so when conjoined with hypocrisy it is bolder than one of the people would think, and more adroit than even an astute man would apprehend The hypocrisy of the monks was crude, and they discoursed of divine things, if at all, in coldest fashion. But these men further act in such a way that they do not persuade or induce those whom they find thrown in their way; they assail and rush on them. So these wretched fellows just undertake I know not what beyond their powers; they assail the magistrates in terrible fashion; they devote to destruction the ministers of the gospel; on all sides they act like Alexander the false prophet—he would not have Epicureans or Christians at his tricky performances. For as those in the magistracy command great wisdom and kowledge of affairs, so also they who worthily preside over the ministry of the gospel ought to be established in sound doctrine, so as to be able to overcome the contumacy of those who contradict it. Now see the astuteness of these men. They revile especially the ministers, both of the church and the state, so that if ever one in accordance with duty even whispers against them they straightway are able to say they are hostile to them because they have assailed their vices. Now any one of the people who hears this will suspect the ministers of the church and the magistrates before he does these many-colored deceivers: aroused to fury they charge forward at their command, ignorant whither they are rushing or to what end they will come. Impudence and audacity increase, so that he who to-day is a simple hearer will to-morrow abuse the magistrate to his face. When it is seen whither their increase is tending and resistance is made, straightway he who is the instigator departs from the midst and leaves the miserable people to be mangled by the executioner. And they present a parallel to Ate :* whithersoever they turn all is woe; they overturn everything and change things into the worst condition possible. Some city begins to think more soundly about heavenly teaching; thither they proceed and bring confusion; they do not introduce the Lord to those which do not receive the word. Who does not discern from this whose apostles they are? Therefore establish your courage, good brethren. The hypocrisy of the Roman pope has been brought into the light; now we must war with hypocrisy itself. And you must do this with the less delay the more you see those apostles of the devil, although they promise I know not what salvation, seeking nothing but disturbance and the confusion of affairs, both human and divine, and destruction. So much about their division and betrayal of the church. They have gone out from us, for they were not of us. Yet I may add this one item: there is a small church at Zollicon† where the catabaptists set up their teaching under inauspicious beginnings. This church, though small (for it is a part of the Zurich church, only five miles out), is admirable in its constancy. For now they have about overcome the catabaptists born among them, having ever embraced

* The daughter of Zeus, who induced gods and men to do rash and inconsiderate things.

† On the north shore of the Lake of Zurich, and five miles from the city.

the word with simplicity and placidity. This opportunity these [catabaptists] had eagerly looked for, hoping that on this account the men would the more readily yield to their hypocrisy because they displayed such great simplicity and eagerness.

Now I return to their tricks, and thus I respond: When you say that the family of Stephanas is one of Zwingli's bases for insisting on infant baptism, you show great disingenuousness. For where, pray, have I ever postulated this, which you assert, as a foundation? Have I not written a special book to the unfaithful Balthasar,* the apostate, in which I briefly showed upon

---

* Balthasar Hubmaier was born at Friedberg, near Augsburg, about 1480, educated at Freiburg in South Germany, became professor of theology at Ingolstadt, and D. D., 1512. In 1516 he went to Regensburg as cathedral preacher and led the attack on the Jews, whose synagogue was destroyed. On its site a Christian chapel was erected, and he was its first chaplain. In 1521 he removed to Waldshut, near the border of Switzerland, and this brought him in contact with the Swiss Reformers. He embraced their teachings and introduced the Reformation into Waldshut, 1524. In that year Hubmaier came under the influence of Thomas Münzer, who confirmed him in the Baptist views he had previously independently imbibed from his Bible study. His accession to the ranks of the Baptists was a great gain of them. He was quickly recognized as their leading theologian. Driven out of Waldshut in December, 1525, when the city was captured by the Austrian troops and the Reformation suppressed, Hubmaier fled to Zurich. But his Baptist views made him suspected there, as the Baptists, or Anabaptists as they were commonly called, were charged with disturbing the public order and were under the ban of the State. Hubmaier was put in prison, tortured, compelled to recant, and finally driven out of the city. He went to Constance, to Augsburg and finally into Moravia, everywhere proclaiming with eloquence and success by voice and pen his Baptist views. There was in those times, when religious liberty was a term unknown to Protestants and Roman Catholics, and when Baptists especially were hunted to death by all non-Baptists, only one possible end to such a career as his. He came into the hands of King Ferdinand of Austria, was taken to Vienna, 1527, and there burnt at the stake, March 10, 1528. He died like a hero. His wife, who courageously exhorted him to firmness, was herself put to death three days later, only it was through the waves of the blue Danube and not through fire that she entered the presence of the Master who looks with pity and forgiving love upon His followers' vain attempt to bring in His kingdom by the sword. The life of Hubmaier has been written from the sources by Johann Loserth, Brünn, 1893.

what bases I strive in defending infant baptism? In this book do you not read:

On the Baptism of Infants.

I. The children of Christians are no less sons of God than the parents, just as in the Old Testament. Hence, since they are sons of God, who will forbid their baptism?

Circumcision among the ancients (so far as it was sacramental) was the same as baptism with us. As that was given to infants so ought baptism to be administered to infants.

II. But perhaps you have not read it, for in your superstition this is the first point, that he whom you wish to render doubly worse than he was may not unite with that church that has as bishops those who defend infant baptism. So I do not doubt that they have placed under interdict my books. My mention of the household of Stephanas, Lydia and of the keeper of the prison came about in the following way: I was giving you many warnings not to argue unskillfully thus: We do not read that the apostles baptized the infants of believers, therefore [infants] ought not to be baptized. First, because of the absurdity, because we might just as well argue, the apostles are nowhere said to have been baptized, therefore they were not baptized. And when you replied, it is most likely they were baptized long before they baptized others, then I replied: It was too true what Christ set forth, that some see a mote in a brother's eye and are deceived as to the beam in their own. But when I had said that it was more likely than not that the apostles baptized believers' infants, what laughter and mockery did not the faithless apostate Balthasar excite against me? Those are the columns, he says, and they bring no other Scripture but futile conjecture; we demand clear Scripture. See the crafty fellows! In the sam matter they reply by conjectures and laugh at others who adduce conjecture simply as conjecture; nay, they falsely assert among themselves that we use conjecture as a foundation. After that I very properly adduced as exampes, which showed it was more probable than not that the apostles baptized infants, the families of Stephanas, Lydia and of the warden of the prison. And these examples you will never be able to do away with, as I shall clearly show. You then continue to answer my examples thus:

Catabaptists. We reply first that Zwingli says in his book that an act of the apostles can prove nothing, which is not true. Second, grant that it is true; the obscure testimony which he alleges concerning the act of Paul, 1 Cor. i. 16, and concerning Lydia, can therefore by his own admission prove nothing.

Reply: I myself recognize my own words, and I will not permit them to be twisted by your violent appropriation of them otherwise than as they were said. It was in this sense that I said that the act of the apostles proved nothing. Everywhere we read that they baptized; by that fact we cannot prove that they did not baptize those whom Scripture does not assert to have been baptized by them. For otherwise it would follow that the divine virgin mother was not baptized, for Scripture does not relate her baptism. I would say: By a fact a not-fact cannot be proved. We read that Christ was at Jerusalem, Capernaum and Nazareth; it does not follow that he was not at Hebron because Scripture does not say so. We read that Christ taught at Nazareth, therefore he did not teach at Bethlehem, for we do not read that he taught there. Again, who does not see that the acts of the apostles are most pertinent as a defence of our acts, provided we do them in the same way under the same law? Peter thought nothing external should be placed on the necks of the disciples; James allowed that something should be imposed, principally because of the Jews who had believed. It therefore follows rightly, if it can be obtained, that all ceremonies be abrogated entirely; if this can not be done with public peace, those can be tolerated on account of the weak which do not involve impiety. For while the apostles permitted certain small details, such as abstinence from blood and things strangled, they in no way permitted believers to be circumcised. For he who is circumcised becomes a debtor to the whole law; not so he who eats not blood or things strangled. It does not follow: The apostles are not said to have eaten pork, therefore they did not eat it. So our reasoning here is: It cannot be proved that believers' infants were not baptized by the apostles because this is not written, for there are many things done, both by Christ and by the apostles, which were not committed to writing. The lawyers call this a question of law, not of fact. Something may exist in law that never issues in fact. It was lawful for Paul to draw bodily nourishment from the field where he sowed spiritual seed. For Christ had said that the laborers were worthy of their hire. Now as he did not use this lawful right, the reasoning does not follow: Paul did not receive remuneration for preaching, therefore no one should accept it. Where again, not to pass over this, your audacity ought to be considered. For when you cry out among the simple populace against the ministers of the gospel that they ought not to gain a living from the gospel: Paul with his hands provided support for himself and for others, in this, as in all other matters, you act with malicious unfairness. For he himself (Paul), I say, taught that it was right for those to receive support who in turn nourished by the word. The condition of affairs at that time admonished him, so that he did not do what was permissible, as the impious and the false apostles were assailing him. Read 1 Cor. ix. and you will learn how much Paul discussed on this matter of fact and right. You will see that it is not only foolish, but impious to argue thus: This is done, it is therefore done under warrant; this is not done, therefore it is not right to do it. I would say then by this expression nothing else than this: The acts of the apostles cannot prove anything more than that the apostles did not baptize infants— to grant for the time that they did not—but it does not follow that they are not to be baptized, or that a negative follows from the affirmative, as the apostles baptized adults and believers, therefore infants are not to be baptized. You may argue neither in divine nor in secular matters from the fact to the right; then only may a fact be adduced for the law when an act has been proved done by the law. For example, at Zurich it was permitted by the goodness of God to abolish all externals without compromising public peace. Since this was done legally it is not lawful to do away with all at Winterthur and Stein if only love as a judge permits it as right. At Jerusalem things strangled and blood were interdicted because of the weak. Now at Bern and Basel certain things which are not most wicked can be borne to a certain extent if love warns that this is right; impious things, such as the mass, idols, false doctrine, are not to be suffered. Therefore the acts of the apostles are to be a law to us so far as they were done under sanction of the law. So it is only things false and wicked that right forbids both them and us to do, apart from whether they themselves have ever done them. For when you have done that which was permissible you have done right, even though no apostle had done it. My words therefore must be understood as dealing with right and with fact. To wit, infants may not be denied baptism because it is nowhere expressly said that the apostles baptized infants. Also there is the consideration that, as we shall show clearly, the fact that they baptized may not have been put down in writing, and the acts of none may prejudice the right, much less acts not committed. So that if it were down in plain words somewhere: The apostles did not baptize infants, it would not (even then) follow that they are not to be baptized. The inquiry would have to be made whether they simply omitted the performance or whether it was not right to baptize. This we prove by John iv., where you read: Although Jesus himself did not baptize. Here you have an example of fact or non-fact. Christ did not baptize; must we therefore, according to you, not baptize? This would follow if you are to argue from a fact to a law. And you can not say:

But it says in the same place that the apostles baptized. For we should at once reply: Oh, if the apostles rightly baptized, even though Christ himself did not, we, too, rightly baptize infants, though the apostles did not. There is no difference in the cases, or rather our case is the stronger; we have Christ's not baptizing, yet the legitimacy of baptism; you have the apostles only, who did not baptize infants (supposing we grant that they did not), yet none the less, infants are to be baptized. For since baptism is legitimate, though Christ did not baptize, so is baptism of infants, though the apostles did not baptize them, unless it is forbidden by another necessity which prevents the baptism of infants. As to your reply in the second place to the examples and facts which I adduced, as follows: Grant that it is true (*i. e.*, that nothing can be proved by the deeds of the apostles unless it is clear that they acted legitimately), the obscure testimony which he adduces concerning Paul's act cannot therefore even in his own opinion prove anything. In this you have a fine answer; you turn the tables upon me beautifully. For if by acts one cannot prove legitimacy, but one must examine what is legitimate, then that Paul baptized infants in the families of Stephanas, Lydia and the jailor, cannot prove infant baptism. For I was not here intending by these examples to confirm as upon a foundation the baptism of infants, but showing how rash and false was your argument when you said that the apostles never baptized [infants], for you have no testimony to this; and then to prove that it was more likely than not that they baptized, I laid as the foundation the saying: The children of believers are as much within the church and as much among the sons of God as are their parents.

Catabaptists. Third. Just before this fundamental argument of Zwingli's Paul says: Some of the family of Chloe tell me that there are strifes and contentions among you, etc. [1 Cor. i. 11.] As here infants announced and could announce nothing (for they could know nothing), so the infants of Stephanas' family were not baptized, if indeed there were infants in that family. For Zwingli thrusts them into it, in spite of the testimony of Scripture?*

Reply. Who does not see that the church never had such impostors? They dare to reason as follows: No infant of the family of Chloe could make announcements to Paul, therefore no infant of Stephanas' family was baptized. What is there here but imposture for those who are ignorant of argument? Who was ever so unskillfully malign or so malignly unskillful as to argue thus? It can only be that they rely upon the foolishness of men. As if I should argue: No infant announced to Christ about the tower that fell, or about those whose blood Pilate mingled with the sacrifices, therefore Christ embraced no infant. Or: It is written of a certain family that it announced certain tidings, so who could not announce could not be of that family. As if announcement or any other deed made one of a family. What insanity is this?

Catabaptists. Fourth. All testimony that mentions families excludes children. This is self-evident.

Reply. Therefore when Christ was a boy he was not of the house and family of David. Then why is the family of his foster-parent Joseph so diligently written down? So when peace was given to the family of Zaccheus, if there were infants in it, were they excluded from peace? Ex. i. 21: Moses asserts that the Lord had built a house for the children of Israel, *i. e.*, given them family and posterity, when the midwives pretended that the Hebrew women had skill in helping on progeny. So those children were not children, or the women bore adults and men; for infants, according to you, are not of the family. Ex. xii. 30. There was not a house in which there was not one dead, therefore no infant was dead. But why do I plead with the aid of testimony, as if there were need to tear away with testimony of truth things said most foolishly? But that is fine which they

---

* That is, Zwingli claims that there were infants in the family although there is no plain scripture proof of it.

add: This is self-evident. As if any ass ever gaped so at a lyre as to believe him who asserted that boys did not belong to the house or family.

Catabaptists. Fifth. According to the reason, opinion and sentiment of man no one ought to baptize or do anything else, but according to express Scripture or fact, as the mass of testimony of divine Scripture proves. Just as Zwingli himself has often exclaimed against the vicar * and other enemies of God, and will not admit anything which depends upon human judgment or the custom of the fathers. But now he hastens to do what the enemies of truth have thus far done.

Reply. I am always of the opinion you ascribe to me, and have never held or will hold a different one while life lasts. But when you impute to me what the enemies of truth have done until now, you speak from that spirit which has from the beginning been false and has not been based on truth. For what else have I ever done but confirm by testimony of Scripture all that I have given out? Not by authority, though I have some modicum of this; not with clamor or hypocrisy. This will appear to my readers in the progress of the discussion.

Catabaptists. Paul teaches that what is not in the gospel or in the discourses of the apostles is anathema.

Reply. Where, pray, does Paul teach this? I suppose you refer to what he wrote in Gal. i. 8: But though we or an angel from heaven preach to you otherwise than we preached let him be anathema. I will expose your words here a little diligently, for your ignorance and your malice will both be manifest. Your ignorance because you suppose that when Paul wrote this the gospel records and apostolic letters were already in the hands of the apostles and authoritative. As if even then Paul attributed to his own letters (for they are not the least part of the books of the New Testament) that whatever was in them was sacrosanct.

---

* Faber, vicar general of Constance. See note on p. 46.

Not that I would not have his productions sacrosanct, but that I would not have monstrous arrogance imputed to the apostles. As often as they, either Christ or the apostles, refer to Scripture they mean not their own letters or the gospel records, which were either not yet written or were then in process of writing, just as the times demanded; they meant the law or the prophets. You cannot escape by saying that you do not refer to the gospels or the discourse of the apostles in writing, for you say: Whatever is not contained [therein]. You use the word "contained." And this must refer to documents [monumenta]. Here is stretched forth the finger of your malice and inconstancy. You have finally come to the point of denying the whole Old Testament, just as also at Worms Denk and Haetzer with Kautz deny in no obscure terms a full satisfaction through Christ, which is nothing else than trampling upon the New Testament; with us at Grüningen they deny the whole Old Testament, as I have seen with my own eyes.* For they have written to our senate: The Old Testament is antiquated and the testimony adduced

* These persons were prominent Baptists. Hans Denk, born at Heybach (Habach), Upper Bavaria, about 1495; was educated at Ingolstadt; and in Augsburg received into the circle of the Humanists (1520); in Basel was proof reader for Cratander and Curio, and thence in the autumn of 1523, on Œcolampadius' recommendation, went to Nuremberg as principal of a classical school. But his stay was short, for his advocacy of the views of Münzer and Carlstadt made him so detested by the local clergy that he was driven out of the city on January 31, 1524, and ever after was a wanderer. He is found in Muhlhausen, St. Gall and in Augsburg (September, 1525–October, 1526), and there he met Balthasar Hubmaier, and there he was baptized and baptized others. He was now recognized as a leader by the Baptists, which meant that he was a shining mark for persecution. He went to Strassburg and made a stir, quite captivated many people, so the authorities requested him to leave, and he did, on December 26, 1526. On January 20, 1527, he is found in Landau holding a disputation upon Infant Baptism; the next few months he passed at Worms, and there in connection with Haetzer, another Baptist scholar, made a translation of the Prophetical Books, which is still esteemed (published by Peter Schöffer at Worms, April 13, 1527). Again the zeal of the Baptists in defending their views in a public disputation (June 13, 1527,)

from it is void, and so can prove nothing. Here I look for your spirit, I say, if you assert it to be a true one. For it at the same

led to his expulsion from the city. He visited his brethren in South Germany and Switzerland, everywhere at the peril of his life. At last, wearied in body and mind from incessant wanderings and debatings, he came to Basel in the autumn of 1527, and threw himself upon the gentle and generous protection of Œcolampadius, who cheerfully received him and conscientiously, though vainly, strove to convert him. But soon he was attacked by a power no earthly protector could cope with—he fell sick of the plague and died in Basel, November, 1527. He was a pure, honest and noble man and fine scholar.

Ludwig Haetzer (or perhaps oftener written Hetzer, *i. e.*, baiter, as being an objectionable form, and therefore more suitable for a hated "Anabaptist ") was born at Bischofszell, near St. Gall, Switzerland, about 1500; educated at Freiburg im Breisgau, and became proficient in Latin, Greek and Hebrew. He lived in the circle of the early Swiss Reformers, and showed himself a brilliant though excitable youth. When chaplain at Wädenschwyl, on the south shore of the Lake of Zurich, and fifteen and a half miles from the city, he published a widely read pamphlet advocating the destruction of the images in the churches, the consequence of which was that on September 29, 1523, the crucifix in one of the city churches was destroyed. In the Second Zurich Disputation (October 26–28, 1523,) he came into prominence, and drew up the official report. In Zurich he remained for months occupied in literary work, but there he joined the radicals, who eventually became the first Swiss Baptist party. In the end of June, 1524, he went to Augsburg, with a letter of recommendation from Zwingli, but returned at the end of the year, and then allying himself with the Baptist party he was ordered from the city, January 21, 1525. He went again to Augsburg, and found employment with the printer Ottmar. But his associations with the dreaded and detested Baptists caused his banishment in the autumn. By way of Constance and Basel, where Œcolampadius received him as he had Denk, he came once more to Zurich and won at length the return of Zwingli's confidence. But he had not altered his opinions, although out of prudence he concealed them, and when he published a book revealing his Baptist views Zwingli did not stay his banishment from Zurich. So in March, 1526, he was back in Basel. Then, at Strassburg (whence he was banished in the end of December, 1526), and later in Worms, he translated the prophetical books of the Old Testament from the Hebrew, and with Denk issued the volume as already mentioned. The two were expelled (June, 1527,) and Haetzer went again to Augsburg, whence he had to go, in the spring of 1528. These repeated and now long-continued experiences of persecution seem to have broken his spirit. He went to his native village, time takes away from us the Scriptures of the Old and the New Testament, for at Grüningen you tread upon the Old Testament

thence to St. Gall, and finally, in the autumn of 1528, to Constance. There he married Anna, the widow of his Augsburg patron, George Regel. But he was charged with having married also her maid, and so he was arrested for bigamy, and on February 4, 1529, beheaded. But then the Baptists were popularly believed to be capable of all the sins and crimes in the calendar, and the probability is that Haetzer really was innocent of the accusation and died for his faith. Anyhow, his death was considered by many as that of a martyr, and was surely faced with religions ecstacy and commemorated by the Baptists.

The last person to be mentioned in this connection is Jacob Kautz, called by Zwingli under his Latinized name Cucius. He was born at Bockenheim in Prussia, three miles northwest of Frankfort on the Main, about 1500. He entered the priesthood, but a little later accepted the Reformation and preached it at Worms. He took his coloring rather from Zwingli than from Luther, and so was on bad terms with both the Roman Catholic and Protestant clergy in the city. When Denk and Haetzer visited Worms in 1527 they made his acquaintance, and he joined the Baptist company there, which had become quite numerous, and it was he who on Whitsunday (June 9th), 1527, gave out in German the Seven Articles (printed in Zwingli's Works, viii., 77, both in German and Latin,) as topics for a public debate on June 13th. These Articles of Kautz were as follows:

"I. The external word is not the true, living or eternally abiding Word of God, but only the testimony or indication of the inner to satisfy the demand for external things.

"II. Nothing external, whether word, sign, sacrament or promise, has power to assure, console or make certain the inner man.

"III. The baptism of infants is contrary to the teaching of God given us through Christ.

"IV. In the Lord's Supper neither the body nor the blood of Christ is corporeally present.

"V. All that was lost in the first Adam is and will be found more richly restored in the second Adam, Christ; yea, in Christ shall all men be quickened and blessed forever.

"VI. Jesus Christ of Nazareth suffered on the cross and made satisfaction for us in no other way than that we should stand in his footsteps and walk in the way which he has opened, and obey the command of the Father, even as the Son did. They who speak, think or believe otherwise of Christ, each in his own way makes out of Christ an idol.

"VII. Just as the literal bite of the forbidden fruit would have harmed neither just as much as at Worms upon the New. If you admit it not to be true, what boldness is it to simulate the divine Spirit with

[Adam] himself nor his descendants if he had not eaten of the same with his mind, so also the bodily suffering of Jesus Christ is not real satisfaction and reconciliation with the Father without internal obedience and the greatest desire to yield to the eternal will.

"Of these articles thus formulated, no one must be judge except only He who speaks and testifies in the hearts of all men, as Scripture says. For no man has been commanded by God to call the truth into judgment, but only to testify."

It must be confessed that some of these Articles were repugnant to the prevailing orthodoxy, but in a less strenuous time they could have been debated without persecuting those who held them.

There were at that time close connections between the Reformed in Worms and in Strassburg, and many of the Baptists in the former place had come from the latter. Accordingly the Strassburg Reformed pastors issued, on July 2, 1527, a pamphlet entitled: "A faithful warning of the preachers of the gospel in Strassburg against the Articles which Jacob Kautz, preacher at Worms, has lately issued concerning the fruit of the Scripture and the Word of God, Infant Baptism and the redemption of our Lord Jesus Christ, and other doctrines."

There is no evidence that the purposed debate ever came off, but the city banished Kautz, along with Denk and Haetzer, and henceforth he was a wanderer. He went first to Augsburg, then to Rothenburg and in the beginning of 1528, to Strassburg. There he had a debate with Capito and Butzer, June, 1528, and remained at liberty till January, 1529, when he was cast into prison for street preaching. He was released only to be banished. He is heard of only twice again. In 1532, he applied in vain for permission to return to Strassburg; in 1536, he was teaching school in Moravia. The date and place of his death are unknown.

The allusion to a Baptist denial of the whole Old Testament at Worms is to that by the company of Baptists already mentioned as gathered in that place. Grüningen, which is also mentioned in that connection, is a village in the Canton of Zurich, and twelve miles southeast of that city and some three miles back of the north shore of the lake. It was an early Baptist important center and, therefore, a scene of ruthless persecution.

Capito in his letter to Zwingli of June 9, 1527 (see latter's Works, viii, 76–78) reveals the attitude of the Strassburg Reformed clergy towards the Baptists, to whom he had for a while inclined. He charges them with fantastic belief and fanatic conduct. It is very likely there were mystics and fanatics among them, but testimony from violently prejudiced quarters should be received with caution, for from all that appears, the rank and file of the Baptists were good and God-fearing people.

such persistency and wantonness! But in vain do I offer you this alternative, for you will never admit your spirit to be a lying one. I will arraign it then by the very power of him who silences the kind of spirit in which you abound, so that it does no more dare to assert: Thou art the Son of God. For as falsely and faithlessly as you did they say: Thou art the son of God. For as often as you confess Christ (by "you" I mean your leaders) you make a confession worse than the demons. For pain constrained them, for they so experienced his power and might that sincerely they confessed that he is the Son of God. But if you ever confess him you do it with pretence, for as soon as you hope for such an increase of your forces that you may speak disdainfully of him without being called to account, suddenly you assail his kingdom and goodness. For does he who denies that Christ has thoroughly made satisfaction for the sins of the world by one offering of himself—does he say aught but: Christ is false, he is not God, he is not our souls' salvation? Of this enough has been said above, I think. But it is time to prove your spirit. You openly teach that felicity can come to none but by works of righteousness. So Christ, whom the Father sent into the world to become a victim for the despairing, is made void. Of this victim you have no need, for you trust in your righteousness But do you truly trust? By no means. For not only does divine Scripture teach that all men are liars and that all things are under sin through the law; even the human reason of wise men reaches the same conclusion, so that it sees that man thinks and does nothing except by his favor. I have adduced the testimony of Cicero in my *Commentary* for this purpose—it would take too long to repeat this here.* So the oracle attributed to Apollo, "Know thyself," makes clear to us that man within and at heart is worthless and evil. For man is not told to inspect himself that he may con-

---

* Allusion to his *Commentary on the True and False Religion*, see Works, iii., 171.

template himself with pleasure, but that he may descend into himself and weigh both himself and his [works]. He will find such corruption that he will not rashly think highly of himself whom he finds so low, or have a low estimate of another than whom he sees himself no better. Since then even human reason perceives, when it is quite frank and thrusts itself into the hidden recesses, that man is altogether evil, with what boldness do you assert trust in human innocence? Or will you perhaps say that we must not trust at all? According to your opinion then we shall all be adjudged to ultimate condemnation. For if felicity must come by our innocence, and this innocence is wholly denied us, then felicity for us has perished. Then why do you simulate innocence? Why do many of you take to themselves these words of Christ and boast: Which of you convicteth me of sin? I therefore judge that this is the result, whether you assert that innocence is man's and from this innocence (which the apostle calls righteousness) felicity [flows], or whether you deny it, your hypocrisy is made clear. For if you insist that felicity follows from our deeds, reason and common sense oppose. What have you to do with sacred Scripture, which you so hold as a supplement or appendage that you lay it aside whenever you please? If you deny that it [innocence?] can be obtained, why then do you pretend that what you see can pertain to no mortal, that you hold with both hands? Read again and again this refutation, I beg, and you will come to know yourselves, unless you are more obstinate than the demon. What then? At Worms you deny Christ, and lead the way back to trust in works, because the men there who have recently become interested in religion are little trained in the wiles of hypocrisy, and so are susceptible to your tricks. For when they see your squalor and hear also your sounding words about innocence they assert that you have assumed this squalor that you might the more put on God; they therefore receive you as men of God, and supply richly what they possess. For what chest is so firm that it will not yield to such sanctity, what pouch so close as not to open to so vehement a spirit? Worshippers of the belly! At Grüningen you deny the Old Testament, for you see there many who are not affected by a pretence of sanctity, and detest the boldness with which you talk about "spirit" when Scripture does not suffice. Since therefore you see that catabaptism, from which you hope as from a fountain to derive all your counsel, is proved by no Scripture; while infant baptism can be defended by the Old Testament, you reject the Old Testament. Since then you disparage part of the Old and part of the New, you only show that you are the very worst and most fickle of men, indeed atheists. For while you draw from the records which are written about Christ the matters that concern baptism, you make Christ himself of no account. So it is known to all that you do everything for contention's sake, however much in hypocrisy you simulate sanctity and simplicity. Further, since you reject the Old Testament for the reason that you cannot endure what is deduced from it in reference to infant baptism, you clearly evince that you make of no account him who is God both of the Old Testament and the New. Let me not seem too immoderate, dear reader. You will see that in all matters the case of these people is worse than my pen can show. What hidden ulcer is that they cherish—but why do I say hidden ulcer, when it is not hidden that they deny both the Old Testament and Christ himself? Weigh a little carefully their words, which we copy here. Paul, they say, teaches that whatever is not in the gospel or discourses of the apostles is anathema. You see how openly they reject the Old Testament. You see them as wishing to appear to strive by Scripture, yet distorting Scripture as they do here by Paul, even making that Scripture lie which Christ called in as testimony. And have the apostles taught anything that they had not drunk in or proved from this Scripture? A fine and learned saying that: "Whatever is not in the gospel or in the discourses of the apostles, let it be anathema." The oracles of the prophets or of the poets [*i. e.*, poetical books of the Old Testament,] are not contained to the word in the gospel and apostolic commentaries, so they are anathema. Thus ought they to speak who make themselves masters of all. Who, pray, thus speaks? Do not all who base their speech on this axiom speak thus: Whatever is asserted without the testimony of the Old and New Testament, let it be anathema? But now I will restrain my chiding, for I think that you, most devout reader, see clearly this hidden ulcer.

Catabaptists. John xvii. 20 gives a good reason through the mouth of Christ as he says: Neither pray I for these (*i. e.*, the apostles,) alone, but for them also which shall believe on me through their word. The apostles have their word from Christ, but Christ has [his] from the Father.

Reply. Unite these words, reader, to those immediately preceding, that you may see how trained a sense they have in citing Scripture and how excellently they square what they thus caw out before an unskilled people. What will they of the authority of Christ? Is it that he is to be believed because what he has said and taught he has drawn from the Father and his disciples from him? Then why do they not believe Christ, who just before said: For their sakes I sanctify myself, that they also might be sanctified through the truth, *i. e.*, really and truly sanctified?' By which words he means only what Paul does when he says, Heb. x. 14: For by one offering he hath perfected for ever them that are sanctified. Why do they not believe him when he says: God hath not sent his Son into the world to judge the world, but that the world might be saved through him. He who believeth in him is not judged, etc. And: No one cometh to the Father but by me. Why do they not believe his apostles? Peter, *e. g.*, saying: Ye yourselves are built up as living stones into a spiritual house, a holy priesthood, offering spiritual sacrifices acceptable to God through Jesus Christ. And Paul: Through him we have access to God. And: He is our redemption. In fact whither does the whole teaching of Paul tend if not to show that through Christ alone sins are done away and salvation is given. Why do they not believe John? Little children, he says, I have written these things to you that ye sin not. But if any man among you sin, we have an advocate with the Father, Jesus Christ the righteous. He is the propitiation, not for our sins only, but for the sins of the whole world. These people then have not the purpose of proving that faith is to be had in Christ's words and his apostles', for they have none themselves; if they had they would not assert justification by works.

Catabaptists. Sixth. By the same rule by which Zwingli thrusts infants into the family I thrust them out, but by Scripture; this Zwingli does without Scripture, for infants cannot be counted among the baptized families.

Reply. First, I ask by what rule do you think I thrust children into families. By none. Do you not see then that men are born of men, that parents support and protect children? You see how those angel messengers of the devil have put off all human sense. Their head in hell knows that a demon is not born of a demon. So having become his slaves they suppose that this has become obsolete among men viz., that man should beget man and foster what he has begotten. Hear therefore what I mean, and how I would say: It is more likely than otherwise that the apostles baptized infants. For in the sacred Scriptures we have whole families baptized by them, in which it is more than likely that there were children. So to you this does not seem the more likely? Show the reason, and teach us how it is more likely that there were no children in those households, of which we mentioned three. But I will throw them out by Scripture, he says. But who, pray, are you that throw them out? I throw them out, he says. He must be a man of great authority among you to promise that, yet he shows none, neither baton nor scourge. For however he promises, he furnishes no evidence by which he may demand that he be believed. . . Himself said it, forsooth! Children, he says, cannot be reckoned among the families baptized. Here is Scripture for you! That master of ours thinks they cannot be reckoned in; who will dare to contradict him? Zwingli, he says, thrusts children into the family without Scripture. What then if upon you, you raging wild ass (for I would not call him a man who I think was baptized among the shades on the Phlegethon,* both because it seems funny to strive with ghosts and because I am not sure, even though I am led by certain assured conjectures to conclude who is the author of so learned a confutation †)—upon you I should bring down loads of proof from Scripture, from which you may learn that children are to be reckoned in baptized families. In Acts ii. 44 we read: And all that believed were together, and had all things common. Here I ask: Did the believers have their children with them or not? If they did, were they not in their families? If not, how is it we nowhere read that they were anxious because he who believed could not have his children with him? Was the spirit that impelled them so cruel as to dictate the abandonment of their children? Oh! You do not mean that they did not have them and nourish them, but that these did not belong to the Christian family! I ask then what you mean by family? You will doubtless say: Those who had come to such an age that they knew what law is and what sin is, for he must repent who wishes to be baptized, but since infants cannot repent, they cannot be included in the family. Thanks to God that you have learned to make so fine a rope of sand, twisting out lie from lie.

* Phlegethon was one of the five rivers of Hades.

† The document is generally attributed to Conrad Grebel, who had been converted by Zwingli from a licentious life, and who became one of his ardent followers. He joined the radical party in Zurich, and when Zwingli would not go their lengths he turned against him, and in letters to Vadian, his brother-in-law, abuses him. See *Die Vadianische Briefsammlung*, ed. Arbenz, *passim*. Grebel belonged to a prominent Zurich family. His father was beheaded as a traitor (November, 1526), and he himself was banished from the city for his Baptist faith in 1525, and died of the plague the next year at Maienfeld, in the canton of St. Gall and a couple of miles north of Ragatz.

For having persisted in the statement that none is to be baptized but he who can repent, you will rightly assert that infants may not be baptized. But here there is need of a law forbidding, and you have no law. You therefore are the law, and where the lion fails you, patch on the fox. And why not? What one of your brethren weighs how correctly or incorrectly you reason? But we, who are accustomed to assert nothing not abundantly founded and supported by divine testimony, we know that Isaac, even when an infant, belonged to Abraham's family so completely that he compelled his father to send forth the servant and the child born of her. Does not this seem so to you? But Paul joins Moses in saying: The son of a maid-servant shall not be heir with my son Isaac. He was heir, and doubtless of the family. For even they who are not heirs, such as slaves and freedmen, are of the family. I do not care to plead here that by lawyers this son whom you disinherit here is declared a member of the family. I hasten to this: Ex. xii. 48 we read—we who go to the Old and the New Testament as to two lights to prevent us from being deceived, while in the meantime you support yourselves on your own spirit—as pearls do on their own absorption when nothing flows into or moistens them from outside—we read, I say: And when a stranger shall sojourn with thee and keep the passover of the Lord, let all his males first be circumcised, and then he shall rightly keep it. Why is said here: All his males? Does this pertain only to adults? Why then the precept to circumcise every male on the eighth day? Yet infants are not of the family. To me the opposite seems true, for they possess heirship. But it is yours to prove by Scripture that they who received the sign of the church of God in accordance with the rite and religion of the parents belonged not to their parents' family. But that you will as soon do this as cut through an isthmus I will show by other evidence. In Acts xxi. 5 Luke writes: And after some days we went on our way, all bringing with us wives and children, etc. Were the children here only adults? And if not adults, were they not of the family? What miracle is here, or what is the special attention, if the fathers of the family brought the apostle on his way with wives and youths or almost adults? This was the special attention, that fathers with their wives carried or dragged with them the children, as is customary during such eager times. Now they took with them not others, but their own sons; these were therefore in the family. There is no reason to admonish you, good reader, that I am exposing some trick or guile. For what difficulty will there be in discovering this to be malice, in that they do not reckon the infants of believers with the father's family. For it cannot be foolishness, since they themselves are counted in the families of the Denks and Hetzers and Kautzs (wonderful flock) to their finger-nails.

Catabaptists. Seventh. Grant that there were infants in these families, the truth yet does not favor that those infants were baptized. But it follows with insult to truth and divine wisdom.

Reply. Who can wonder enough at the assurance of the man? He grants that children were in those families, but says they were not baptized. Yet in the first passage the words are: But I baptized also the house of Stephanas. In the second: But when she was baptized and her house. In the third: And he was baptized and all his house. How could he say in general, in the first place, that he had baptized the house of Stephanas, which he did not do if there were children in it whom he had not admitted? The same must be said about the second. But in the third case, when he asserts that the whole house was baptized, how is it that they do not see that in the beginnings the same custom obtained as with Abraham and his descendants, who circumcised the whole class of his servants, as well those taken in war as the home-born slaves and those bought, not to say the children, as appears from the passage just cited from Exodus? There it is expressly commanded to circumcise every male of the family, and there is never any mention of believing or knowing God, which yet ought to be the especial care of all It follows, he says, with insult to the truth and wisdom of God. Though they know neither, they affirm insult to both. But what contumely is it to either God's truth or his wisdom that Hebrew infants were circumcised and included in the faithful families? But these words of theirs are high-sounding; this is their merchandise—bombast and words a foot and a half long. To words of this sort, which they use in great rotundity, the unskilled mob erects its ears and then applauds.

Catabaptists. Eighth. The last chapter of this epistle shows that the apostle neither knew nor baptized children. Zwingli dishonestly keeps this back; it makes against his foundation of glass. Paul describes this family to the learned when he says: Ye know the house of Stephanas, that it is the first-fruits in Achaia, and that they have addicted themselves to the service of the saints—that ye submit yourselves to them and to every one that helpeth with us and laboreth. A family of this sort pædobaptism and pædobaptists do not recognize; they do away with it, for it is against them.

Reply. As in many other places so here, we easily catch the author of this frivolous confutation, although the greatest proof is the Swiss tongue, in which it is so written that it has no foreign or imported words. Yet, as I have said, since the man now doubtless burns among the shades as much as he froze here through his catabaptist washings, I have concluded to omit his name.* What impudence is this, O shade, in that you assert that I wish to ignore these words of Paul. Were these words

---

* The editors of Zwingli's Works think that here, as on p. 155 and elsewhere, is an allusion to Balthasar Hubmaier because, as they say, Œcolampadius announced to Zwingli on July 19, 1527, that there was a rumor that Hubmaier had been burnt at the stake. The rumor was false and the editors made a slip, as this treatise of Zwingli's is dated July 31, 1527, and the letter of Œcolampadius is really dated August 18, 1527. (*Works*, viii., 85.) But the allusion probably is to Conrad Grebel, as already stated on p. 155. To burn among the shades it was not absolutely necessary to have been burnt at the stake first.

not cited by Haetzer in the first two debates? Did not I reply that they were synecdochic, like 1 Cor. x. 1 : All our fathers were under the cloud? But there were infants also under the cloud, yet no individual mention is made of them. All crossed the sea. Yet the infants could not have crossed. Therefore they crossed who did not, but were borne by those who did. So in the family of Stephanas there were those who were the first believers of the Achaians; there were also those who at the same time belonged to the church, who in actuality, because of age, not yet believed or took part in the ministry of the saints. All were baptized unto Moses. He speaks throughout of the fathers, the ancestors and forefathers, by which we understand that they who were then infants Paul now calls fathers, for out of these was the people of Israel. Therefore not only adults, but infants also, were baptized unto Moses. For if they who were infants at the crossing of the Red Sea were not baptized, the apostle did not speak correctly in saying : All were baptized unto Moses, for they were, as I have just said, the fathers of their posterity. Whither do you turn now? Not to pass this by : Infants are written of by the apostle as then baptized. But you say it is a figure. Very good. It was a figure like this : As those infants then belonged to the family of their earthly and their heavenly Father and were sealed by their sacraments, so now also they who are children of Christians, since they are also sons of God, use the sacrament of God's sons. You will find no crack by which you can escape. For you argue foolishly to the negative from facts and examples, or rather from neither fact nor example. For what do you but say : The apostles are not said to have baptized infants, therefore infants are not to be baptized? Does not your whole strength turn on this one hinge? But we cannot so strive, but only by facts, if only one has to stand and judge by examples, as follows : The Hebrew children were all baptized in the cloud and in the sea, just as are ours. Paul, in the passage cited, tends in no other direction than to prove that they are as much initiated by our sacraments as we ourselves. It follows therefore, first, that in Paul's time it was the custom of the apostles to baptize infants; second, if any one contradicts it he vitiates the opinion of Paul. What does this man here than the like? He says we are not superior to them, and they are not inferior to us. He attributes to them then the same sacraments as we have, and to us the same as they had, as in Col. ii. 11. Those ancients could not all be baptized exactly as we are unless we were all baptized with our families. All these therefore being baptized and made equal with us, it is clear that as all their infants were baptized in the sea unto Moses, so also in the time of the apostle believers' children were baptized unto Christ.

Now I return to the point, and assert that the children are spoken of by synecdoche in: All crossed the sea. For to be accurate crossing occurred only to those who were of an age and strength to cross, and that all ate the same spiritual food when those alone ate who were spiritual, yet none the less it is said of all that they ate. So also in this place, if Paul had used the word "all" and had said: *All* of Stephanas' family have given themselves to the ministry of the saints, yet by the very force of synecdoche the infants also would be understood to be of the family, and [likewise] that they who then had believed had given themselves to the Lord. For this is the nature of synecdoche, that when as to any body that has different parts, and those parts are similar in some respects and different in others, anything is predicated of the whole body, it is understood of a part, and what is said of a part is understood of the whole. Here is an example of what I mean. All Judea went forth to him. You see that "All Judea" is put for those who went out, and the synecdoche is two-fold. One puts the container for the content and the other the whole for a part: the Judean region for the inhabitants, all the inhabitants for a good part of them. On the other hand see Is. iii. 16: Because the daughters of Zion are haughty. Here the daughters of Zion are a part of the whole, yet they are put for the whole people, especially for the princes who erected haughty crests wickedly against the Lord. Ex. xvi. 2 : All the congregation murmured against Moses. But how did the children murmur? They were ignorant of what was done. But if they did not murmur the whole congregation did not murmur, for the children were also of the congregation. You see what sort of critics you are, laboring in logomachy and desperately ignorant of what you most trust in. For you cling to the letter alone, and are ignorant of what is of prime importance in expounding the letter. Tell me, pray, to whom was it said : Thou shalt not take the name of the Lord thy God in vain, and thou shalt not steal, and the like? Was it not to the ancients who were the people and church of God? But those things cannot be said to infants ; are these then not to be of the church and people of God? God forbid ! The children were members of the people of God, the fathers indeed of the people. Gen. xxv. 23. It is clear therefore that what is said with reference to some body or whole when there is a part of that whole to which what is said does not relate, that part none the less belongs to that body, even though what is said does not fit it. Again, if anything is said of a part of this body or whole which yet does not belong to that part at all, yet it so relates to the whole body that it touches and admonishes those parts that are subject to what is said, as is clear at once from the examples cited. " Thou shalt not steal " is not said to the infants, but to those who are under its responsibility. Again, the threat that Isaiah makes against the daughters of Zion pertains to all who oppressed men by their violence and haughtiness. So also I replied, though not in so many words, to that passage that Haetzer adduced from Paul, by which he would exclude the children from the family of Stephanas. Yet that family appears to have been pretty large, if we worthily weigh the generously ample words in which Paul treats of them. Children remain therefore till now in believers' families and are baptized, and when mention is made of those families, or they are written or spoken of, whatever is said or told pertains to that part to which it is applicable. I might adduce numberless examples, for the Hebrews use almost no figure more extensively, but I think a taste has been given by which you will easily tell all the rest. " Israel my inheritance." To whom was this said, if not to the Israelitic posterity? But children can not receive this. It does not follow therefore they did not belong to the inheritance or the peculiar people. But although there is a part that cannot understand what is said, that part none the less belongs to the whole body. So when Christ said: Go ye, teach all nations, baptizing them, etc., the apostles taught all who were accessible to the doctrine, and they baptized all who were fitted for the sacrament of baptism.

Catabaptists. Paul, a man of truth, wished in this first chapter [of First Corinthians] to show that he had baptized but few at Corinth, but Zwingli and his witnesses make Paul a liar, and say that he baptized many when they assert that he baptized infants in the house of Stephanas.

Reply. Because we say that doubtless there were children in the families does it follow? Therefore they make Paul a liar, who asserts that he baptized but few. As if, though infants were baptized, they who were baptized by him could not be numbered still as a few! What, pray, can you do with such a stupid kind of men? What kind of a church do you think that which—I will not say believes, but—listens to a man asserting such things?

Catabaptists. Tenth. How the reality is, this text shows which says: Let no one say he was baptized in my name and thence be puffed up on my account. If infants then should speak and be factious (as those Zwinglians would have it) they were rightly baptized.

Reply. See how fine they are at a syllogism! Let no one say, says he, infants can not speak nor be factious, therefore they were not baptized. As if none could be factious but those who said they were of Apollos, Cephas or Paul! Then, as if we had not just shown that by synecdoche that is to be understood of any part which is suitable to it.

Catabapiists. Eleventh. It is not true that Paul baptized Corinthian children.

Reply. Gently, I beg of you.

Catabaptists. Why? Because he baptized believers alone or saw that they were baptized by others.

Reply. Now you argue finely, for it follows at once: Believers only were baptized, therefore children could not have been baptized—provided you can establish that exclusion, that believers only were baptized by the apostles.

Catabaptists. As we shall establish it from Acts xviii. aud xix., to the confusion and disproof of the misleading pædobaptist contention.

Reply. The mountain is laboring.

Catabaptists. It is thus in the Acts, xviii. 8. When Paul was at Corinth, Crispus, the ruler of the synagogue, believed in the Lord with his whole house, and many Corinthians who heard at the same time (I translate faithfully and literally, perverting nothing, however those fellows struggle and stammer even in the German tongue) believed and were baptized. Infants could not hear, they could not then believe, much less be baptized. For the hearing faithful were baptized. And here the whole house was rendered faithful, from which infants are excluded, and they were so excluded because there were none there, or if there were they were not counted in it and accordingly not baptized, for the faithful families were baptized.

Reply. Infants could not listen [to the word], but it does not follow that consequently they were not baptized. We have nowhere the prohibition not to baptize infants of believers unless they hear and believe. I require a prohibition forbidding. But you add beautifully: And here the whole house was rendered faithful. I grant it. You continue: From which infants were excluded. This I ask you to prove from sacred Scripture. I hear it said: Infants are excluded, but nowhere by a divine oracle. Here the whole dispute hinges. There was a strife among the apostles whether the gospel should be preached also to the Gentiles or not. This strife rested partly upon a false inference, partly upon probability. The fallacy was this · To us the Christ was promised, therefore not to the Gentiles. But who is so unskilled as not to see that it does not at all follow: The Messiah was promised to us Jews, therefore not to the Gentiles. For it may be that he was promised also to the Gentiles, and the Scriptures testify to this in various ways. So in the present passage: The writings of the apostles testify that they who heard and believed were baptized, but it does not at all follow that children were consequently not baptized by them. For it may at the same time be true that the apostles baptized believers, and the apostles baptized children. Just as it is true: The Hebrews circumcised adults, they also circumcised infants. For when adult, nay, decrepit, Abraham inflicted upon himself the wound of circumcision and upon the infants Ishmael and Isaac. You are mistaken therefore, O Catabaptists, when you make an indefinite proposition exclusive. An exclusive is either, no one ought to be baptized except he who first believes, or infants ought not to be baptized. But from: The apostles baptized believers, and from: The apostles are not said to have baptized believers, it does not follow. For "The apostles baptized believers," and "No one may be baptized unless he first believes" are not equivalent. So also with: "The apostles are not said to have baptized infants, therefore these were not baptized by them and may not be by us." For it may be that they baptized both believers and infants, and also either that they baptized infants, but the fact was not recorded, or that they did not baptize them, and still these were baptized by the ministers of the churches or may be rightly baptized. For [the apostles] were sent above all to preach, not to baptize. If you impute sophistry to me here, as the boldness of the calumniator suggests, recognize that the following is your syllogism, or rather paralogism: The apostles are not said to have baptized infants, therefore they did not, and these are not to be baptized. So that we are compelled to turn your weapons against yourselves. This is probably what led the apostles to think that the gospel was not to be preached to the Gentiles. In the first mission this interdict was given: Go ye not into the way of the Gentiles, from which it was possible for them to assert most strongly that it was intended by Christ that he should keep himself for the Hebrews alone. If you had had such a deliverance, ye gods, with what impudence would you have rushed upon us! Consider therefore these two commands: Go ye and teach all the Gentiles, baptizing them in the name of the Father, etc., and: Go ye into all the world and preach, etc. Here we have the abrogation and annulment of the interdict: Go not into the way of the Gentiles. For they had before taught and baptized. They who thus far then had been shut up to the enclosure of Judea found opened to them the whole world. Thus, I will say in passing, you find these latter passages opposed like an antithesis to and abrogating: " Go not into the way of the Gentiles." You have not therefore yet proved the negative: " No one may be baptized but the believer."

Catabaptists. So also Acts xvi. 31 has: Believe in the Lord Jesus and thou shalt be saved and thy house. And that his house was saved with him follows on: And they spake unto him the word of the Lord, and to all that were in his house. Then further: And he was baptized, and all his, straightway. He heard the word of the Lord, and so he was baptized, and all who were in his house; they, too, heard and so were baptized. Where again infants are excluded, for they could not hear and believe, as follows on: And he rejoiced with his whole house, because he had believed in God.

Reply. To pass over some things translated into the Swiss tongue not with entire fidelity, I briefly say: This whole knot may be cut by the one axe of synecdoche. For if there were infants in that family, what is said about faith and doctrine we apply to those who could receive and believe, but what is said of baptism, to those who belonged to the family of the believing master, but through age or weakness neither heard nor believed. For when God said: Hear, O Israel, the Lord thy God is one God, he spoke to all who were of Israel. But because the infants neither hear nor understand he does not exclude them so that they are not of the congregation of the people of God or should not be circumcised with all who hear and believe.

Catabaptists. Twelfth. Philip preached to the whole city of Samaria, where doubtless there were infants. Yet Luke speaks in these insuperable words: And they were baptized, men and women. Men and women, says Luke. But if some sciolist should say, as a certain Wittenberg sophist lately did: Under the word women girls are also included, and under " men " males, this is fiction. For preceding these words we find: Philip preached, they believed. They, the men and women, I say, believed and were baptized. So here falls synecdoche, Zwingli's other basis. This synecdoche is a comprehensive mode of speech to the effect that where Scripture speaks of believers baptized, infants, too, are included among them, as he strives to prove by perverting the Scripture passages that do not contain this.

Reply. I pass over, O shade, what that Wittenbergian did with you while you were in the flesh. But this is sure, that this passage does not exclude infants, even though it does not mention them. For that does not exclude which does not explicitly mention; for to pass over is one thing, to exclude, another. That may be omitted which is in no way excluded. The excluded can never come into the account. Since then the omitted, as well as those expressly mentioned, are included by synecdoche (as has been sufficiently shown), we are still waiting for you to prove that exclusion of yours by which you assert infants are excluded. For we have proved that by comprehension (*i. e.*, synecdoche, unless the Latin word is less appropriate than the Greek,) they are included. In that you promise to show how I had asserted synecdoche only by twisting Scripture, again you are rich in promising, but poor in fulfilment. For when you would tear away synecdoche, you establish it most firmly.

Catabaptists. As in Acts ii. 44: All who believed were together and had all things common. Here, says Zwingli, if believers alone were there, whither had they removed the infants? If they had cast them off, they would have been fine believers to disown the children against the command of the Lord. So the children of believers were also numbered with believers and were baptized with them. To which we reply: Zwingli speaks rightly when he says that they would not have been believers if they had cast off the children. For how could it be that these who had all things in common did not have the children common nor educate them in common, according to the precept of the Lord? Infants then are not numerated or reckoned among the believers, but are included in this, that the believers had all things common.

Reply. You see, good reader, whither the lie turns itself. They would rather enumerate believers' children with their animals and baggage than with the parents, lest they be compelled by synecdoche to include them with believers. For they will not include them with: All who believed were there, but with: And they had all things common. Among them therefore children are not like dear pledges, are not our flesh and blood. For what else will they when they deny that they are included among the believers, and put them in what all have common? What tiger, pray, is so cruel? Surely to this pitch of insanity ought they to come who have put off not only the sense of piety, but also all human sensibility. Here I beseech you, pious heart, not to take offence at what I am about to say. For here it must be put down (not that I yield so much to passion, but that those things ought not to be ignored by all which those people secretly perpetrate, like what Alexander the coppersmith did to the divine Paul), so that we may the more easily guard ourselves from this pestilence. In describing their deeds I shall be free and brief. They have their wives common in such a manner as to desert their own marriage partners and take others; so with the children, as to desert them and leave them for others to support. These fine fellows, when lust persuades, make common a brother's wife, even his virgin daughter. Though the very force of nature requires that they cherish their children by the sweat of the body, they make them common to others.

We have a man named Figella (Hafner ?), who lives about a mile from the city. He most contumaciously protected their teaching, and had got together for his house provision wherewith to spend the winter, and as often as meal-time came around the idle flies were present, prophesying finely about God, for they think their babblings worthy the name of prophecy. The father, wife and children were held fast by these wonders until the provisions were exhausted. The man then, least expecting what would happen, hoped to provide other food with the aid and assistance of his table companions; he warned them that it was time to get to work providing nourishment. He talked to the deaf, for when he was compelled to lay the warp and set the woof (for he was a weaver), and looked for their help in some part, they began to praise God that his providence prepared and promised all things for them as it were unsown and untilled, and laid hand to no work. Meanwhile he learned from his wife that they had attempted adultery with her under the pretext of piety, and [when] he saw that they were bellies, and not the angels he had a little before supposed them, he drove the scoundrels from his house, recovered his eyes and returned to the Church of Christ. Here you see how public they would have things. The lost fellows would have the goods of ordinary men common, but their own, if they have any, in no wise. If they have none they make all common in this way: they distribute the labor to others; they enjoy leisure so as to do nothing, then they eat in common. So with wives, not to do away with the *Republic* of Plato,* they make common not their own, but others. This is proved by the following: One of their leaders lived in a village about five miles out of the city,† a man of considerable wealth. His wife came to him in haste when he was going away that he might leave something for the children. She asked blood from a stone. Meanwhile the wife remained for the night, perhaps hoping that her blandishments would win something from him, and when the hour arrived she sought the couch of her husband, and the spiritual man replied to her: Did I not tell you that you came only for lust? He then cast her off, and called to him a Catabaptist girl. When the wife, foreboding evil, opposed this, he devoted her to evil. " You are carnal," he said, " and so you think and suspect carnal things. You will be damned eternally." Since her suspicion was in no way shaken by the maledictions, she came to us and told us what her husband, elsewise so impatient of lust, imposed upon them to believe—*i. e.*, about spiritual marriage. For there was room for the suspicion, since he had gone with the same girl on several occasions to St. Gall, and alone with her had passed not only through groves and shady places, but had occupied her couch during the night. Now finally he disclosed the mystery—there was a spiritual marriage between them—to which statement the wife gave no credence. So this fellow would have left his wife common to others that he might leave something common (he never touched her afterwards), unless she had kept her marriage vows with better faith than he, and took a common girl, or rather, made her common.

I will give also another example. There were elsewhere also those who contracted spiritual marriages after a similar fashion; by silver rings they purchased of jewelers they bound girls and women spirits to them. There were such in the school of Valentine,

* Allusion to the teaching in Plato's *Republic*, Book v.

† This village probably was Zollicon, which was five miles out.

as Irenæus testifies in his first book.* At St. Gall public charges were made against two girls who had been of unblamed modesty until they had gone over to the Catabaptists, but whose modesty had suffered shipwreck when their bodies were immersed in catabaptism. They affirmed that they were betrothed in spiritual marriage, the rings being accepted, and in one night on one couch two Catabaptists had so loosed their virgin belts that the couch, groaning for a long time, at length, impatient of the burden, threw on the floor with one crash the two marriages. Those who heard the downfall swore solemnly that those spirits made such a sound that it appeared as if four bodies had fallen from on high. I beg you, reader, not to go away before considering that the force of hypocrisy surpasses even the attack of lust. By which they may be the less self-complacent who, even if they were chaste (which I do not myself believe), yet were such in order to lay up for themselves this glory among mortals. For those very girls had before been tempted to the crime, but in vain. Hypocrisy is therefore more potent than the flesh, for under the pretext of the Spirit and by deceit it has carried the tower of virginity. Why should I speak of the open adulteries, which, although many, are few in comparison with those concealed by their skill? But who can fittingly tell of the awful murder which a brother perpetrated upon his own brother in St. Gall? † What ability in words can worthily set forth so great

* Irenæus, *Adv. Haer.*, I., vi., 3. The passage is as follows:

"Some of them are in the habit of defiling those women to whom they have taught the above doctrine, as has frequently been confessed by those women who have been led astray by certain of them, on returning to the Church of God, and acknowledging this along with the rest of their errors. Others of them, too, openly and without a blush, having become passionately attached to certain women, seduce them away from their husbands and contract marriages of their own with them. Others of them again, who pretend at first to live in all modesty with them as sisters, have in course of time been revealed in their true colors, when the sister has been found with child by her [pretended] brother." (*Ante Nicene Fathers*, Chr. Lit. Co., ed. i., 324.)

† Thomas Schinker upon his brother Leonhard.

atrocity? Or who is so dull as not to see that God has set forth this example for the good of all, so as the more to deter from this pernicious sect? A brother calls in a brother who is thinking of no such thing into the presence of his father, mother, sisters and the whole family, and orders him to kneel in the midst. The fanatical fellow obeys, thinking his brother is going to show some wonder. Doubtless the parents had the same expectation, for almost daily among them something new is born, as in Africa. But when this one had kneeled, the other seized a sword which he had brought for this purpose, drove it through his neck and cut off his head, which rolled to the feet of his parents, and left him lifeless. From his trunk poured a great quantity of blood. All there fell and became [as] lifeless in madness. The murderer himself ejaculated: The will of God is fulfilled. Like a madman he came into the city and cried out to the Burgomaster: I announce to you the Day of the Lord. For at that time they were appointing as the day of the Lord that Ascension Sunday that passed two years ago. I cannot jest here at that murderous sect, for the deed was too atrocious to admit any mirth. They assert for many other, but especially for this reason, that a Christian may not exercise the magistracy, that a Christian may kill no one. And at the same time they all deny that they can judge that crime I have been describing. A parricide therefore is not charged among them, while a homicide is.

Now I return to the matter. Not without reason will they not reckon among believers the children of believers who live with the church; they put them among the things that are common, for they make a man as valuable as a beast—nay, a beast loves more truly a kindred beast than that murderer his own brother. What is there wonderful then about their using virgins and matrons as they do beasts and baggage animals? Among them it is no crime to lay murderous hand upon a brother; how much less will they hear an accusation of adultery and lewdness! Those who are rebaptized unite with a church that denies, if they themselves commit it, that adultery and harlotry is a crime. For to that purport once he who is now a shade said to me, when they were asserting that they were without sin: They would at once shut out from the church him who committed any wrong. I at once reminded him of the man who had committed adultery at Wesen;* he replied: Even though he committed adultery, he did not sin. They who are in our church cannot sin. Then I said: So adultery is not sin among you? There is no adultery with us, he said: I will not say whether [adultery] is sin or not, but that is not adultery which you think is. For since we have one and the same spirit nothing can take place with us which is sin, for as we have one spirit so also we have one body. This sentiment they now preach in open terms. Those who are rebaptized unite also with a church that does not know to judge parricide [fratricide]. But the most noble senate of St. Gall— a city that is most regardful of the glory of Christ— executed the parricide [fratricide] at the prayers of parents and kinsmen, and thereafter, a sign being given by the Lord, suppressed so prudently this evil that nowhere are there fewer Catabaptists, although in the beginning their number was very great. For that whole family had been immersed, and the house itself was the meeting place of the Catabaptists—the house where a brother dipped his murderous hand in his brother's blood. From this one might rightly say that it was stricken with death by divine justice, both on account of the family and the Catabaptists.

Catabaptists. Otherwise Zwingli would be compelled to admit because of the following context that infants sold their goods and distributed them, which is impossible, and has nothing to do with them, for the property was their believing parents'. And from the context it would follow that the infants who are reckoned among believers, and so baptized, were obliged to celebrate the

* At the west end of the Lake of Walenstadt, no mean rival of Lake Lucerne, some twenty miles southeast of Zurich. There Zwingli had passed his boyhood in his uncle's house.

Lord's Supper because they were baptized. Similarly they must have prayer with the other believers, for the preceding and following context is as follows: And they continued steadfastly in the apostles' doctrine and fellowship, and in breaking of bread and prayer. Who steadfastly continued? All that became believers. If then infants became believers, or were numbered with them, they also broke bread, which no reason can make out, and they were also not baptized. For if they were baptized, they also broke bread, which Zwingli himself will not maintain. Now see how synecdoche hangs together!

Reply. Why do you charge me viciously with a skill in arguing which I never assumed, but [which] is deceitfully attributed by those who cannot sustain the force of the truth on which I rely, since this whole paragraph is only vicious reasoning? For when you oppose synecdoche, you make clear that you do not yet see what synecdoche is. For you do not yet understand that there is no synecdoche where the words are received in their simple and true sense. For where this is the case there is no figure. That discourse is figurative which does not bring us the sense which the first aspect of the words carries. Synecdoche is a figure, so where synecdoche is some other than the open meaning is hidden. Hence when you thus infer: If infants were numbered among the believers, they broke bread, prayed, sold their goods and distributed to the needy, you take everything according to the letter. What then? Do you wish to eliminate synecdoche from the passage? Why not say then: This passage does not admit synecdoche, and then prove it by argument and evidence? But this cannot be done, since I have proved more than sufficiently above that infants belong to the family of the parents, and that you act not only impiously, but inhumanly, when you prefer to include believers' infants among baggage and goods rather than among believers. If, however, you have come to the poin of confessing this discourse to be figurative indeed, but here require of synecdoche that whatever is said of the whole body be true of all its parts (as every one sees you do think when he looks closely into your teachings), you are wholly in error. For that is not synecdoche where, as we have said, what is said of the whole is true of each part, for then there is no figure. But that is synecdoche when a part of any body is received for the whole, or the whole for a part. I have shown this by the clearest examples. Still, that you may be supplied with all abundantly, hear this. In Ex. xxiii. 17 it is written: Three times a year all thy males shall appear before the Lord thy God. Notice this word "all." Tell me, then, were infants in the cradle from all Palestine carried thrice a year to Jerusalem? If so, then according to your argument, they ate unleavened bread for seven days, sowed the fields and offered the firstfruits. But since they did not do this it follows that [all] males were not included. If they were not brought it is not true that every male appeared thrice a year before the Lord. "All males" is therefore synecdoche, and however on first appearance it seems as though every male is ordered to be present at the three feasts, they alone are bound by the law who were so old that they could receive the instruction or offer firstfruits or bear branches of trees, according to the variety of the feast or manner of celebration. So also when Deut. xxxi. 11–13 speaks of appearing at the reading of the law at the celebration of [the feast of] tabernacles it appears that those boys came who were beginning to understand what was read. So also Luke ii. 42 shows from Christ, who when 12 years old was a participant at the Passover, that they appeared who could themselves make the journey and understand what was done. At the feast of Pentecost it appeared that they alone went up who offered the firstfruits, a duty of the father or his representative. Here therefore is synecdoche. Again, Ex. xxxiv. 19: Every male that openeth the womb shall be mine. This can not bear synecdoche. For it so pertains to all the firstborn [males] that none is left exempt. I think you now see how crude and unlearned is your argumentation, since you do not deny synecdoche in the passage: They who believed were together, yet contend that all must be predicated of each part that is contained in the whole of which the synecdoche treats. But you do not consider the composition of the word itself—*sun* and *ex* with *dechomai*, as if you would say: When I take the whole body I understand something separate from among those things which are together included in that body. Or: When I take some part of the body I understand the whole body. So that the Latin comprehensio does not quite correspond with the Greek. Then when you contend thus: If then infants were counted among the believers, or were made believers, they also broke the bread, a thing that cannot at all be, and so they were not baptized. For if they were baptized, they would also have broken the bread. You reason wretchedly, so that it is clear to all who read your productions with judgment that you are all impostors. For since you leaders are not so untaught as not to see how wretchedly you reason, and since none the less you offer to the untaught vicious syllogisms, you cannot be saved from being impostors even by the Saviour himself. For what constrains it to follow here that they who were baptized also broke bread? Were there not among the ancients circumcised infants who yet did not tear the lamb nor eat unleavened bread? Or because thrice a year they were not present, were they therefore not of God's people? Learn then that infants were counted among believers and were baptized, and that of believers those actually believed, prayed, distributed property, broke the Lord's bread, who had come to such age and understanding as to be fitted for this and subject to the observance, as is clear from the examples drawn from Exodus and Deuteronomy. Every male was directed to be present at the feast, the women and boys at the reading of the law; but however the letter reads, by synecdoche is understood every class according to its manner and understanding. What have squalling [infants] to do with the reading of the law, or adolescents with the offering of firstfruits, unless the father directs them?

The thing itself compels me willy nilly, good reader, to cease to give the vain words of the Catabaptists and to draw to a close. So hereafter I will act thus: I will untie every knot, and whatever is said by them that has any force I will adduce with such fidelity as I have thus far in rendering it literally into Latin. And for this reason in particular, that what they have thus far adduced against the figurative sense has been in great part refuted. What they have argued about the Testament will be so treated and torn away when we reach the Testament.

The arguments against the synecdoche in 1 Cor. x. 9: All our fathers were under the cloud, they all crossed the sea, all were baptized unto Moses, all ate the same spiritual food—the arguments, I say, that they bark out against these synecdoches are so foolish and impure that they are not to be taken into account. For they say they know that they ate, drank, crossed the sea, went to stool and urinated, but it must be proved by us by clear Scripture that infants were baptized. After that they insult us this way: See now how Zwingli stands with his synecdoche, which he affirms with his own peculiar cunning and sophistry, lest by acknowledging the truth he may suffer the persecution of the cross of Christ. What can you do with these men? That I might expound synecdoche correctly I adduced these examples, which they are so far from tearing away that he who will may use them, not only as examples of synecdoche, but to show also that in the apostles' time believers' infants were baptized, as I have indicated above. They approach the matter with bitterness, since they can do nothing by the sharp energy of the word of God. They charge cunning and sophistry, which I so express my abhorrence of that all my writings can free me from the charge better than any oration prepared for this purpose. But I recognize and cherish the truth. And I should have to endure nothing if I should adopt your opinion, unless you are most mendacious, for you have promised oftener than I can say that all will eventuate happily if I join you. But you had to have recourse to calumnies and shouts when you undertook to overthrow synecdoche, for you saw this to be impossible. This remains, and will ever remain, synecdoche: The fathers were all baptized, the fathers all ate the same spiritual food with us, as was shown in the foregoing sufficiently and will be treated again in the following. Thus far I have replied to the first part of your refutation, to the rest I will do the same in the course of the disputation. Now I proceed to the second part.

SECOND PART.

This part is to overthrow the foundations of your superstition; although you have never published them, yet hardly any of your people exist who have not a copy of these well founded laws, as you call them. Why, pray, do you not publish what are so divine and so salutary? But counsels evilly conceived fear the light, and are terrified at the judgment of learned and pious men. For this reason you do not publish the dogmas, articles, principles of your superstition. I therefore shall expose them to the world, translated faithfully and literally into Latin. As in the first part, your position shall come first, then the refutation.

TITLE OF THE CONSTITUTION OF THE SECT OF THE CATABAPTISTS.

Articles which we have drawn up and to which we agree, viz.: Baptism, abstention, breaking of bread, avoidance of abominable pastors in the church, [of love], sword and [of wrong] oath.

To this article I say the same as the apostle in Col. ii. 20 : If ye be dead with Christ from the elements of the world, how is it that you set forth decrees or dogmas as though you were in the world? But I know what you will say: These are not human dogmas, articles, principles, but divine oracles. To which I reply: Why then do you say you have drawn them up and agreed to them? If they are divine, why do you call them the articles of your conspiracy? Why do you smear the mouth of the divine word with your human ordure? If not [divine], why do you impose new decrees upon the necks of your brethren? You would therefore rule in the Lord's stead, secretly lead into captivity, and place a check on brethren's liberty. For however you turn you need no new articles; divine providence does not need your consent, which is nothing else than conspiracy. But thus heavenly wisdom orders all things. As often as we apply to you the term "sect," because you have withdrawn from the churches that confess and embrace Christ, you at once reply that you cherish no sect. And now you yourselves produce this beautiful offspring of yours. Is not he a heretic who has conspired unto particular articles, though you with a more respectable nomenclature denominate it an agreement? But now I turn to the overthrow of the foundations of your articles, so that the world may see that what you affirm to be divine is fanatical, foolish, bold, impudent. This is not too severe.

Catabaptists. First learn of baptism. Baptism should be administered to all who have been taught penitence and change of life, and who believe really that their sins are done away with through Christ, and in general who wish to walk in the resurrection of Jesus Christ, and who wish to be buried with himself into death that they may rise again with him. So we administer it to all who demand it and require it of us themselves after this manner. By this all baptism of infants is excluded—that chief abomination of the Roman pontiff. For this article we have the testimony and support of Scripture; we have also the custom of the apostles, which we shall preserve in simplicity and also in firmness. For we have been made sure.

Reply. Behold, good reader, in how many ways these jugglers impose upon the judgment of the simple. For, first, who does not know that baptism should be administered to all in Christ, both penitents and those confessing that remission of sins is found? There is no contest here, but whether it may be given to those alone and not to their infant children. Second, they conceal justification by works, and though they admit remission of sins through Christ here, they clearly deny it elsewhere. For they who trust in works make Christ of no effect. For if justification is by the works of the law, Christ has died in vain. Third, they yet do not conceal it so thoroughly as to betray their opinion by no sign. For when they say that remitted are the sins of all who wish to walk in the resurrection of Christ and to be buried with him in death, they elevate free will, and next to that justification by works. For if it is in our choice or power to walk in the resurrection of Christ, or to be buried with him in death, it is open for any one to be a Christian and a man of perfect excellence. Then Christ spoke falsely the words: No one can come to me except the Father who sent me draw him. Finally here is discovered their chiefest evil: When they refuse an oath to the magistrate who asks it, they plead this reason: According to the word of Christ a man cannot change a hair of his head to make it shine white or be dim with blackness. But here they say: They who wish to walk according to him, and then: Who themselves demand of us; after, of course, they have promised that they will walk according to the resurrection of Christ. Will he then who makes this promise be able to walk according to the stipulation or not? If so, why then will he not swear to do this or that when he is able? If not, you in like manner ought not to demand that he promise to walk according to Christ lest he become a liar, as you forbid him to swear lest he become a perjurer. Fourth, where in the Scripture do you read that baptism is to be given none except to him who can make a confession and demand baptism? Of yourselves do you assert this, for circumcision was most often given to those who could neither make confession nor demand. But you reject the whole Old Testament. This is what you clearly betray in the former confutation. This point ought to have been treated by me, but it has fallen out. It therefore comes in properly here when you say: There is no need for me to seek baptism in the Old Testament. By which do you not despise the Old Testament? And yet Christ submitted himself and his teaching to it, and the apostles used no other Scripture, indeed they could not, since until after the beginning of their preaching there was no Scripture as yet other than that drawn from [the Old Testament]. Here therefore your error, in which you do not consider the analogy of the sacrament as does the apostle Paul in 1 Cor. x. and Col. iii., so that we ought not to neglect his example—your error, I say, causes you to deny that in all Scripture the sign of the covenant is given to any except to one who makes confession and demand according to your way of thinking. But is not this deciding dogmas and ordinances? Fifth, you say: We have the testimony and support of Scripture for this article. Who lies? to use a German taunt. Produce that Scripture testimony of yours, and all strife will be laid. Sixth, where do you find this custom of the apostles to baptize no one who had not made this confession of yours and forthwith demanded baptism? Seventh, they say: Which we simply and at the same time firmly will preserve. For we have been made sure. Why do they promise to do what is not in their power? But if they refer to baptism, *i. e.*, that they will baptize according to this rite, again they dogmatize, *i. e.*, make decrees. This they themselves recognize, for they add: For we have been made sure. If they could show from Scripture the firmness of these ordinances, they would doubtless adduce it. But since they cannot, they have recourse to revelation and the confirmation of the Spirit. We are made sure, they say—himself said it. Here we ought not to omit in passing the fact that this has caused their error about the resurrection—they do not see that Paul in Rom. vi. 4 uses an argument from the external sign in order to exhort the more ardently to the imitation of Christ. But wherever they find the word baptism, even though the discussion is not about the sacrament, the truth striving to the contrary, they twist it to some perversion.

Catabaptists. Second. This is our opinion regarding abstention or excommunication: All ought to be excommunicated who after they have given themselves to the Lord that they may walk in his precepts, and who have been baptized into the one body of Christ and are called brothers or sisters, yet either slip or fall into sin and imprudently are thrown headlong. Men of this sort ought to be admonished twice in private; the third time they should be corrected publicly before the church according to the precept of Christ. But this ought to be done according to the ordinance and command of the divine Spirit before the breaking of bread, so that all who break and eat one bread and drink from one cup may be together in unison in the same love.

Reply. If I am silent as to this law I shall seem to approve it, but if I touch on certain things I shall appear captious. Since then it is all so crude that it smells of nothing but a three days' theologian, I will myself suffer that in this place ignorance be called simplicity, and will note in a few words a few things which ought not to be winked at. They err then in this when they say: The third time they ought to be corrected publicly before the assemblage. For the third time they should be admonished by the church, not corrected. Then if they hear not the church as it warns they should be expelled. Second, they err again when they say this should be before the breaking of bread, unless you understand by this the denunciation customary among the ancients, which only forbade to the excommunicated who had before been cast out the breaking of bread with them. Excommunication did not take place then unless the occasion demanded it, but access was denied the excommunicate to the feast of the church. This I say because it is the Catabaptists' opinion that they should refuse to celebrate the communion unless those who are to do it first confess or bear witness that they are about to pronounce excommunication or banishment [from the communion]. I do not think this is according to the custom of the apostles, who seem to have celebrated the supper of the Lord without interdict of this sort. But where one had been convicted of a great crime he was already banned. And I think it sprung from that usage that before the Lord's Supper the excommunicate and banned were publicly interdicted. I do not think it came from the institution of Christ that some ancients and some moderns had and have the custom of thus warning: Let no homicide, usurer, adulterer, drunkard, etc., approach. For if an adulterer or drunkard, or one addicted to any other crime, defile the church he ought to be warned according to the command of Christ, and if he refuse to confess after the testimony of witnesses before the church he ought to be shunned or to be excluded from the church, but so only if contumacious. But if only rumor travels around (it is sometimes mendacious), or he who is under suspicion can rightly ward it off, so that he appears to carry himself honestly, then he ought not rashly to be excommunicated, unless the thing is absolutely certain for which he is excommunicated. This I say not of myself, but after comparing carefully and weighing the words of Jesus on this subject. For when he says to Peter that one is to be forgiven seventy-seven times, and in another place orders the tares to be permitted to grow until harvest, he evidently shows that there are some things at which fraternal love may wink. But when, on the other hand, he commands to expel straightway after the reproof of the church has been despised he surely means in those matters which are manifest and may defile the church. For there are some, sad to say, too ready on one side or the other. Some who think that nothing reaches to the point of requiring dismission, perhaps because they labor under the same or an equal disease; there are others who, if some passion persuades them, at once cry out: Why is he not excommunicated? Moderation therefore in this matter with the greatest diligence (which is to be sought from the Lord) is to be observed here. But what reason is there why the Catabaptists should say aught to us about excommunication when they have not considered the judgment of, or how they ought to judge, the murder that took place in St. Gall, when a Catabaptist murdered a Catabaptist and a brother a brother?

Catabaptists. Third. In the breaking of bread we thus agree and unitedly determine that they who wish to break one bread in commemoration of the broken body of Christ, and to drink of one cup in commemoration of his shed blood, shall first come together into one body of Christ, that is the church of God, in which Christ is the head. And this is particularly through baptism. For, as the divine Paul teaches, we cannot be at the same time participants of the Lord's table and the demons', nor can we be participants at the same time of the Lord's cup and the devils'. *I. e.*, all who have communion with the dead works of the shades have no communion with those who are called from this world to God. All who are settled in evil have no part with the good. Therefore it ought to folow that they who have not the calling of their God to one faith, to one baptism, to one spirit, to one body with all the sons of God, they cannot unite in one bread. But doubtless this must be done if one wish to break bread according to the precept of Christ.

Reply. Hither, doubtless, all this superstition tends, that the untaught people, that rises to every novelty, be led away into catabaptism and to an evil church. You admit no one to the Lord's Supper unless he have first united by baptism into the one body of Christ. So by baptism as by a cement each one is united to this body. Why then do you strive so mightily that no one be baptized unless he first believe and confess with his own mouth? See how consistent you are ! But you would not speak here of the church's baptism, but of heretical baptism, *i. e.*, your sect's, and this, as it is born outside the church, is justly called pseudo- or catabaptism (some prefer " anabaptism "). Since then you do not recognize rebaptism or contrabaptism, though nevertheless against the standing custom of Christ's church and against the divine law, by your baptism you crucify Christ again (for as he was once dead and once was raised from the dead, so he desires to have once baptized him who loves Christ) ; you do not dare to call your rebaptism catabaptism, but you call "baptism" that which is rebaptism. And while your words appear as though you were unwilling to admit any one to the table of the Lord unless he has been baptized, what you mean really is that no one in your evil church should hope to be a participant at the table of the Lord unless he has been rebaptized. This is what you mean, I say. Behold the tricks of the impostors, my reader. They talk simply about baptism, but will not be understood about simple but about double baptism. To this the confirmation of their law bears witness when they add: For, as the divine Paul teaches, we cannot at the same time participate at the Lord's table and at demons'. By which they mean only that initiates who were baptized in youth belong to the demons, though they beautifully cover up this error so as not to be compelled to answer a new question which is beyond them, *i. e.*, whether the baptism which we as children received is not sufficient? For they were vanquished by us when they at length declared this baptism to be from the Roman pontiff, and so from a demon. Nevertheless they carry around a long document in their church, in which they show from the decrees of the pontiffs that infant baptism was begun under popish rule—wicked men that they are, since I showed them before that in Origen's time, who lived about 150 years after Christ's ascension, baptism was in common use, and afterwards in Augustine's time, who flourished about 400 years after. For both testify that infant baptism had remained to their own times from the custom of the apostles. But in those times the name of pope, and also monarchy or tyranny, had not come into the churches. And I refuted their statement (that you may lose nothing of our side, reader,) that the baptism of the pope is not Christ's, but a demon's, in the following way: If baptism were of the pope alone, I would not object to their calling the pope's baptism either "not Christ's" or a demon's. But the baptism of Christ is not the pope's, even though the pope were the arch-demon himself and used Christ's baptism, for when the devil used the prophet's word in the temptation of Christ, the prophet's word did not become the devil's; and again, when the demons cried out: "Thou art the Christ the Son of the living God," so salutary a confession was no less salutary because a demon made it; so when the pope baptized not in his own name, but in that of the Father and Son and Holy Ghost, it could in no way be vitiated so as not to be the baptism of Christ's church. In the second place Christ himself said: "He that is not against us is with us." The pope therefore has this much of good, that he baptizes in no other name than that in which we were baptized; in this he is with us as was he [with Christ] who expelled a demon by the power of Christ's name, although he neither followed nor cherished Christ. Finally the apostles have left us in the matter of matrimony a fine example, both in this matter and in others which pertain to disputes about externals. For as some had married among the Gentiles before the apostles had carried to them the salutary teaching of the gospel, so they [the apostles] left those marriages intact. This is clear from the testimony of Paul in 1 Cor. vii. 13, where he commanded the faithful wife to dwell with the unbelieving husband, provided she did what was pleasing to him. This is nothing but the confirmation of the marriage laws which each nation had, even of those marriages entered upon in idolatry. Equally therefore we may not repudiate a baptism which is not only not founded upon the pope's invention or authority, but depends upon the authority of Christ himself and the apostles. For the popes baptized in no other name than that of the Father, Son and Holy Ghost. But in whose name do they suppose marriages among idolaters were made? Yet the apostles left these marriages whole and intact, no matter what the laws and gods under which they were undertaken. The more therefore will baptism be untouched by us when it is given in that name in which we give it, even though the pope have administered it. Then they offered as objection too hatefully the matters of salt, butter, saliva, mud and that class of things, nay, even the prayers made over infants, on the ground that neither John nor the apostles are said to have begun or celebrated baptism with prayer. To which I replied, first as to ceremonial: Christ restored some blind men to sight by the medium of touch or of mud others by the words " Receive thy sight " alone, and they saw no less distinctly who regained sight by the medium of touch or mud than they who did by the words alone. But we care nothing for those externals if the church orders them to be abolished, and it has been brought about that it forthwith gave the order, we who preside over the church not being ignorant that in the beginnings of the church there was need of these things, though not so much was attributed to them as in our times, whence we cut them off without difficulty. As to the prayers which they attempted also to tear away, I replied: The Lord Jesus himself prayed over the infants brought to him. What madness is it then to be unwilling that we pray over infants! I had the best of it in this part, the Catabaptists in the other. All this, I say, they know and conceal in their false church, or rather their conspiracy. And so, to return from my digression, since they know from these reasons and this basis of Scripture that it is not the pope's baptism, but Christ's, in which we are baptized, and yet they contemn it, it is clear that they act by no right or reason, but in violence and fury—by which they call, though not truly yet plausibly, their own rebaptism baptism—so as to be able to draw the hearts of the untaught to a rebaptism.

Finally, lest by their words it may be manifest whither they tend, they bring finally an exposition of this their baptism and separation, *i. e.*, they say: All who have communion with the dead works of the shades have no communion with those who are called from the world to God. You will consider diligently all this, reader, and I am sure you will discover by what wiles and stratagems they allure to their conspiracy untaught men. Do you not see that in this exposition they wish to seem to intend only that they who most impudently sin ought not to attend the supper of the Lord? But while you see this most clearly, do they not do this same thing under the action of the law of excommunication or banning that immediately precedes? Therefore whither reaches the treatment of one and the same cause under two constitutions? You infer therefore with no trouble that by this principle they wish—no matter what string of words they put together—that he who would come with them to the table of the Lord must also be rebaptized in their catabaptism, and that they who were baptized as infants these men consider to be of the devil's table. This is therefore the sense of their exposition —men who have gone over to the church of their rebellion and conspiracy belong to those who have been called of God from the world, but they who will not with them betray the church of Christ belong to those who communicate with dead works. For their words and daily abuse testify to this. For when they see marriages or public feasts celebrated among us they straightway cry out: They are Gentiles, and are of the world, not of the church. And they accept as satisfactory neither that Christ and the apostles appeared at a marriage nor that the tribes of Israel celebrated joyously three times a year, nor that the Lord's Supper would have perpetually remained a friendly feast if the Corinthians had not abused it—or indeed anything else. You see how on the one side what unjust judges they are, in that as soon as they see those things done among us which Christ himself did not abhor, they traduce, curse and condemn. And on the other hand, how sincerely they act when they think of themselves so finely that they boast that they are the people who have been called to God from the world. As if indeed lewdness, adultery, murder, hatred, envy, arrogance, hypocrisy—in which these people excel—all mortals were not worldly. I am not speaking of the immoderate expense, voluptuousness and wantonness of marriages and feasts, but I am so far from condemning joy in moderation that I think he who takes it away from the pious will have to restore it with interest. In a word, by this law they mean that no one shall approach their supper unless he has been rebaptized, unless he has been called to God from the world, *i. e.*, unless he is of the church and heresy of the Catabaptists. For whatever they do or say, a conspiracy it is, according to the word of the prophet in Is. viii., and a most wretched pretence. For what iniquity is equal to his who prefers himself to others on account of his innocence and who winks at no slip of his brother's, when he ought to forgive seventy and seven times, even if he were really most innocent who so acts? But what do I? They were not of us, therefore they have gone away from us.

Catabaptists. Fourth. We thus decide about the revolt, separation and avoidance, which ought to be manifested as to that evil planted by the devil—that we have no commerce with those nor agree with them in the communication of their abominations, *i. e.*, inasmuch as all who have not yet yielded in obedience to faith, and have not yet given their name to the Lord as wishing to do his will, are exceedingly abominable in the sight of God, therefore nothing is done by them that is not abominable. Now in the world and in all creation there is nothing else but good and evil, faithful and unfaithful, darkness and light, worldly and those out of the world, the temple of the Lord and idols, Christ and Belial, and no one of these can have part with the other. Known to us also is the precept of the Lord in which he orders us to separate from evil, for then he will be our God and we shall be his sons and daughters. Hence he commanded us to go forth from Babylon and the Egyptian land lest we share their evils and penalties which the Lord is going to bring upon them. From all of which we ought to learn that what is not united to our God and Christ is nothing but an abomination which we should shun. Here we understand are all the popish and secundo-popish works and the contentions of idolatry, processions to churches, homes of feastings, states and alliances of unbelief and many like things. They are held by the world in esteem, yet nevertheless they fight and lead directly against the precept of

Christ according to the measure of wickedness that is in the world. We ought to be alien and separate from all of these; they are pure abominations, which make us hateful to Christ, who has freed us from servitude to the flesh and made us fit for the service of God through the spirit of God which he has given us. By the strength of this constitution there fall away from us the devilish arms of violence, such as swords and other arms and things of this character, and all use of them for either friend or enemy by reason of this word of Christ: Ye must not resist evil.

Reply. What they mean by so confused a statement, which is so torn and patched that it contains nothing sound and fresh, you would hardly divine if they had not said in the title of the work that they dealt with the avoidance of abominable pastors in the church. First, they have so heaped together those statements of nothing in the world but good and evil, Christ and Belial, and the other matters these divine men have piled up together, that they would be very fine, and would give a reason for not assembling in our churches. You must not suppose this is horror of popish pastors. It is against us they rail in this fashion. For they meet with the popish and do not shun their meetings. We who stand by the gospel are assailed here. The reason is that we alone show up and shun catabaptism and their wholesale sedition. By the papists we are called heretics, by the catabaptists secundopapists, because we preserve in the church infant baptism and some other things which they will have nothing of. So are we exercised in the Lord's glory that we may bring to him a victory the more excellent the more numerous those are by whom we are assailed. I will show in a few words the deceit they conceal in the words of this article. What they allege from Scripture about separation is not said in the sense to which they wrest it. For otherwise we should be compelled to retire not only from the world, as Paul says, but also from the church. For there is nothing human so holy and blameless that it does not fail in some part. We ought therefore first to be separated from ourselves, of which Christ also speaks. Who hates his own life in this world, he says, saves it for life eternal. This separation results when we daily set forth a desire for betterment, and with our might exhort the brethren to this by example and prayer. But according to this we do not seek to be separate from those who have infirmities in common with us. The thing itself warns us, if only we be truly pious and cherish God, how far in each case we must bear. Nay, we should hear piety alone in this matter of condemning or seceding, so that establishing another law is neither possible nor due. Second, we are separated from those who are not weak, but malign, a thing that both piety and love will teach. For Christ himself also taught that the contumacious and impudently wicked man ought to be shunned only when he had reached in obstinacy the point of not respecting the church. But I know whither tends this supercilious avoidance. As soon as they have allured one to their faction, above all they forbid him to go for a month at least, if they cannot get it for all time or for longer, to any assemblage where one teaches who is opposed to their sect. And this order is at the beginning strongly suspected by those who are not yet wholly demented. Indeed, many who return to a good mind testify to this. For they immediately think of the apostles': "Prove all things." In order that by the figure of anticipating arguments they may cut off consideration of this among foolish men, they show great diligence in inculcating separation. They therefore condemn conventions, even those in which for the most honorable purposes the city holds assembly, for there are always found men who arraign the audacity of the men. And it is strange that they have omitted here what elsewhere they have urged as a prime objection. In the assemblies of the city [they allege] murders often take place—as if this did not happen more frequently in the market place and the country. According to that we must not assemble in the country or the market place. They condemn also the processions to the churches; they do this with such a form of words as might seem to apply to those votive processions which we formerly engaged in to the image at Lauretum, Baden, Oetingen and elsewhere, while really they condemn the processions to the churches appointed for certain days. These grieve them, for they prefer those where many meet in some wood by night rather than by day, when the way home has to be felt out through the dense darkness by the more comely girls and matrons, and they consummate spiritual marriages with carnal copulation; or where two or three meet at the house of a man who is a little better off, and eat and chat, lead astray the women, and in a word do many things you would hardly dare imagine. By this hunting they find much greater booty than if their auditors should hear in the assemblage of the churches what is against their doctrines. For who will protect the foolish girls and women and countrymen and simpletons from wolves of this sort when they never openly appear, nor after the manner of the apostles go to the synagogues first and disclose the sources of their doctrines in the Scriptures.* But for some months they will waste the time with some worthless idler and contaminate the whole family not only with error, but with harlotry also, and then appear in some spot. And as soon as they are asked to give the reason for their doctrine they fly away and leave the featherless chick to the hawk. Thus they are at variance with both the word and institution of Christ, who both said: "In secret have I said nothing," and commanded that what they heard in the ear they should preach upon the housetop. Now see these circumcised! Having gained permission of some house owner they ascend the roof, and there caw out that they are now fulfilling what Christ said: preach upon the housetop, etc. But when a traveler or policeman is seen at a distance they turn tail, as is recorded in the fable of the little fox. Now they condemn states

* The authorities, with Zwingli's assent, first forced these oppressed people into holding secret meetings, if they met at all, and now Zwingli taunts them for their secrecy! Alas.

also, not seeing that Paul preserved himself from violence by this one means. Is it not clear now that they have come to the point of obscuring all things, of dissolving all friendship and all union? Who ever forbade one to be a citizen? These learned men have spoken of alliances of unfaithfulness in place of alliances of the unfaithful after the Hebrew style. Alliances then are to be given up, unless we are not ready to make shipwreck by their baptism. Do you see whither they tend? For they add that they are sheer abominations which make us hateful to Christ, who has freed us from the servitude to the flesh, etc. What is this servitude of which they speak? Of course it is obedience to the Christian church, assemblage in all honesty at public meetings and in private interests of brotherhood for the sake of order and quiet, where obligations that are lawfully undertaken and cannot be left undischarged without injury and similar observances are preserved. Freedom from these and all obligations, I say, these pious interpreters in this matter assert in somewhat obscure terms at present they have received from Christ, but they will preach this openly as soon as they have gained a church upon the strength of which they suppose they can rely. So that new tragedies are to be looked for by us. I do not greatly condemn that carrying of arms which some nations have always done as a custom *—such as the German and Swiss—but I detest murder. This, however, does not always come through the sword, but sometimes by spear or rock. Therefore you will have mountains and forests removed, for out of these weapons are obtained. One man dies from the seed of a raisin, another from a goat hair in a glass of milk. I myself saw a man among my people of the Toggenburg who died from the sting of a single bee. Are then grapes, goats and bees to be done away with? But I know whither this also points. The power of every magistracy is particularly hateful to them, and they are not content with what the

---

* In Switzerland it was the custom to carry side arms in the senate, courts, popular assembly, and even at baptisms. (Edd. Zwingli's Works.)

apostle commands: Fear not authority, but do what is right and lawful. Not applicable to the magistracy is the saying of Christ: Resist not evil, nor that other; you ought not to rule. This has reference to apostles and bishops and each private individual, for authority is of God. It belongs to those to fear legitimate authority who seek the confusion of all things. Hence they snarl out I don't know what foolish statements all the time about laying down arms. Not that I either approve or assail this custom of carrying arms. But I do condemn the disposition toward slaughter beyond all mortals so thoroughly that nothing do I hate more.* I, too, teach that arms are to be laid aside, but I teach that the sword is to be drawn by which they may be struck who have done injury, those be relieved who have suffered, and those praised who have done their work well.

Catabaptists. Fifth. We thus determine about pastors of the church of God, that there be some one pastor of a flock according to the order of Paul in all things, who shall have good testimony from those who are outside the faith. Let it be his duty to read, warn, teach, instruct, exhort, correct or communicate in the church, and to preside well over all the brethren and sisters, as well in prayer as in breaking of bread, and in all things pertaining to the body of Christ to watch that it may be supported and increased, that the name of God be cherished through us and be praised and the mouth shut to blasphemy. But support ought to be supplied him from the church which elects him, if he lack. For he who serves the gospel should live by the gospel, as the Lord ordained. But if a pastor have done aught worthy of blame or correction, action should not be taken against him unless by the testimony of two or three witnesses. When they sin they should be publicly reproved, that the others may fear. But if a pastor be either driven out or be led by the cross to the Lord another should succeed him at once, so that the people and flock

* He refers here to his antipathy to the foreign military service of the Swiss, which he assailed and condemned. (Edd. Zwingli's Works.)

of God be not scattered, but receive consolation and be preserved by exhortation.

Reply. We have seen in a former paragraph how perplexingly and confusingly, captiously and obscurely they treated of separation from abominations, for their cause had little justice in it. Here we see how clear they are when they deal with their church (it is wonderful, the effrontery with which they call it a church) and their pastors. There they were after this one thing—to show their treachery legitimate, both because of the morals of men and the bishops, and they were torn by conflicting emotions, and, as is said, held the wolf by the ears. For if they extravagantly blamed the morals of the faithful they would incur the charge of evil speaking and malevolence, but if they thought moderately well of them, those whom they had brought over to themselves would not be sufficiently aroused to their secession. So since they dared not speak freely, both because of fear and caution as well as because of the injustice of their cause and malice, they concluded to speak obscurely and suspiciously, so that none attacking in open contest might easily catch the oily and chameleon-like adversary. For when you were going to say: Why do you encourage secession from the churches of the faithful, they would be ready to reply that they taught only separation from the evil, and that legitimately. When you objected that you do not denounce separation from the wicked, but that they seem to speak of separation from those whose life is wholly endurable, they could reply by heaping up, in dramatic forestalling of objections, what they can in no way correctly defend—the world, those out of the world, good and evil, God and the devil, Christ and Belial, etc. By this you could be led to reason thus: It is true what they say; all things known are either divine or worldly, and so if you found aught worldly in yourself you would condemn yourself, even if you should have commerce with worldly matters, and so being aroused would go over to the betrayers, not reflecting that when you had gone over to them you would at once find human misery there, too, just as much as among those who as citizens do as the law directs, meet in assembly, attend marriages and public feasts, bear arms and do the other things which those men blame as the very worst possible. Nay, you would find worse misery, for they are steeped in abominable crimes—to use their own vocabulary. They render his own to none, they defile wives, fail to judge parricide, take away the magistracy, eliminate obedience. But I return to the proposition. When in the former paragraph, I say, they encouraged defection, they purposely said everything in obscure terms, chiefly for the reasons I have assigned. But how plain and clear are they when they speak of the pastor of their own church! They concede, then, under this rule the support to the pastor of a heretical church which they deny to the bishop of the Christian church. Where now are those words: "They eat at the table of Jezebel; they themselves devour the homes of widows," though at that time none of us had more than seventy gold pieces, and we all said that it is much better to live from those goods which were first among the churches, or from the tithes or returns that might be collected, than, leaving those to I know not whom, weigh down the churches by a new begging of support. But thanks be to God the leaders * have thoroughly disclosed themselves here. Now they mark out support for the bishop of their own church. Where, pray, will they get it? Do you not cry out that you are more than sufficiently burdened, and probably with justice, under the innumerable contributions, taxes, giving and other exactions? But this is sweet—what they add in the marking out of support: If a pastor need aught! As if all those leaders were not most lost vagrants, who either save their soul with their feet when they owe anything or are so slothful and idle that they will not provide support by their hands. What then do you suppose they lack? A part of support? They who are so slothful and lazy that when you have

* Zwingli calls them *Coryphaei*, the name given to the leaders of the chorus in the Greek drama.

supplied all support they are hardly able to endure the labor of living. The atrabilious men! It is bile, and not the spirit, for which they sell themselves. Do we not know that it is from bile and an evil admixture that the crazy commit suicide? And are we ignorant of those atrabilious fellows who labor with their own impatience, and shall we trust their lies about the spirit? I know that all is not borne along of its own will, but is governed and disposed by the providence of God, but at the same time I see also that by his providence these monsters are led like wild boars into our liquid pools to prove us, so that it may appear whether we are faithful or not. That they have sewed together in this article of theirs a patchwork from many passages of Scripture— this I do not think needs exposition.

Catabaptists. Sixth. We determine or decide about the sword as follows: The sword is an ordinance of God outside of the perfection of Christ, by which the evil man is punished and slain and the good man defended. In the law the sword is ordained against the evil for punishment and death, and for this the magistracy of the world is constituted. But in the perfection of Christ we use only excommunication, for the admonishing and exclusion of the sinner, for the destruction of the flesh alone, as admonishment and warning that he sin no more. Here we are asked by many who do not understand the will of Christ toward us: Can a Christian use, or ought he to use, the sword against evil for the defense of the good or from love? This reply is therefore revealed to us unanimously: Christ teaches us to learn from himself. But he is mild and gentle of heart, and we shall find rest to our souls. So Christ said to the woman taken in adultery, not that she should be stoned according to the law (and yet he had said: As my Father hath commanded me, so I speak), but he spoke to her with commiseration and indulgence and warning not to sin again, and said: Go and sin no more. We must in the same way observe this according to the rule of excommunication.

Reply. I will not interpret the whole of this paragraph in its prolixity at once, but divide it into parts, and confute it as briefly as possible. Therefore when they say that the sword is an ordinance of God outside the perfection of Christ, etc., I would know to what they refer the perfection of Christ, to the head or the body, *i. e.*, do they mean to say: Christ himself is so perfect that he needs no sword (*i. e.*, the magistracy,) to chastise or punish himself, or do they mean that Christians need no sword or magistracy? If the first, I assert that the Lord of lords and King of kings is so far from needing magistracy that all magistrates draw their authority down from heaven through him. If the second, I strive with all my powers against the proposition that Christians need no magistracy. For I grant this, that it is easy for them to say that a real Christian needs no magistracy, for of faith he omits none of those things that ought to be done and does none of the deeds that are not right. But it is our misfortune that among men we do not find so absolute perfection, and may not hope to find that all who confess Christ are wholly happy, as long as we bear about this domicile of the body. Therefore the saying: The sword is an ordinance of God outside of the perfection of Christ is true in this sense—wherever the members of Christ do not arrive at the measure of the perfection of the head there is need for the sword. But they mean something else entirely, *i. e.*, that the heretical church of the rebaptized needs no sword, for it is within the perfection of Christ. For the foolish men assume what the monks used to assume, viz., that they are in a state of perfection, although they do not use those words. For when they separate from the world, crying to brethren of the same kidney, "Go ye out from them," do they do anything but guard themselves from being defiled by some filth from us? Afterwards when they say: But in the perfection of Christ we use excommunication only, etc., you see how they assert that they have perfection within their church when they say: *We use*. These most seditious men therefore would take away the sword so that they may the more freely throw all into confusion. There is no need for you to say that there are so many impious that there is no danger of taking away the sword by their preaching. For they do not go to the impious. But when they see those who have embraced the gospel—even now so great a number that if they should undertake to do what those do who defend the pope they might hope to come off superior— if they could draw these to their faction, all magistracy and obligation will be abolished. Well known is the cry of that Catabaptist when he returned to Christ: If we had been as superior to you as you were to us, you would have seen whether we had swords and oath or not. And when they would free us from all fear, and promise that all will come out as we desire it, whither, pray, do they look, if not to the multitude, for when they have gained this they will sail into port? They consequently desire to cajole those who have received the gospel to lay aside the sword. For among them the authority of the word is valid. If you repeat six hundred times the words of Christ to others, the tyrants and the impious popes, they are not all disturbed. In the perfection of Christ, viz., in their evil church, they would have the sword removed, so that they might more freely associate with harlots, defile matrons, seduce with their blandiloquence the women, confuse all settled conditions, nay, overthrow cities and men's dwelling places. For thus a little band of robbers will be able to compel the making common the goods of those who are unwilling to put them to common use. So that the more the sword ought to be preserved even on their own account, since they assail with so many stratagems the public peace, the more they deny that it can be employed among Christians. When therefore they lead us to Christ, who offered himself as an example to us of gentleness and humility, they wish to appear to have done right; indeed they would in our judgment also have done right if faith were with them. For if it were, they would continue to be mild and of humble spirit, even though none followed them, but now since there is nothing bitterer or more harsh [than they], it becomes evident that gentleness is taught by them just as we have heard that temperance was taught once by a most eager glutton. For when any edible was brought in of which he was particularly fond, he used to warn his table-companions not to swallow it hurriedly and hastily, but quietly to dwell upon it and to masticate it for a long time, and so increase the pleasure by lengthening it, in order that he might gorge himself the more abundantly. So since there is nothing harsher than these (for what age has ever seen such evil speaking?) they refer others to Christ to learn gentleness, while they themselves go as far from his example as possible. Then they adduce the example of Christ when he dealt with the woman adulterer, *i. e.*, he did not hand her over to be stoned, but regarded her with compassion, and said: Go and sin no more. Indeed they write all this charmingly, so that you may the more easily understand that those spirits are even now propitious to adulterers. But look here, you slothful and over-sensitive fellows, have you not read that Christ gave all sorts of precedents in accordance with the diversity of occasions? How often do you read the most cruel things? Here then learn to recognize a divine and punishing justice. How often, on the contrary, do you read the most gentle? There recognize pity. Then in a word learn this, that he whose first coming had nothing harsh in it, with that same one there is also the most complete justice, but since in that first coming his purpose was not to judge or condemn, but to save, he preserved the limits of his mission. Unless you show me that somewhere during that advent he assumed the authority of a judge, you will never move me by that example [to believe] that the magistracy is not lawful for a Christian. This you cannot do, for he fled when once they wished to make him king. But now that that mission has been completed, and he has sat down at the right hand of God, see whether or not he has destroyed cruel murderers and given his vineyard to other workers.

It is no strange thing that so many sects are born daily; it is wonderful that more are not produced, especially when we have so wise interpreters of Scripture that they do not yet discriminate between Christ's omnipotence, providence and divinity, by which he ever governs all, and his mission which he performed here. For when they behold that which he did in accordance with his mission here immediately they found upon those laws. Here he did not take upon himself the functions of a judge, for he did not come for that. Let no one therefore be judge. By no means. For that is to confound divine and human law.

Catabaptists. Secondly, the question is asked about the sword, whether a Christian may pronounce or give judgment in secular matters, between force and force, strife and strife, in which the unfaithful differ. To which we reply: Christ would not decide between brethren who quarreled about a bequest, but drove them away. Consequently we must do likewise.

Reply. I think it is clear enough why Christ put away this case; he had not come to prepare a kingdom for himself in this world, but that he who was Lord of all might subject himself to all. And I assert that the words of the Saviour prove this. For who, said he, made me a judge and a divider over you? Behold how he rejected the office of a judge! For although Christ was lord of all, yet in the dispensation of his humanity he never proclaimed himself king. When then he denies that he is a judge, he denies that this case concerns him; but meanwhile, when the occasion offers, does he not discuss the rendering to each of his own?—something that he almost never omits. If ever a reason is given for discussing necessary matters, he always passes from the gross to the spiritual. But here in passing by this he openly teaches that there was some judge to whom they could refer the case, but Christ was not he, so he made no decision. Therefore we see the office of judge rather confirmed than done away, even among the devout. So Paul's admonition to bear injury rather than litigate with a brother does not involve that a Christian may not be a judge; it urges us not to be litigious. So also Christ warned against lawsuits because of the danger, since it often occurred in fact that he who hoped to return from the court a winner was thrown into prison till he could pay the whole debt. But this is excessively Christian when they say: In the lawsuits which the unbelieving engage in—meaning by the unbelieving all who are not of their heretical church. For they assert that a Christian may not exercise the office of judge in external matters —yet this is a divine matter if rightly performed. While they arrogate to themselves the judgment of the inner man (for they call all unbelieving who of a whole heart cherish the true God and the one Jesus Christ, provided these do not follow their erring flock). And they do this openly. For often two of them pass by good and devout men and one of them, the other being left to go on, stops to chat with our people; then the one who has gone on, turning about, cries out to the other: Brother, what are you doing among the unbelievers? Go away from them! Gentle men, indeed, who occasion some damage as often as opportunity permits! Which class seems to you, reader, to be the gentler and more humble—they who think nothing but violence and injury or those who overcome all audacity by sweetness?

Catabaptists. Third, about the sword it is asked whether a Christian ought to hold office when it is appointed to him. We reply that Christ was about to be made king, yet he fled and did not look back, according to the ordinance of his Father. So ought we to do, *i. e.*, follow him, and we shall not walk in the darkness. For he said also: He that would follow me must deny himself and take up his cross and follow me. He even interdicted the power of the sword, and thus denounced it: The kings of the Gentiles rule, but ye are not such. So Paul says: Whom God foreknew he also predestinated to be conformed to the image of his Son. Peter also said that he had suffered, not ruled, and left us an example that we might follow in his footsteps.

Reply. That Christ would have been king if he had not fled has been discussed above. For he came not to be tended and ministered to as tyrants are, but to minister; not to give the whole world for the redemption of his own skin, as you Catabaptists do, betraying all your brethren when peril threatens, but to give his life for all mankind. He came for this, I say. Yet he never forbade a Christian and one worthy of empire to become a king even. "Who would follow me must deny himself and take up his cross and follow me"—this was not said by him to indicate that no one could take office because he did not. For many kings have despised themselves and followed him, though retaining their royal authority until the end. If Saul had done this he would not have rendered the mountains of Gilboa illustrious by his calamity. "The kings of the Gentiles exercise authority over them, but ye are not so," was not said to interdict from the magistracy. We ought to consider the occasion by which he was led to express this sentiment. The apostles had been contending about the leadership. Let us then recognize that it was said to them. For as he had come not to rule, but to redeem, so also he sent the disciples: As the Father, he said, hath sent me, so I also send you, *i. e.*, to preach, not to rule. So since the apostles acted in Christ's place, they ought to restrain their desires to rule after the pattern of their archetype Christ. He commanded them therefore not to rule; nay, to each private individual he implied that he should not put himself forward. I will prove this by the testimony of the apostles themselves. Peter ordered slaves to obey their masters, not only good and humane ones, but even the perverted. Behold how he opposes the perverse to good and humane! He means by the good those who were faithful; by the perverse, not the harsh and unkind, but those not in the faith. Therefore there were faithful masters. Peter also baptized Cornelius the centurion. The high functionary of the Ethiopian Candace was baptized by Philip. But if, according to your opinion, a Christian may not exercise the magistracy, and penitence and confession of faith are required before being baptized, then Peter and Philip did wrong in baptizing these before they had resigned office, or a Gentile who has been placed in office may also be baptized and received into the church. But in Paul we find mention of a Christian Quaestor and faithful master. For in writing to the Ephesians he says: Slaves who have faithful masters. And to the powerful of the Colossians he writes that they should act justly to the slaves whom they possess. I pass by Sergius Paulus. Now neither Peter nor Paul in writing to magistrates and masters discourage them from mastership. But when they write to the bishops, how often, pray, do they advise not to compass lordship in their duty, *i. e.*, in the inheritance of the Lord, not to circumvent the brethren or throw a snare or be violent or the like! Clear, therefore, is the word of Christ: Ye are not such. Even the apostles understood it only as directed to themselves. What these cite from Paul respecting conformity to the image of Christ applies equally to kings and beggars; nay, they are more conformed to the image of the Son of God who in the height of power place themselves among the lowest, as did the Son of God, than we who creep upon the ground. Peter, they say, asserted that he had suffered, not ruled. He did that for which he was sent, as has been said often enough.

Catabaptists. Finally we learn that a Christian may not be a magistrate from what follows. The magistracy is a carnal office, a Christian is spiritual. Magistrates' home and dwelling are corporeal in this world, all Christians' are in heaven. The first are citizens of this world, Christians of heaven. The arms of the former are carnal and against the flesh; of the latter, spiritual and against the machinations of the devil. Earthly magistrates employ brass and iron, but Christians put on the armor of God—truth, righteousness, peace, faith, salvation and the word of God. In short, just as our head is disposed toward us, so ought all the members of the body in their entirety to be disposed through him, that there be no strife in the body to destroy it. For every kingdom divided against itself perishes. Since therefore Christ is as he is described, the members must necessarily be such that the body may remain sound and whole, to its own preservation and upbuilding.

Reply. You stupid seducers, for what more appropriate words can I apply to them? The magistrates' office is carnal, say they. They might say at least that their power is directed toward the carnal and external. For are those things carnal that are mentioned in Ex. xviii. 21 : Provide out of all the people able men, such as fear God, men of truth, who hate covetousness. Therefore a judge ought above all men to be rightly affected to all and unwavering, giving no decision in partiality or hatred or fear or violence. But who can better do this than a most devout person? But because he has to do with those who do whatever they please, according to the impulse of the flesh, does not make him less spiritual than those who think themselves so mightily so. It actually occurs that a father has to judge his son, as occurred to Saul, Brutus, Manlius and others. In such cases what are we to think a judge has most need of? Firmness, surely. But the flesh does not supply that, but either desire for glory or contention, and then it is not firmness, but persistency—such as that livid kind of yours—or from love of righteousness, which can be from God alone. A judge of this sort is more spiritual than those gentle little fellows who preach to us a kind of womanish gentleness, especially since there is so much evil among mortals. A judge of this sort is of more advantage to the glory of God and the advancement of the public peace than the whole Catabaptist heresy, though it should include its thousands of thousands. Consequently a judge or magistrate ought particularly to be a Christian and a spiritually-minded man. So God himself deigned to call them by his own name Elohim, because they should be most like God as high priests of righteousness, equity and firmness. "Their home" (*i. e.*, judges') "and habitation are corporeal and in this world; Christians' are in heaven." As if those words sounded to us of heaven! Where are you, pray, when you say these things? In the world, I think! So you, too, are in this world. If then a Christian may not be a magistrate because his habitation is in this world, then you are not Christians, for you are in the world. But how is a Christian's habitation in heaven? In that he lives there in contemplation and moves thither in possession and in fruition, no doubt.* Therefore a judge, since he is ever engaged in contemplation of God, since he is every moment considering the safety of the people under him and the rendering of exact justice to each, is he not in heaven, so far as contemplation is concerned, rather than all the Catabaptists, who, if they honored God, would not engage in counsels so foolish and audacious. Finally, a judge who fears God will ascend after this life unto him whose name and office he bears here, when those seducers will all be sunk in the depth of their own evil baptism. Here meanwhile, magistrates and judges, be ye mindful of your duties, for not otherwise is horror of you conceived than because those who render right to every one are so rare among you, especially in this time when all abounds in violence and cruelty. But I have not time to pursue this here. After this manner I reply to their grandiloquent words—the citizenship of these is in this world, of Christians, in heaven. For the Catabaptists thus far have no citizenship here, no church in which they may live and watch, as a bishop and pastor should, but they are like wolves that lie in wait in the forests, that seize the prey and flee, that burn and then escape. The arms of these are carnal and against the flesh, they say, but Christians' are spiritual and against the forts of the devil. They do not need me as a teacher here, for we see clearly enough that their wars are not against the flesh, for in all they yield to it. So earthly magistrates, they say, are armed with brass and iron; Catabaptists with hypocrisy and evil speaking, lies, injury, discord, faithlessness, disaster and the word of the devil—to give them altogether the gifts that are theirs in

------

* *I. e.*, transfers his real possessions and interests thither.

place of what they claim for themselves. "We ought in all to imitate Christ"—who denies it? But what prevents a pious judge from being, through the goodness and grace of God, as like Christ as is a Catabaptist? Rather, as I have said, he is the more able as he is the more like him, since when he was placed aloft he thought of humble things. But the Catabaptist ever assumes the highest in his own impudence. And the kingdom of Christ is not divided when a Christian exercises the magistracy; it is built up and united. This is clear from one example of Scripture, many times repeated, where cohorts of slaves are said to have embraced the faith of their masters. And it has been repeated by many cities in these times of ours, for as soon as the gospel began to be preached they gave opportunity to hear it to the people entrusted to them by the Lord, just as when faithful Jehosaphat ordered the law to be expounded by the priests and Levites, supported by several cohorts, throughout all his dominions. They opened a door by public command to the gospel and its ministers. And they have shut the door upon the wolves and false apostles, whether they have proceeded from the court of the pope or from the dens and caves of the Catabaptists. By this deed, glory to God, great growth of the gospel has at once been seen. But, as I have said, among the Christians they keep agitating these perverse teachings about not exercising the magistracy or taking the oath, so that if possible they may sow their errors without punishment or fear.

Catabaptists. Seventh. We thus decide and determine concerning the oath: 1. An oath is a confirmation among those who litigate or make promises. And the law directs, 2, that it be done by the name of God alone truly, and not falsely. But Christ, who teaches the perfection of the law, forbids all oaths, whether true or false, whether by heaven or earth or Jerusalem or oneself. And this for the reason which he adds, saying, 3: For ye cannot make one hair white or black. So notice! All swearing is prohibited because we are unable to perform any of those things we promise with an oath, for the very least of our possessions we cannot change. But some do not believe the simple precepts of God, saying, 4 : Since God swore to Abraham by himself who was God, at the time when he promised to be kind to him and to be his God, if only he kept his precepts, why may I not also swear when I make a promise to any one? We reply: Hear what Scripture says—when God wished to offer a promise to his heirs, with surety that his counsel would not change, he interposed an oath, that we might hope. Listen to the import of this Scripture: God has the power of taking an oath, which he prohibits to you, for to him all things are possible. God gave an oath to Abraham, says Scripture, to show that his counsel would not change, that is, since no one could resist his power, so it was necessary that he should preserve his oath. But we cannot, as was shown above by the word of Christ, keep an oath or do what we have sworn to do, so we ought not to swear. Again some say that it is in the Old Testament, not in the New, that we are forbidden to swear by God; in the New it is forbidden to swear by heaven or earth or Jerusalem. To which we reply: Hear the Scripture, 5 : Who sweareth by the temple or heaven sweareth by the throne of God and by him who sitteth therein. You see how to swear by heaven is forbidden, for it is the throne of God; how much more serious to swear by God himself! O blind and foolish, which is the greater, the throne or he that sitteth thereon? Some even dare say: If it is wrong to swear even when the Lord's name is used to support the truth, then Peter and Paul sinned, for they swore. To this we reply, 6 : Peter and Paul only testify to this, that by God himself a promise was made to Abraham by an oath, but they themselves make no promises, as the examples clearly reveal. For testifying and swearing are entirely distinct. When an oath is taken something is promised for the future. 7. To Abraham when an old man Christ was promised, whom we received after a long interval. But when one testifies he testifies to something present, whether it is true and good or not. Just as Simeon said to Mary about Christ and testified: Lo, this one is set for the fall and rising again of many in Israel, and for a sign to be spoken against. After this manner Christ taught us when he said: Let your speech be yea, yea, and nay, nay, for whatsoever is added to this is of evil. Christ warns us thus: Your speech ought to be yea, yea, that we may not understand him as permitting an oath. Christ is simply yea and nay. And all who seek him simply shall find him the Amen.

Reply. So far you have discussed what you decided about the oath. I will then reply to each error in order by its number, to avoid eternal repetition of your remarks. 1. Who, pray, has given you this definition of an oath? You have indeed touched on the practice but the essential nature of an oath you either do not know or maliciously pass by. You tell only what an oath we use, but what it is or how taken you say nothing of. If you should tell this frankly, an oath would cause no great dread in men, but this would not suit your designs, for you wish to destroy the magistracy and the power of which it consists. Take away the oath and you have dissolved all order. The burgomaster summons a senator who does not obey. You say: Let him have the policeman arrest him. How will he obey? The burgomaster sees a Catabaptist inciting the people to rebellion, and, wishing to see that no evil befalls the state, he orders him not to teach in secret (for they who are on the side of the gospel in sincerity easily overcome him when he teaches openly). Or he forbids him to teach publicly or privately, and orders the Catabaptist to be arrested when he despises every order. But the policeman does not obey. Who will arrest [the Catabaptist]—the burgomaster? But the other is stronger. You see, good reader, all order is overthrown when the oath is done away. Still, if the Scriptures required this, I would not oppose, for he by whose providence all is governed will never fail the house of Israel. But he wills not this confusion. Give up the oath in any state then according to the Catabaptists' desire, and at once the magistracy is removed and all things follow as *they* would have them. Good gods! What a confusion and upturning of everything! For no one is so destitute of all wisdom in an emergency as this class of men. They would have everything rectified by their shouts, just like that physician, or rather quack, who runs to his single cureall for every sickness. But, to come to the point, an oath is an appeal to God in deciding or vouching for something. This is not our definition, but his through whom we swear. Ex. xxii. 10 thus commands: If a man deliver unto his neighbor an ass or an ox or a sheep or any beast to keep, and it die or be hurt or driven away by robbers, no one seeing it, then shall an oath of the Lord be between them both, that he with whom it was left hath not put his hand to his neighbor's goods, and the owner of the beast shall accept the oath, and he with whom it was left shall not restore aught. Here you see an oath is an appeal to God, for it says: An oath of the Lord (or of God), for the word is יהוה, [Yahweh.] But this appeal is nothing but a vowing of himself to the extreme punishment of the divine wrath if he is wrong. For since he calls as witness him, of whom alone he confesses himself to be a worshiper, and [of him] who can by no means be deceived, though man may, he bears witness under penalty of losing him whom alone he worships and who alone knows the hearts of men, that he is not deceiving and will not deceive. This authority of Exodus deals with the deciding [judicial] character of the oath. In Gen. xxi. 23 we have the words of Abimelech to Abraham, as follows: Therefore swear unto me by God that thou wilt not harm me nor my posterity, etc. And afterward Abraham says: I will swear; and again: There they both sware. Here again we have an attestation by God to do something. For Abraham swore to do no harm, which oath he kept. This, I say, is an oath when you define it. The Catabaptists call it a "decision," and omit the appeal to God, that the simple may not reason thus among themselves.

How is it that God is not to be invoked when the safety of a neighbor is in danger? An oath is therefore a divine thing, a sacred anchor to which we flee when human wisdom can go no farther. For who knows what is in man except God alone? He therefore betrays him who swears falsely by him. For a man is believed for the faith and religious trust which he has in God to have spoken [truly] and to be ready to fulfill. And it is through him that he deceives. For the benefit, then, of one's neighbor an oath is commanded by God. And since the whole law and the prophets hang upon these two commands: Thou shalt love the Lord thy God with all thy heart and all thy soul and all thy mind, and thou shalt love thy neighbor as thyself, then the oath itself is an appeal to God, whom you uniquely love and serve, and is for the advantage of the neighbor. Who then will dare against all the authority of Scripture to deprive the people of God of the oath? God cannot be offended by an oath, for he is called as a witness, so that if we are not believed yet we may be believed, since we will on no account betray him. For all will be praised who shall swear by him. And the neighbor also will not be hurt, for the oath is given for his advantage, that he may either know that to be true which he did not know, or may be sure that what he deprecates will not be done by his neighbor or what he asks will be granted. So far from a devout man not being able to take an oath, he will be impious who refuses when a matter worthy this attestation demands.

But the whole source of the error arises from their not seeing the opinion of Christ in Matt. v. 33; indeed they do not know the very words. For the German word "schwören," to which they suppose the Greek ἐπιορκεῖν, the Latin "jurare" is similar, has another signification than what they suppose. For when we say in German "Der schwört," *i. e.*, he swears, it is uncertain whether a formal oath is referred to or whether one is just swearing offhand. The signification of this word is twofold. The Latin "jurare" is always used in a good sense, *i. e.*, for asking a sacred obligation.

But "dejerare" is used for swearing, either truly or falsely, outside of sacred obligations, which we might translate into German by a new word, "zuschwören," equivalent to the Greek word ἐπιορκεῖν. So the Latin has three words, "jurare," "dejerare" and "perjerare;" the first means a sacred obligation, the second to swear off-hand to anything either falsely or truly, the third to swear falsely. Christ would not forbid us to swear ["jurare"], but to swear lightly or offhand ["dejerare"]. But as these men do not, or will not, see this (I have often set it forth to them), they willingly and wittingly stumble. But to show this is the sense of Christ's words I will examine the words themselves, as follows: Ye have heard that it was said by them of old, Thou shalt not ἐπιορκεῖν, *i. e.*, "dejerare," or swear lightly. Our translation has it, "Thou shalt not commit perjury," which is not wholly bad. For the word "perjerare," though never used in a good sense, does not always indicate the violation or transgression or pretended fulfilment of an oath, but sometimes it means "dejerare," when "dejerare" is used in a bad sense. For "dejerare" is sometimes used in a good sense, as I have sometimes observed. While therefore the words of Christ are: It was said by them of old, Thou shalt not commit perjury, you will nowhere find among the Hebrews this interdict of perjury, nor among the Greeks. But you will find in Ex. xx. 7: Thou shalt not take the name of the Lord thy God "temere," which our translator translates "in vain." You will find, Lev. xix. 12: Ye shall not swear by my name falsely, where the Greek interprets: οὐκ ὀμεῖσθε τῷ ὀνόματί μου επ' ἀδίκῳ, *i. e.*, Ye shalt not swear by my name to that which is wicked or false. The Latin translates: Non perjurabis in nomine meo. You see how elegantly the divine Jerome has used here the word perjurare for falsely "dejerare," not for violating an oath. It was therefore forbidden by them of old (2) to take the name of God rashly, *i. e.*, as it is expounded in the passage from Leviticus—not to swear to a falsehood. So in them this opinion rose out of this understanding—if the name of God were taken to that which was true no harm was done even though this was in ordinary and daily discourse, but that it was not permitted to apply it either as "adjurare" or "dejerare" to a light, vain, false, fictitious or lying matter. This opinion it was that Christ combatted, thinking that they ought not "dejerare" either to the true or false in ordinary discourse; everything was to be said and done so truly that if one said *ναὶ*, that is, Yea, the neighbor should know that what the other had said was true, or if he said Nay, the neighbor should know that for truth. About the official oath nothing is said here. For the passage runs: Ye have heard that it was said by them of old, Thou shalt not forswear thyself. Where is this said? Why, where the discussion is not about perjury, but of "dejerare." There it was permitted to take the name of God in asseveration of the truth. There follows: Thou shalt pay thy vows. Whither does this point? If the discussion is of official oath, where then does the former passage, Thou shalt not forswear thyself, hold in this sense: Thou shalt not fail thy oath? It is clear therefore that he speaks about those oaths in which people undertook off-hand to do something, just as if he had said: All that thou hast sworn to do must be done correctly and lawfully, in order that by this he might deter from rash vows and swearing, on the ground that there was danger that the Lord would require it if you undertook anything lightly. Then he follows with: But I say to you, swear not at all. But of what swearing does he speak? Why, of that which was lawful for the ancients when he wished to call upon the name of God for some matter true and important. For we ought not in a matter true and important adjure, dejure or promise anything of our own private authority. Here no mention occurs of the oath required by public authority. What follows establishes this. He says: Neither by heaven, for it is God's throne, nor by earth, for it is his footstool, nor by Jerusalem, for it is the city of the great king, nor by thy head, for thou canst not make one hair white or black. These examples show that Christ did not refer to the oath [required by magistrates]. For which of the Hebrews ever took [such] an oath by heaven, earth, Jerusalem or his head? On the other hand, who does not swear off-hand by these? One man promises something by the cross of Christ, another asseverates by heaven and earth. This then is what Christ forbade. To this he directs the wind-up of his whole discourse. Let your speech be such that yea means yea, and nay, nay. There you have it. He does not speak about our oath; he does not touch upon the forum or court or magistracy, but upon daily conversation in our familiar intercourse.

Perhaps I seem to some to argue for this opinion tamely. But if they weigh as often as I have done the passages from Exodus xx. and Leviticus xix, in the Hebrew, the Greek and the Latin, I know they will think as I do. You see now whether enough can be said against the Catabaptists, since they have not considered the double sense of the word, but have made a misunderstanding the basis of their error.

(3) Nor is this a good reason for refusing to make oath, that we cannot change a hair, for if it were legitimate we might not reply with even a yea to our neighbor. I have answered yea to many who asked me whether I were going to lead an army against the Catabaptists, yet at no moment was I secure from him who knocks equally at all doors. Still I was right. Yet I was uncertain that I should live, much more write, but no one will accuse me of falsehood. A brother promises another to be on hand to-morrow. But because, taken down with fever, he does not come, he is not accused of falsehood, nor does any one blame him, for God gives him the excuse of necessity. So also when he is summoned to an enquiry by the magistrate under oath, his reply is not such that the power of almighty God cannot rightly exempt him. For when Abraham swore to Abimelech himself, did he not swear to do something? Why then did he do it? Especially when the Catabaptists declare that he could not do anything, and assert that Christ meant that? Under the

law, they say, it was permitted to make oath. But Abraham made this reply on oath 430 years before, and he was not under the law, but under faith. For the apostle makes him our father by faith. It is clear then that Christ spoke against that insanity under which many swear of their own motion so frivolously and promise something as of their own authority, or swear not to do what they could not avoid. They also call to witness for any sort of thing, not only the names of heaven and earth, but also of the living God, thus bringing contumely upon God to their own evil.

(4) When they seek to weaken that example of God swearing to Abraham himself, do they not weaken themselves? How often have they said in the foregoing that we are to do what we see that Christ did? But they add, this is possible to God—to do what he promised—but not to us. Must not the same be said of Christ? So I say: Christ could love his enemies, I cannot. So I must not. You see, good reader, that although they try and move many things, yet in all it is shown that they have laid the foundations of their error in some marked arrogance or malice or at least ignorance, as in this case. For in their persuasive discourse from the words: "For thou art not able to change one hair," they infer that by this Christ would take away the solemn obligation known as an oath.

(5) They reason from the less to the greater: If one may not swear by the throne, how much less by God himself who sitteth upon it? Not inaptly do they infer, if they speak of perjury or of swearing lightly. For if God forbids swearing lightly by his throne because it is his, how much less should we swear lightly by him? But if they speak of the obligation [of the oath], they infer wrongly that if we may not assume an obligation by his throne we may not by himself. An oath is not legitimately taken and as it ought to be, "any created thing," but "by God" himself. An oath is a religious matter; he who makes oath binds himself to the sum of religion; in religion the chief thing

is adoration. Just as it would be illegitimate to infer: The throne is not to be adored, therefore God is not. So it is no less illegitimate: By the throne oath is not to be taken, therefore not by him who sits upon it.

(6) When they speak of the testimonies of Peter and Paul, they do not know of what they chatter. They have not yet learned that the word "testify" is in most elegant use among the Hebrews for proclaiming a thing boldly and constantly. That one may give testimony is clear from 1 Tim. v. 19: Against an elder receive not an accusation but before two or three witnesses. I ask first whether the apostle speaks here of Christian witnesses or the unbelieving? If of the unbelieving, then every moment bishop and church are in danger. For the more holy and innocent one is, the more do the perfidious assail him; and Paul seems to have ill advised for the church and the bishop when he has given the unbelieving the opportunity to testify. But if he speaks of witnesses within the church, it results that a Christian may give testimony. My second question then is—were they who gave testimony sworn or not? If unsworn, again the bishop is in peril, for there are many false brethren, many who the more vigilantly the bishop watches, the more hostilely aim at his deposition. In short, it is the fact in human affairs that there are few whom you can believe unsworn; indeed they say that among the Romans in reality Cato was the only one whom they could believe without an oath. In fact it is not very likely that within the church witnesses were ever received without oath, for under the spirit and prudence that was powerful with them they easily saw that if men unsworn were accustomed to speak against the bishop, daily empty accusations and movements would be aroused against the bishop. If you had weighed this testimony a little more carefully, ye immersers not only of bodies, but of souls, you would not teach that an oath may not be taken. But what good do I hope from you? For whatever you assert you affirm willingly and wittingly against the Scripture.

(7) When an oath is taken, they say, something future is promised. But what is promised for the future when he with whom his neighbor's ass has been left swears that he has not put his hand to his neighbor's goods? See how learned and prudently you dispose your trifles. At first an oath was a decision only between litigants; now it is only a promise. What is this but babbling forth whatever comes into your head? When any one testifies, they say, he testifies regarding the present, whether it is true and good, just as Simeon testified: Lo, this one is placed for the fall and rising again of many in Israel, etc. What if the apostles testified regarding a past event—the crucified Christ—throughout the world? And ye shall be my witnesses, not only in Judea and Samaria, but to the ends of the earth. The apostles testified therefore to a past event. Also Simeon testified to the future when he said that Christ was to be a sign to be spoken against. I myself now testify to you of the future, and faithful is the word, *i. e.*, it is sure. I testify to you, whether you accept the monitor or not, that the time will come when they who are now led astray by you will recover their sight and will be aroused against you like shepherds against a wolf or a mad dog. Do not I also now testify? Why do you not insert in those laws of yours something of your sweet attestation? That you may not be ignorant of this, reader, listen to this: At Appenzell they use the following tricks: Some Catabaptist throws himself down just as though he were an epileptic; as long as he can he holds his breath and pretends to be in ecstasy. Those who have seen it say he presents a horrible appearance. Finally, like one waking up, he begins to testify about what he has heard and seen while in ecstasy. They have all seen especially that Zwingli is in error about catabaptism, and this opinion one pronounces gently and another violently. They saw that the day of judgment was at hand two years ago, and that catabaptism was a righteous and holy thing, and all that kind of foolishness. You must not suppose that these tricks are concocted by their com-

mon people; the leaders are the authors, as you may know from the following example: At S. Gall there was a Catabaptist girl of about 12 years or a little more. She was the daughter of a right thinking man, as they say. He was preparing one day to carry some provisions (he is a provider of grain) when his daughter warned him to remain at home, for he would see something wonderful. A little after she fell down in the way I described above. And when she was waking up she babbled out those empty ravings of theirs. You see how she knew when she was going to fall. Why did she not fall down at once when she saw her father leaving? Why, she had not been taught all she should say when coming to consciousness, nor been told of all that there was need of in accomplishing the affair. Every now and then they use these tricks still at Abtzell. And they call it an attestation, though it applies to things past and future, so that those vain seducers of old women cannot say that when any one testifies, it is of the present. Oh, how sweetly and gently do they arrange everything. Ye gods and goddesses above, below and in between, be propitious to them!

(8) They rightly tell us that Christ taught that our speech should be ever yea or nay, yet they do not seem clearly to understand it, or if they understand they do not act upon it. For though in many places they have said yea, it has never been yea. When those leaders are banished against whom I write especially, and are asked for an oath, they will not take oath, but say that through the faith which they have in God they know they will never return, and yet having been seen returned, they say the Father led me back through his will. I know very well that it is the father of lies that brings them back; they pretend to know it is the heavenly Father. This is worth telling: When that George (whom they all call a second Paul) of the house of Jacob [Blaurock] was cudgeled with rods among us even to the infernal gate, and was asked by the senate's officer to take oath and lift his hands [in affirmation], at first he refused, as he had

often done before and had persisted in doing. Indeed, he had always acted as if he would rather die than take an oath. The official of the senate then ordered him to lift his hands and make oath at once when put to the question, "or do you, policeman," said he, "lead him back to prison." But now, persuaded by rods, this George of the house of Jacob raised his hands to heaven and followed the magistrate in the reading of the oath. So here you have the question confronting you, Catabaptists, whether that Paul of yours did or did not transgress the law. The law forbids to swear; he swore, so he transgressed the law. Hence this knot: You would be separated from the world, from lies, from those who walk not according to the resurrection of Christ but in dead works. How then is it that you have not excommunicated that apostate? Your yea is not yea with you, nor your nay, nay, but the contrary. Your yea is nay, and your nay, yea. You follow neither Christ nor your ordinances.

(9) Be these things said about oaths which they would abrogate from human affairs only for the sake of sedition and tumult? For in promising to the untaught the liberty of the flesh, which neither Christ nor the apostles preached, they use these arts of rebaptizing, separating and refusing an oath. Meanwhile they do not consider what Paul says, Heb. vi. 16 : An oath is confirmation and the end of all strife. In saying this it is clear that the divine apostle said not of those who are not within the church, "an oath among them confirms or decides everything," but of those who are not without the church. Among these therefore he declares that all is confirmed or decided by an oath. Nor do they consider, as I have warned them, what was said above about witnesses testifying about a bishop, nor this, that neither Christ nor the apostles ever taught that the statement that every word stands or falls by the utterance of two or three witnesses had been made void, as is easily seen by Matt. xviii. 16 and Heb. x. 28. From these they might have learned that an oath was never abolished, although they had no word but:

Render to Cæsar what is Cæsar's and to God what is his. So they are told to render to Cæsar what is his. But they owe the oath. Therefore Christ orders it to be given.

But before we leave this a warning ought to be given the tyrants of this world, who though they falsely boast in the name of Christ yet do all to beat down his gospel, that they must not suppose that by this defense of the oath, which I have furnished, an opportunity is given for finding a defense of their own cruelty, because nothing has been said thus far of the atrocity of abusing an oath. To give in brief the sum of my opinion, I myself do not think an oath ought to be demanded, or can be demanded, without disturbing conscience, except when either all human attestation fails or the safety of a neighbor is gravely imperilled, and then only in case that in no oath that we take is the name of God blasphemed. This opinion of mine you will easily extract from what has been said. I think that those trifles of the Catabaptists have been quite thoroughly refuted. Now I go to other matters.

PART THIRD.

In this part I undertake to treat of two things—the covenant or testament, and election, that it may stand firm. Here I shall show with sure testimony and argument that it was the custom of the apostles to baptize the infants of believers. On the covenant then I speak after the following fashion: Although the Architect of the universe created this great world that it might have man as a cultivator, yet before any colony was sent out to any part, nay, before the future colonists were born, the one hope of the whole race, the father of the human race, rebelled against his Maker. But God was too merciful to visit the betrayer according to the magnitude of his fault, and at the same time too just to pass so daring a deed unpunished. So whom he might have utterly destroyed he made wretched and full of misfortune. When he drove him from Paradise he did not forbid him to become a father, but simply that he should not be the father of so noble a race as would have been if he had not betrayed his trust. So then it came about, that such as the offspring was, it was disseminated, as the cultivator, in all the corners of the earth. But, however, it grew and multiplied, and became divided into the various races of men, yet divine Providence in a peculiar way designated one to be among all peoples as especially sacred, as if it were a venerable priesthood among all. Divine Providence selected this race for this purpose, that when it would clear the world's sin by the death of his Son, this Son should take a body in which he could die from this nation. And this nation he followed in all times with his great blessings, nay, he so cherished and preserved it in every crisis that by observation of this alone one might learn that God was about to accomplish through it something exceedingly wonderful. So that whenever it was reduced to fewness in numbers it suddenly sprang up anew; however it was afflicted, it was ever restored. Adam believed that the son born to him was he of whom God had said not long before that he should bruise the head of the devil; so also his mother said : ["Cain"] I have gotten a man from the Lord, *i. e.*, have obtained or received the man whom God promised.* When she had another son, she named him Abel, *i. e.*, superfluous, not out of scornful pride, but of gratulation, because God had abundanty given what he had promised. As if she would say : That munificent God has done more than he promised.† But in a short time she who had deemed herself more than happy in her sons was bereaved, for he who as the firstborn was the hope of his parents, arose and killed his brother, who merited and expected no such thing. So all fell out that everything depended upon one; Abel was slain; Cain, the murderer, showed clearly by the working of his conscience that out of him should not arise the one who was to repair the fall of his parents. But God in his goodness succored them in this calamity, and he sent them another son, as a

* The name is commonly interpreted "acquisition."

† Modern scholars made the name "Abel" mean "breath" or "vanity."

branch from whom posterity should flourish. So his name was Seth, *i. e.*, one placed or given, for the Hebrews often used the word to place or give in the sense " given of God." * From him then posterity was derived up to Noah, who was the most just and unoffending of all in his times. And when the human race was borne along by its cupidity and violence, and by its boldness left nothing undone, he destroyed all in a flood, since they would not hear Noah, who had been sent by God. But Noah and his family alone were saved in the ark. The covenant was renewed with him, in whom the whole human race was renewed and spreading to all parts of the earth in order to its cultivation. Meanwhile God was not unmindful of his counsel, and so passing by all the rest, even the best of them, he embraced Abraham and selected him out of all for this purpose, that from him might come the posterity that would save not only the Jews, but the whole human race. With him then he renewed the covenant he had compacted with Adam, and made it clearer, for the nearer approached the time of his Son's advent, the more openly did he speak with them. Therefore he promised him first his own goodness, that he would be his God, and he required of him in return that he should excel, *i. e.*, should walk before him in right doing. He then promised that he would give him that blessed seed that was to bruise the head of the old serpent and should raise to an unfailing hope of safety the head of man bowed down by the serpent. He promised also an innumerable posterity to be born to him not only after the flesh, but also according to the spirit. Finally he promised him Palestine. And as the sign of this covenant he ordered circumcision. And the stranger and sojourner so grew that they who had knowledge of the man could easily see that God was with him. And God did all that he had promised. And when his posterity had increased to an enormous multitude in Egypt, he selected not one tribe alone, nor one man, as before, with which or whom to keep the covenant he

* " Seth " is now interpreted " substitution."

had made, but although Judah the son of Israel was designated as he from whom the Saviour should be born, yet the rest of the tribes which came of Abraham were not excluded from the covenant or from his friendship that he had given to their father Abraham. Just as he did not change anything with those who afterwards were of Judah, yet not of the house of David, who was himself peculiarly marked out as the father of the coming Christ, all were regarded as under the covenant who had descended from Abraham. Now to return to the point. This, I say, is the Israelitic or Hebrew people whom the Lord marked out as his own peculiar people from all races and peoples, so that it should tower above all peoples, just as the colleges of priests stood forth prominent among that race and all races, as he testifies in his words in Ex. xix. 5 : Now, therefore, if ye will obey my voice indeed, and keep my covenants, ye shall be my excellent people, *i. e.*, my own peculiar and sought-out people of all peoples although the whole earth is mine. And ye shall be a kingdom consisting of priests to me and a holy race.

Here then the Catabaptists have a medicine or plaster for their whole error, if they would suffer it to be applied. If ye will hear my voice and keep my covenant, he says. Here is God speaking synecdochically ! For when he addresses the whole people : If ye hear my voice and keep my covenant, etc., which can be referred to those alone who hear and can have desire to keep the covenant, yet he no more excludes infants because they do not hear or understand what is to be kept than they who were bound in sleep or mentally. For they who are of one body are considered together. But since infants are of the people of God, they are not excluded because they cannot hear or understand. For that they are members of one and the same body of God's people is clear from this, that circumcision, the sign of the covenant, is given them. For God with his own mouth named both the covenant and the sign of the covenant, because he who was of the covenant was sealed with this sign. Paul in 1 Cor. xii. 13

says: In one spirit we are all baptized into one body. But you Catabaptists yourselves argue that if one comes to the Lord's table, he must first through baptism have become of Christ's body. I do not say this because now or hereafter I wish to teach that circumcision or baptism introduces one into Christ, but that I may show that the circumcised or baptized are in the body of God's church, although I take no exception to the change of form: We are baptized into one body, instead of: We who are of one body are baptized in one baptism, for by nature being of the body precedes bearing the mark of the body. So also Paul says: In one spirit we were all baptized into one body. The grace of the spirit by which we are admitted into union with the church precedes the sign of union. For no one is sealed unless he has first been enrolled in the army or service. I therefore am coming to this: If they who are baptized in one baptism have come into one body, doubtless they who were sealed with one circumcision, the sign of the covenant—they were also gathered into one body. Hebrew infants were sealed with circumcision, the sign of the covenant; they were therefore under the covenant. Since they were under the covenant, and God spoke with that body which was joined with him by the covenant, whether we will or not we are compelled to confess that the words: "If ye hear and keep "are a synecdoche by which infants are not excluded, even though certain things do not apply to them. I will give another example, to try if they can in any way be made to see the truth. Plutarch teaches in his book, "On the delay of the divine justice," * that a people, a city or a tribe is one, even as a man is one. It therefore makes no difference if races, cities and peoples are not punished as soon as they transgress, for no

* Eng. trans. *Plutarch on the delay of the Divine Justice*, trans. A. P. Peabody. Boston: Little, Brown & Co., 1885. The Latin title is *De sera numinis vindicta*. It is one of his *Opera moralia*; Eng. trans., *Plutarch's miscellanies and essays;* trans. revised by W. W. Goodwin, Boston, 1872-74, 5 vols.

one can escape the hand of the deity. So it follows that some people are punished many years afterwards when none are living of those who sinned. But this is just the same as if those who sinned themselves suffer punishment, for a tribe, a city or a people is one body or, as it were, one man. So consider it in this place that the children of Hebrews and of Christians are of the same body as their parents, and when it is said " Hear, O Israel "—and infants cannot hear—does not say that they are not of the people of God. For although to-day they cannot, yet some time they will act, hear and understand. And those are no less regarded by God himself as among the sons of God who are destined to this, if when he speaks to their elders they themselves do not understand. About which in the following, when we come to election.

There follows "Ye shall be my own peculiar people, sought out." The Latin interpreter says: In peculium eritis mihi. Peter said an acquired people, or, according to the Hebrew scheme, one of acquisition. This is therefore the singular people of God, which he bore upon his shoulders, which he lifted above all peril, just as an eagle flies above all peril. By which metaphors the divine prophets mean this: This people was ever loved by the Lord above all peoples of the earth, was preserved and fostered, just as a father lifts his children upon his shoulders and bears them, or a hen gathers her chickens under her wings. But this is not to be so received as though the Hebrew infants were not of the people of God, since they bore the sign of that body not without the order of him who was the author of the covenant.

Of all peoples. By these words God secretly implies election. For God has not bound his own choice or the freedom of his will to any external or sign or deed. But in every nation he who fears God and does what is right is accepted and is pleasing to him. Acts x. 35. Whence from his selecting the Israelites out of all peoples it does not follow that no one not of that people was to be saved (for the election of God is ever free), but that for his Son's glory he would make that people wonderful above all and peculiarly loved.

For the whole earth is mine, or, *even though the whole earth is mine*. This also refers to the privilege and glory of this people, and asserts election. For although all peoples of the whole earth are the Lord's, yet he selected Israel to be his part, possession and lot. Is. xix. 25. Blessed be Egypt my people, and Assyria the work of my hands, and Israel shall be my inheritance.

And ye shall be my sacerdotal kingdom, or as I have interpreted it, *Ye shall be to me a kingdom consisting of priests*. For the Hebrew has *kingdom of priests*, though to avoid the ambiguity is the sense given rightly in the shape I adopt. Just as the ambassadors of Pyrrhus or some other prince said that the Roman senate was composed of kings because of the solemn dignity and majesty of the senators, so the whole Israelite kingdom is said to be a kingdom of priests or consisting of priests, both because of its system of ceremonies and the excellence of its law and its prophets, and because of the covenant and friendship which the Lord had with and for this state. Therefore the Israelitic people excelled all others on the earth, both in those matters which pertain to God and in those pertaining to nobility of race. For as they were all sprung from one, so from them sprung he who was made the only king and emperor of all nations. What greater nobility or what equal grace is discoverable?

Was it not the greatest glory if one were sprung from that race, since God had cherished it above all others, had made it his own and made a covenant with it? And although all these matters are most noted throughout Scripture, and everywhere treated, yet Paul above all treats it in brief but clear words in Rom. ix. 3: I could wish, he says, that myself were accursed from Christ for my brethren, who are my kinsmen after the flesh, who are Israelites, to whom pertaineth the adoption, the glory, the covenants, the giving of the law, the service, the promises, whose are the fathers and of whom is Christ as concerning the flesh; who is above all God blessed for ever. See how he makes out the Israelites to be adopted as sons of God, even though very many of them had displeased the Lord. He says theirs is the glory, for what majesty is equal to theirs, that they are the people of God, sons of God, and that from them was born the Saviour of all? Theirs are the covenants also, for whatever the Lord has covenanted with the human race has been done through this people. *Whose is the giving of the law*, for the highest and best was not satisfied to enter into covenant or alliance with them without fortifying his people by divine and righteous laws. Theirs, too, was the *service*, for God showed them how worship could best be done, in righteousness, equity and innocence. But it is not to be believed that the service of animal sacrifice which he had pointed out to them displeased him, though it meant only discipline, circumspection and foreshadowing. He willed the discipline of this service among them that they might have rites by which they might less revolt to the service of idols than if such rites were absent. But he wished to indicate by animal victims that there would come some time a victim that would cleanse their souls. For he wished to accustom them by bodily victims to the idea of a victim for perfection and for their souls, that when they saw beasts commanded for the external purification of the flesh they might learn that a victim would come to purify their souls also. For they could all understand that God's care was first for the souls and then for the body. Theirs was the service, whether it represented the true service or was itself the true service, for from them was born he through whom all true worshipers and adorers should approach to God. *The promises* also were made to them alone; I say nothing about the sibyl's poems, whether they were produced among them or introduced. Still this people of God stood for this, that whatever good he wished to bestow upon the human race he gave or promised through this quasi priesthood. It was then the special people whose were the promises, even though he spoke also through sibyl prophetesses among the Gentiles, that we might recognize the liberty of his will and the authority of his election.* But theirs *are the fathers* also, men filled with God, some of whom, though almost the whole world was living a bestial life (for where God is not worshiped what difference is there between man and beast?) and was following its own raging affections, alone honored God, believed his word and submitted themselves to his will. Others boldly announced the good things which through the in-breathing of the Holy Spirit they saw coming to the obedient and God-fearing, or the evil in store for the rebellious, impious and contumacious. These, I say, were the fathers, whom we call patriarchs and prophets, to whom the promises were made, and they came of the Israelites, the people of God.

In short (for why should we use much testimony in so clear a matter?), I mean this: The Israelites were God's people with whom he entered into covenant, whom he made especially his own, to whom also he gave a sign of his covenant from the least to the greatest, because high and low were in covenant with him, were his people and were of his church. And when, in giving command or prohibition, he addresses that whole people, the infants are not excluded because they understand nothing of what is said or commanded, but he speaks synecdochically, so that so far from excluding that part which could receive nothing that came because of the times or its age he even includes it, just as when a person acts with a man he acts also with all the family and his posterity. So that he often addresses the whole people as one man: Hear, O Israel, and: Say to the house of Jacob, etc.

Therefore the same covenant which he entered into with Israel he has in these latter days entered into with us, that we may be one people with them, one church, and may have also one covenant. I suppose that some will vainly cry out: See how that fellow would make Jews of us, though we have always been told

* This remark shows how extremely liberally-minded Zwingli was.

of two peoples, two churches and two covenants. See Gen. xxv. 23 and Gal. iv. 22. To which my answer is: Whenever there is held in Scripture that there are two distinct and diverse peoples, necessarily one of these is not the people of God. For both when the Jews were God's people and we who are Gentiles were not, and now when we who are Gentiles are God's people and the Jews are cut off, there is only one people of God, not two. In Gen. xxv. 23 we read: Two peoples shall be separated from thy bowels, it is not to be understood as though both were and would be his people at the same time. But Jacob he loved and Esau he hated before they struggled in her womb. Therefore ever one and the same people is that which cherishes the one true and only God, from whatsoever parents it was born. And again, they are diverse who follow a diverse cultus, though one and the same birth-pang produce them. When therefore he spoke of two peoples formerly, one was Jewish, the other Gentile. The Jew worshiped the high God, but the Gentile was impious. Now when we speak of the church of the Gentiles, it is the same now as that former one of the Jews, and the people of the Gentiles or the impious are [now] the people of Israel. For we are put in their place after they have been cut off, not in some place next them. But two covenants are spoken of, not that they are two diverse covenants, for this would necessitate not only two diverse peoples, but also two gods. Since some ancients did not see this, they taught that two diverse gods existed, one of the Old, the other of the New Testament; the one cruel, the other gentle and kind.* So Paul indeed speaks of two testaments, but the one he calls a testament by a misuse of language, when he wishes them to be understood who, although they were under that one eternal covenant and testament, yet on account of the externals which they tenaciously retained betrayed the light and Christ himself. Paul therefore called the way of these a testament, not that it was a true testament, but by a copying or

---

* So taught, *e. g.*, the Gnostics.

imitation of those who so named it. For this is the testament, that that God Almighty is ours, but we are his people. Now before Christ's coming there were many types, but these were not themselves a testament, but were foreshadowings of the light to come from the testament itself.

They therefore who according to the gross nature of man held more tenaciously to foreshadowings than was right, preferred to lose the light rather than the foreshadowings, not unlike that madman who seriously complained that his friends labored for his healing.* After the manner of these then Paul said there were two testaments, one leading to servitude, the other to liberty. For some supposed that they should consider that salvation could be obtained by acts and ceremonies. Yet others saw that by mercy alone was approach to God through him who was to come. But this was the testament, that an appendix to the testament foreshadowing the one to come. So therefore Paul calls the appendix to the testament the testament. For the same testament, *i. e.*, the same mercy of God promised to the world through his Son, saved Adam, Noah, Abraham, Moses, David, which saved also Peter, Paul, Ananias,† Gamaliel and Stephen. Now let me adduce Scripture testimony, by which all becomes clear.

In Matt. viii. 11 Christ says: And I say unto you, many shall come from the east and west and shall sit down with Abraham, Isaac and Jacob in the kingdom of heaven. In these words it is disclosed to us with whom we shall be united—with those whose are the promises, the testament, the covenant, the fathers, prophets, all things, as all things are ours through Christ. It follows therefore that there is one church of them and us.

This way tends that most luminous parable of the master who summoned workmen to cultivate his vineyard, some of whom came early, some seasonably, others after almost the whole day

* Referring probably to some case of recent occurrence and well known to his readers.

† The one mentioned as visiting Saul in his blindness (Acts ix. 10-19.

had passed. Here we see one vineyard, one Master, and (what caused astonishment in the workmen) one equal reward to all. What does this signify to us but one heavenly Father, one vineyard—the church, one reward—Christ, *i. e.*, salvation through him?

But let it not occur to any one that the ancients had access to God, not by Christ, but by observance of the law—a thing that some seem to think because there are two testaments, one that leads to servitude, and the other which is in freedom of the spirit through Christ. They think then that the old requires observance of the law for salvation, not Christ, not seeing that the law even when kept does not save. For if righteousness is through the law, then Christ died in vain. In my opinion, indeed, the law would save, *i. e.*, we should be saved (for the law is spiritual) if we kept the law entirely and according to the will of God, but this is possible to no flesh. Through the law then we learn only our condemnation, for by it we are included in sin and bound unto the penalty. From this it is easily inferred that they also who were under the law saw that by one salvation through Christ both they and the whole world are saved. This Christ himself teaches clearly when in John viii. 56 he addresses the hypocrites of the law: Your father Abraham rejoiced to see my day; he saw it and was glad. Then Abraham desired nothing so much as the coming of him who as promised he did not doubt would be to his great good. Still he had not yet come. When then the time was fulfilled and Christ was in the world Abraham already rejoiced. Therefore as they had one and the same Saviour with us they were one people with us, and we one people and one church with them, even though they came before us a long time into the vineyard. It is also clear what the bosom of Abraham is, about which many have anxiously inquired. For it can be nothing else than the sodality of the early believers to be everywhere preserved for the coming of Christ. For just like Abraham, since they were justified by faith, they desired to see the day of Christ the Saviour. Which bosom (if one likes that word) is now to us the heavenly association with the Son of God and with all who are with him.

Paul, wherever there arises a question about the difference between Jews and Gentiles who had faith, carefully proves that one people and one church arises from both. In Rom. xi. he makes election the basis of this; formerly the Jews were by election the people of God, now the Gentiles are. Yet not in such a way that from the Jews none might any longer be within the association of the elect (since he was an Israelite himself and yet was sent as a minister for the preaching of the gospel of salvation), but that they should last until the multitude of the nations came in. And this Christ meant when he said that the lord of the vineyard would let it to other husbandmen—but it was the same vineyard. They are not then diverse or two churches, not two peoples. They are, indeed, two in name, but unless they were made the same people in one spirit they are not the people of God. In Eph. ii. 11 he thus speaks: Wherefore remember that ye who were in time past Gentiles according to the flesh, who were called uncircumcision by the circumcision which itself was circumcised with hands, that at that time ye were without Christ, being aliens from the commonwealth of Israel and strangers from the covenant of promise, having no hope and being *atheoi, i. e.*, without God, in the world, but now ye are in Christ Jesus who once were far off, but now are made nigh by the blood of Christ. For he is our peace, who hath made both one, the middle wall of partition being broken down, abolishing in his flesh the enmity by the making void of the law of commandments with the ordinances, to make in himself of two one new man, and that he might reconcile both unto God in one body by the cross, the enmity being slain in himself. And he came and preached peace to you that were afar off, and to those also who were nigh. For through him we both have access to the Father in one spirit. Now therefore ye are no more strangers and foreigners, but fellow citizens with the saints and of the household of God, built upon the foundations of the apostles and prophets, Jesus Christ himself being the chief corner-stone, etc. By which words Paul means throughout what I do in the present, *i. e.*, that one people has been made of both through one Christ Jesus, who has united into one both those who once were near and us who were most distant. Weigh carefully, good reader, the words of Paul, and you will find abundantly what we assert here. For there is no need of treating at length so holy and evident a proposition.

Also Heb. xii. 22 : But ye are come unto Mount Zion and to the city of the living God, the heavenly Jerusalem, and to an innumerable company of thousands of angels, and to the church of the first-born that are written in heaven, and to God the Judge of all, etc. By which words also Paul teaches that through Christ we are united to the people of God.

And all the apostles believed this, that there is one testament, one people of God in all, *i. e.*, from the least to the greatest they are considered within the people of God, and that there is one church of God compacted out of all peoples through one spirit into one. For Peter in Acts ii. 36 says: That all the house of Israel may know assuredly that God hath made Lord and Christ this Jesus whom ye have crucified. As he says here that Jesus was made the Christ, that is Messiah, the Saviour to the Jews, therefore also the Jews have salvation. And a little after (he says) : The promise is to you and your children, and to all that are afar off, as many as the Lord our God shall call. Here he asserts that the promise was not only to those who then heard, but to their children also, who were either born or were to be born. So in [Acts] iii. 25 this same Peter says: Ye are the children of the prophets and of the covenant which God made with your fathers, saying unto Abraham: And in thy seed shall all the kindreds of the earth be blessed. Here he makes Christ belong to the Jews; through him alone they as well as we are saved. For he came first to the Jews and then to the Gentiles.

Rom. i. 16. Afterwards in Acts x. 34 he says: Of a truth I perceive that God is no respecter of persons, etc., as I have hinted above. Here Peter proves that Christ is also of the Gentiles. We have therefore one and the same Saviour. Then, too, in Acts xi. 18, where Peter tells how the whole affair with reference to Cornelius happened, it says: When they heard these things they held their peace and glorified God, saying: Then hath God also to the Gentiles granted repentance unto life (for the word repentance is here used synecdochically for the gospel itself, as I have elsewhere shown). We see therefore attributed here to the Gentiles what formerly he said belonged to the Jews and their children.

Also 1 Pet. ii. 9: But ye are a chosen generation, a royal priesthood, a holy nation, a peculiar people, that ye should show forth the praises of him who hath called you out of darkness into his glorious light, which in time past were not a people, but are now the people of God, which had not obtained mercy, but now have obtained mercy. By these words of Peter we see that Christian people are now that elect race which the Hebrews once were, as I have shown above from Ex. xix. [5, 6]. Also the same royal priesthood which is now of all nations, which also belong to God (for the whole earth is his), and which the Lord holds in honor and as of value just as he formerly held the Jewish race as a priesthood of all peoples. *A holy race*, from which infants are not excluded—posterity belongs to the race as much as parents do—a *people* sought and obtained by the blood of Christ. Which people was not a people once (for he alludes to Hos. i. 9), but now is the people of God. Therefore we are they who formerly Abraham and his like were.

All these things, to shorten sail in this part of the discussion, make for this, that we may know that it is one and the same testament which God had with the human race from the foundation of the world to its dissolution. For God is not *prosphatos*, *i. e.*, recent, or of an uncertain wisdom that mends in time what had at first been unwisely begun. He knew that man would perish as he did by his own fault, and he had prepared the healing by Jesus, that is, the Saviour, before man gave himself the self-inflicted wound. God therefore made no other covenant with the miserable race of man than that he had already conceived before man was formed. One and the same testament has always been in force. There is ever one and the same unchangeable God, one only Saviour Jesus Christ, the Son of God not by adoption, but by nature, God eternal and blessed for ever. So there could be no other testament than that which furnished salvation through Jesus Christ. By him alone is access to the Father, so Abraham even came to God by no other way than by him who was promised. One way, one truth, one life, one mediator between God and man, Christ. Through him alone is access to God. Therefore there is one only testament, for the covenant with God tends only that we may have eternal peace and joy.

Yet before I come to conclusion I wish to reply to a question which is perhaps not so fine spun as it appears. What difference is there between the Old and the New Testament? Very much and very little, I reply. Very little if you regard those chief points which concern God and us; very much if you regard what concerns us alone. The sum is here: God is our God; we are his people. In these there is the least, in fact, no difference. The chief thing is the same to-day as it ever was. For just as Abraham embraced Jesus his blessed seed, and through him was saved, so also to-day we are saved through him. But so far as human infirmity is concerned, many things came to them in a figure to instruct them and be a testimony to us. These are therefore the things which seem to distinguish the Old Testament from the New, while in the thing itself or in what pertains to the chief thing they differ not at all. First, Christ is now given, whom formerly they awaited with great desire. Simeon is a witness. Second, they who died then in faith did not ascend into heaven, but [went] to the bosom of Abraham; now he who trusts in Christ comes not into judgment, but hath passed from death into life. Third, types were offered, as is shown in Hebrews. Fourth, the light shines more clearly, so far as pertains to the illumination of the understanding, for ceremonies, while they of themselves made nothing more obscure, yet added much to the priests, and these were not so strong in inculcating religion and innocence as they would have been if avarice had not induced the shortening of ceremonies. Fifth, the testament is now preached and expounded to all nations, while formerly one nation alone enjoyed it. Sixth, before there was never set forth for men a model for living as has now been done by Christ. For the blood of Christ, mingled with the blood and slaughter of the Innocents, would have been able to atone for our faults, but then we should have lacked the model.

Now I state the conclusion. Since therefore there is one immutable God and one testament only, we who trust in Christ are under the same testament, consequently God is as much our God as he was Abraham's, and we are as much his people as was Israel.

The Catabaptists object here that Paul wrote in Gal. iii. 7: "Know ye therefore that they that are of faith are Abraham's children," and like passages from Scripture, all of which it would be "pedantic" or "overburdensome" to put down here. But if they had correctly weighed the discussion that Paul pursues here, or the force of synecdoche, they would raise no such objections. Paul's question is, whether we acquire salvation by the works of the law or does grace come in? And he decides that grace comes in by faith, and not from works. All of these things he says synecdochically, as are all such things throughout Scripture which pertain to this argument. Abraham was justified by faith. Here is synecdoche. If this were not so it would follow that Hebrew infants were not of the people of God, which has been shown to be false, for they did not believe, and therefore according to the Catabaptists' faith they were not sons of Abraham. Therefore they believed who were destined for this by God when age allowed it and they were of the people of God; those who were circumcised grew and advanced until they attained intelligence and belief, and meanwhile they were of the people of God. Not only believers then are of the church and people of God, but their children. And when the Catabaptists admit that sons of Abraham according to the flesh were within the people of God, but suppose that our own sons according to the flesh are not, they commit a great wrong. For how is the testament and covenant the same if our children are not equally with those [of the Jews] of the church and people of God? Is Christ less kind to us than to the Hebrews? God forbid!

The other objections that they offer are either answered in the following or are of no moment. As when they say: Then males only must be baptized, and on the eighth day only. For these constituents have been removed, so that we are bound neither to any race nor time nor circumstance, but under this condition, that in these matters we do not transgress piety. For among the ancients females no less than males were under the testament, even if they were not circumcised.

It results then after all this that just as the Hebrews' children, because they with their parents were under the covenant, merited the sign of the covenant, so also Christians' infants, because they are counted within the church and people of Christ, ought in no way to be deprived of baptism, the sign of the covenant, and the arguments of the Catabaptists, which because of their ignorance of figures and tropes they think valid, are of no avail against us. And we shall not on account of our ignorance compel the Holy Spirit to lay aside its own method of speaking. He has always spoken to the whole church some things which did not fit a great part, but that part was not on this account cast out of the church, out of the people, out of the covenant of God. And the fact that the sacraments, so far as pertains to externals is concerned, were not the same, does not oppose the truth, for so far as meaning is concerned they were the same. For as circumcision was the signature of the covenant, so is baptism; as the Passover was the commemoration of the passage, so is the eucharist the grateful memorial * of Christ's death. Whence the divine Paul, 1 Cor. v. 7–8; x. 18, and Col. ii. 11, attributes baptism to them, and also the eucharist or spiritual feasting on Christ, but to us the Passover and circumcision, and so makes all equal on both sides. So far upon one and the same testament, church and people of God.

On Election.

I am now compelled to treat of election or else forego my promise, but not so fully as the subject demands. For this is beyond my power and purpose. But I shall show election to be sure, *i. e.*, free and not at all bound, and above baptism and circumcision; nay, above faith and preaching. But this briefly. When most of us read Paul's epistle to the Romans we ponder a little carelessly upon the cause of his mentioning election and the following predestination. He had shown that salvation rests on faith, and faith is not a matter of human power, but of divine spirit; who therefore has faith has at the same time the divine spirit. They who have this are sons of God, walk not after the flesh, but whatever they do is a help to them for good. Now arises the query, why then are they acursed or condemned who do not believe? Since he has fallen on this subject, willingly or not, he treats it worthily about in this order and manner: We are saved by faith, not by works. Faith is not by human power, but God's. He therefore gives it to those whom he has called, but he has called those whom he has destined for salvation, and he has destined this for those whom he has elected, but he has elected whom he willed, for this is free to him and open, as it is for a potter to make diverse vessels from the same lump. This

---

* "Gratianum actio" again—"the giving of thanks for."

briefly is the argument and sum of election as treated by Paul. He says therefore, Rom. viii. 28: We know that all things work together for good to them that love God. Now lest you should say: Who therefore love God, or to whom are all things for good? he anticipates and replies: To those who according to purpose are of the called. Do not understand this of a human purpose, but of God's, so that the sense is: Who are sanctified of God's purpose, for *to be called* is here for *to be truly sanctified.* As when it is said: He shall be called the Son of the Most High. Here *shall be called* is Hebrew idiom for *shall truly be.* I return to the argument. *Purpose* is for Paul that freest deliberation by which God is girded for electing, as in ix. 11 we see when he says: That the purpose of God according to election may stand. His purpose is therefore above election, *i. e.,* first by nature. It may happen among men that something is elected, but there is a reason for its election, *e. g.,* it is elected because it seems useful or right. This purpose or deliberation is not free, but depends on that which is elected. Since Paul wishes to show that God's election is born of his free purpose, and not from those whom he is about to elect, he says that the free purpose is the cause why all things work for good to those who love God. Nothing is ascribed to man's merit. For he adds: For whom he foreknew (*pronunciavit*) he also predestinated to be conformed to the image of his Son, etc. I have translated προέγνω by "pronunciavit," which word has the same force as if you should say predetermined or foreordained. This is then the apostle's meaning: I said that all will result in good for those who according to God's purpose are of the called. This I would have understood thus: God freely with himself settles upon, prejudges and foreordains (for by this word the word for " purposing " is expounded) whom he will, even before they are born. Whom he thus foreordains he marks out beforehand, *i. e.,* destines them to be conformed to the image of his Son. As if he should say: No one can be conformed to Christ unless he has been destined for this. Paul proceeds: Whom he predestined he also *called* Here before calling we have predestination or marking out. Whom he called he also *justified*. But are we not justified by faith? Yes, but calling precedes faith. For Christ warns also that no one can come to him unless the Father have drawn him. To draw and to call are here equivalents. But whom he justified he also glorified, for they who believe are eternally honored with him in whom they have believed. Here then is the knot—How does faith bless or how justify? We see that the first thing is God's deliberation or purpose or election, second his predestination or marking out, third his calling, fourth justification. Since then all these are of God, and faith hardly holds the fourth place, how is it that we say that salvation comes of faith, since wherever faith is there also is justification, or rather, each person's salvation has before been so determined and foreordained with God that it is impossible that one so elected can be condemned? But by a light blow of synecdoche * what seems insoluble dissolves. For faith is used for the election of God, the predestination or calling, which all precede faith, but in the same order. So if you say: God's election, predestination or marking out, calling, beatifies, you will ever say right. Why? Because the harmonious order and connections of these are such that you may use one of these without the other and yet not exclude the others; especially is this the case when you take faith, which is inferior and posterior to election, predestination or calling. Since then the justification which is of faith closely follows calling, we see with no trouble that salvation is attributed to faith because they who have faith are called, elected and foreordained.

But why is salvation attributed to faith above the others? Why does Paul use this link out of the chain? I reply, because

---

* This rhetorical figure wherein the part is put for the whole, or a whole for a part, is considered by Zwingli an unanswerable argument. Instances of it are frequent. *E. g.*, the Athenians are often spoken of as if they comprised all the Greeks, and what they did the Greeks are said to have done.

that is best known to us. For each one questions and examines conscience according to Peter's word. If it rightly replies, *i. e.*, if with full assurance he thinks correctly of God, he has now the surest seal of eternal salvation. For who has faith is called, who is called is predestined, who is predestined is elected, who is elected is foreordained. But God's election remains firm. Therefore they who have faith are justified. For this is justification, piety, religion and service of the Most High God. So that no condemnation awaits them, for they are not of those who say: Let us sin that the glory of God may be the brighter, but of those who as often as they sin through weakness return to God and pray: Forgive us our sins. They are not of those who, when they have sinned, are so far from returning to a correct state of mind that they fall into impiety and assert that there is no God, but of those who grieve not so much because they have offended every creature as that they have offended God alone, their own heart and soul and mind, and then say: Against thee only have I sinned and done this evil in thy sight. This, I say, is the justification of faith; to these all things are for good, but the contrary to the impious. Adultery and murder were for good to David, for he was righteous through faith. For he repented his deed and did not fall from hope. It was evil to him who was not as other men, because he had not faith, therefore he was not called or predestined or elected.

I think these arguments are brief, as I promised, but clear and sure. But for what purpose? That I may reply to the Catabaptists. For they argue against me in the tract in which they suppose they have refuted me: " How are the Hebrews' infants of the people, sons, and church of God? We believe the elect are of the people of God, like Jacob, by no means those thrust out or repudiated. For, according to Rom. ix. 11–13, when they were yet in their parents' womb and had done neither good nor evil, God said: Jacob have I loved and Esau have I hated. How then could Esau be of God's people? It is then false what

Zwingli asserts, that the Hebrews' infants were of the people and church of God." To which I think I may now the more advantageously answer, inasmuch as I have said these few things about election and predestination, in about the following manner: It is sure that with God no one is of his people or of his sons except he whom he has elected, and it is also sure that every one is his whom he has elected. But in this way, O Catabaptists, all your foundation has fallen away. For not only believers (as you would understand "believers" in actuality) are the sons of God, but those who are elect are sons even before they believe, just as you yourselves prove by the example of Jacob.

What then shall we do with the saying: Who believeth not shall be condemned? For infants do not believe, they will then be condemned. Again, the elect were chosen before they were conceived; they are at once then sons of God, even if they die before they believe or are called to faith. You see the chain and order! Faith is in that order the last thing beyond glorification, therefore what precedes it is no less certain than faith itself. For as it is true " he believes, therefore is saved," so it is not less true that " he is called, therefore is saved." (I am not speaking here of that calling of which Christ said: Many are called but few chosen. For there he means the external calling, by which many are invited by the preaching of the word. Now I mean that internal calling which Christ calls "drawing.") It is equally true: He is predestined, therefore saved, and he is elect, therefore saved. Do you not see that whatever is in this chain and precedes faith is equally with faith followed by salvation? For "Who is elect shall be saved " is as true as "Who hath believed shall be saved." On the other hand, equal inferences cannot be drawn by arguing from the prior matters to faith unless we accept faith otherwise than for that fact and certitude of mind which regards the invisible things, about which later. For it does not follow " He is elect, therefore believes." For Jacob was elect when he had not yet believed. Nor does this follow, "He does not believe, therefore is not elect." For the elect are ever elect, even before they believe. When therefore it is said: "Who believeth not shall be condemned," it must be that faith is used for that chain already spoken of, so that the meaning is: "Who is not elect shall not be saved." Or else for this, that it means " to be within the faithful people," or (as best approves itself to my reason) that it is said synecdochically of those alone who have reached that point that they can understand language—Who believeth not shall be condemned. For faith is not of all the elect, as now is clear of elect infants, but it is the fruit of election, predestination and calling, which is given in its fit time. Therefore as that saying: Who believeth shall be saved, does not exclude those who are elect, and who before they arrive at maturity of faith join the band of them that are elect, to damn them the more, so that saying: Who believeth not is condemned, does not include those who are elect but do not reach to maturity of faith, to save them the less. By the words, Who hath believed and Who hath not believed, it may therefore be inferred they are not included who by reason of age are not able to hear, nor those to whom the knowledge of the gospel has not come. It may also be inferred that those sayings, Who hath believed, etc., and Who hath not believed, have not the sense of precedence, as though faith necessarily preceded all, *i. e.*, election, predestination and calling. For if this is true, then that antecedent determination or purpose or predestination of God would not be free, but election would follow then finally, when faith had rendered the man suitable for election. For only those could be elected who already believed, the contrary of which is clear. But the words have the " sense of consequence :" Be assured that he who believes has been elected by the Father and predestined and called. He believes therefore because he has been elected and predestined to eternal salvation, and he who believeth not has been repudiated by the free election of God. And here is disclosed to us the power of the keys, so far as they were given to the apostles. When one says that he believes, the apostle promises him: If thou believest from thy heart, be it sure to thee that thou art called, predestined and elected to eternal salvation. Therefore this man of ours is absolved and justified, about which we have spoken above. But when the apostle sees that there is no faith in those that hear, he is sure that they are rejected. They are then ordered to shake off the dust from their feet, that is, to go quickly from such, not as though now first these deserve to be shunned, but because the apostles are now first made sure of their rejection by their aversion to faith; on the other hand, when they see the faith they are sure of their election. So therefore such words were said as: By their fruits ye shall know them. A good tree cannot bear evil fruit, nor an evil tree good fruit. Who believeth shall doubtless be saved, for faith is the fruit of election, so that, ye apostles, ye may have an indication of success. But who does not believe after arriving at years of maturity for receiving your teaching is not elect; he is an evil tree, so you may know among whom your labor is fruitless.

From all this we make two necessary inferences. First, that we are sure of the salvation of those who show faith when they reach that maturity that ought to show the fruit of election; if they do not show this we are contrariwise sure of their rejection. Behold how we recognize salvation or shipwreck by the faith alone of the elect or rejected who have reached that maturity when we may expect faith, the fruit of election. So that infants born to those who are in the covenant and people of God we may not measure by the norm and touch-stone of faith. Second, since those alone who have heard and afterward either believe or remain in their unfaith are subject to our judgment, we err gravely in judging the infant children both of the Gentiles and of Christians. Of the Gentiles, for no law condemns them, they do not fall under that saying: Who believeth not, etc. Then since the election of God is unrestrained, it is impious for us to exclude from that those of whom we cannot judge from the signs of faith and unfaith whether they are included or not. Of Christians, because we not only assail rashly the election of God, but we do not even believe his word, yet he by it has shown us their election. For when he includes us under Abraham's covenant this word makes us no less certain of their election than of the old Hebrews'. For the statement that they are in the covenant, testament and people of God assures us of their election until the Lord announces something different of some one. Therefore also that objection is stricken out: How then were we sure of Esau's election when the Lord says: Esau have I hated? For we follow the law throughout. But if the Lord does something out of the ordinary the law is not thereby abrogated. For privileges do not make the law common. Though indeed it is my opinion that all infants who are under the testament are doubtless of the elect by the laws of the testament. And when it is said: Where then do you put the infant Esau? Under the testament? But he was rejected. I respond two ways: (1) All judgment of ours about others is uncertain so far as we are concerned, but certain as regards God and his law. *E. g.*, when it is said to an apostle: I believe in Jesus Christ the Son of God, the apostle thinks him who says this of the elect because of the certitude of the word. But they sometimes deceive who thus confess, as did Simon Magus and the false brethren who came in secretly to betray the liberty of the gospel. But God himself is not deceived, nor does the law deceive, for God knows the hearts and reins, *i. e.*, the inmost parts, and the law, if all is just and right, does also not deceive, but is eternal. Therefore we ever judge according to the law, as has been said, and the law for the sake of one or many may not be considered the less universal. (2) The other reason is such as all may not receive, but to me it is sure. All of those infants who are within the elect, who die, are elect. And this is my reason, because when I find no unfaith in any one I have no reason to condemn him;

contrariwise, since I have the indubitable word of promise : They shall come and sit down with the God of Abraham, Isaac and Jacob, I shall be impious if I eject them from the company of the people of God. What then of Esau if he had died as an infant? Would your judgment place him among the elect? Yes. Then does election remain sure? It does. And rejection remains also. But listen. If Esau had died an infant he would doubtless have been of the elect. For if he had died then there would have been the seal of election, for the Lord would not have rejected him eternally. But since he lived and was of the non-elect, he so lived that we see in the fruit of his unfaith that he was rejected by the Lord. All our error arises from this, that while we hardly learn all even from the sequel we break in also upon providence. This disposes all, so that not only Esau, but not even a root in the sea, not a weed in the garden or a gnat in the air, lives or dies without it. But what kind of a vessel Esau was or why a gnat has so sharp a sting * we can hardly learn from what is done by them. Since then we learn from the dead mind of Esau that he was rejected of God, in vain do we say : Would that he had died an infant ! He could not die whom divine Providence had created that he might live, and live wickedly. You see then, O man, that almost all our ignorance of Scripture arises from our ignorance of Providence. But I return to my subject. Manifest then from all that precedes are those two inferences. That those two sayings : Who believeth, etc., and Who believeth not, etc., are not a touch-stone by which we may measure the salvation of infants, and that we condemn impiously not only the true children of Christians, but those of Gentiles. They alone are subject to our judgment of whom we have the word according to which we can judge. I think I have also satisfied those who say : If by election we come to God Christ is in vain. For this is election, that whom the Lord has destined to eternal salvation before the world was, he equally

* "Tuba" means "trumpet;" can he mean the mosquito?

predestinated, before the world was, to be saved through his Son, as Paul teaches in Eph. i. 4.

A second pair of inferences also follows. First, they teach incautiously who say that the baptism of infants can be tolerated through love, unless they mean that by love all things are done among Christians, and not by command and by force of law, just as Paul says: Owe no one aught, but to love one another. But if they receive love in the place of complaisance and indulgence, as when Paul through love sheared his hair and undertook a vow (for he did this by indulgence in which he spared the weak), now I think they err seriously who say that through love infants should be baptized. For what do they mean by this other than that now one may not omit for the sake of public peace what some time must be omitted when it is permitted? Let them therefore receive my opinion after considering the distinction of love which I premise. Few ceremonies have been left us by Christ—two or three, baptism, the eucharist and the laying on of hands. The first belongs in general to all who are of Christ's church. The second to those only who can interrogate themselves upon their certitude of faith. For the apostle says: Let a man prove himself. The third only to a few, those who superintend the ministry of the word. Now since these ceremonies have clear methods of performance they are improperly said to be done of love when they are done of precept, even though whatever God commands is most pleasing to you because of your piety. So when it is said: Go and teach all nations, baptizing them into the name of the Father, Son and Holy Spirit, there is here the form of law as much as in "Let every male be circumcised." What the law orders cannot be ascribed to indulgence, but that is done of indulgence when at the celebration of the eucharist certain weak ones are spared, and would be so done if the habit of baptizing infants were being restored and certain weak ones were spared from being compelled to baptize infants after the custom and rite. This, I say, would be done of love.

The eucharist therefore is not celebrated from love in this way, but it is stopped out of love by many. So it would be with baptism. I warn you here, dearest brethren, to weigh again and again my opinion, for some seem to wish to cover up with their astuteness of words the mouth of your simplicity.

The second necessary inference of the second pair. Whether the Catabaptists or others receive or not my opinion on election, predestination, calling and faith—which assuredly is not mine, but the apostle Paul's, nay, that of God himself, if you estimate carefully the providence of God—still baptism is not at all to be denied infants on account of God's election or reprobation, for neither to Esau or any other who was rejected was circumcision denied. So I regard the whole Catabaptist argument as now overturned, and it is demonstrated that election is above baptism, circumcision, faith and preaching.

That the Apostles Baptized Infants.

In the foregoing I said that when Christ and the apostles referred to Scripture, they referred to none other than that of the law and the prophets. For not yet were the Gospels written or the apostolic epistles collected. But in this I would not speak as if I would take aught away from the canonical New Testament, since the books of the Old Testament also were not written at one time, and yet the authority of the later books is not less; but I would show that Catabaptist writers are in error in this, that they suppose the apostles to have directed baptism in accordance with that writing that was not yet written. Nay, they order to be omitted what is verbally omitted in what was written afterward in accordance with the figurative scheme of the Hebrew tongue, but what is affirmed by the implications of speech. Meanwhile the thing itself warns otherwise, and the men who wrote the New Testament testify that they were not able to record all that Christ himself did and taught. I have undertaken to prove a hard thing then, the Catabaptists think, but it is easy if we give ear to the truth. I shall first employ argument and then testimony. But the arguments I draw from no source but Scripture itself, as follows: Every one knows how sharp was the contest among believers about circumcision, which contest is described in Acts xv.; some contended that those must be circumcised who were not entered into Christ, others opposing. But when there had arisen a great strife the delegates from Antioch, the apostles, and the whole church guided by the divine Spirit decreed that circumcision and all the externals of the law, a few exceptions being made in concession to the weak, should be abrogated. Here then I will ask the Catabaptists whether they believe the disciples were less solicitous about administering the baptismal rite than about circumcision? If they say that they were not solicitous, then the piety of the parents which has regard for the children as well as for themselves leads us to think otherwise. Since then a part were anxious that circumcision should not be omitted, a part that they might not confuse baptism, it appears that they were no less anxious for their children than for themselves, especially since in the beginning their infants had been circumcised. It cannot be then that if the apostles were unwilling to baptize the children there would not have arisen some disturbance. But nothing is said of this, so there was no disturbance. So because of believers' opinions children were baptized, and for this reason there is no distinct mention of it. But if they admit that parents were anxious about the baptism of their children, then they conquered and baptized them, for baptism conquered and remained when circumcision became antiquated. For if consideration, strife and anxiety did arise, and yet the opinion of those who thought they ought to be baptized did not conquer, then circumcision would have been strengthened and baptism weakened. And this argument pertains to conjectures and indications, yet it is drawn from Scripture.

II. But the second argument is insuperable, gathered by comparison of Scripture. Circumcision was abrogated by decree of the church gathered in the spirit. Infants were with their parents within the church. If then, according to the Catabaptists' opinion, those infants or little children were not baptized, yet were circumcised, it follows that by a decree of the church children of Christians were cast out of the church and were remanded to the circumcision. For who is circumcised becomes a debtor to the whole law. And there is no reason why we should plead here that account must be taken of the time. For the strife about circumcising believers arose at Antioch, not at Jerusalem, where it is agreed that either circumcision or baptism flourished.

III. The third argument also is from conjecture—that we should consider the race from which the first believers came. They were of a race that so clung to externals that the apostles believed even after the resurrection that Christ would rule corporeally. It is not therefore likely that they left their children unbaptized. I leave the rest to you, reader, for much can be educed from these bases.

IV. The fourth I have touched on in the foregoing, *i. e.*, that Paul in 1 Cor. x. 1-2 makes us and the Hebrews equal. All, he says, were baptized, all ate the same spiritual bread, and since all their children were baptized in the sea and the cloud they would not be equal if our children were not baptized, as has been said. But here the Catabaptists chatter out: If they ate the same spiritual bread, therefore our children will also celebrate the eucharist. This has no weight, for by synecdoche to each part its own property is attributed. But since we have a precept for the celebration of the eucharist: Let each man prove himself, and boys are not competent for this, while they are for baptism and circumcision, it is clear that with Paul infant baptism was in use, but not infant eucharist. Here also is answered the objection they draw from Col. ii. 11, that children cannot be circumcised with the circumcision not made with hands nor lay aside the body of sin, therefore baptism did not come in the place of circumcision, since circumcision is external and corporeal, but this is internal and spiritual. For we learn here that Paul attributed our externals to the Hebrews, though they had the internals alone, but the externals not in the same form but differently. No one denies that they ate spiritual bread just as we, for they, like we, were saved through him who was to come. But they did not carry around the bread and wine in the supper, but used other externals in place of these, manna and water from the rock. Do you see how by analogy he makes the externals equivalents? The internals were the same, the externals different. So he attributes to them that internal baptism, so that they as well as we were cleansed through Christ: external baptism he expresses by the analogy of the sea and the cloud, but to us he attributes internal circumcision, for we are under the same covenant with them and are renewed by the same Spirit, and by it are circumcised. That is, he is speaking by synecdoche in accordance with the age of each class. But he found no other external than baptism, for what cause would there be for making a comparison analogically between baptism and circumcision, when without that he could have spoken of the spirit being renewed, unless he had wished in the same way to make equal the internals as well as the externals, as he did in 1 Cor. x. 1? It must be therefore that Paul entertained this opinion, that our circumcision is baptism; this he would never have held unless he had seen at that time the children of Christians baptized as he had formerly seen them circumcised.

V. Not only three, as above, but many families were baptized by the apostles, in which it is more likely than not that there were infants. This, too, pertains to probability, about which enough has been said above.

Now we come to testimony. You will put together here, good reader, whatever has been said of one and the same testament, people and Saviour. And you will at the same time consider here that in the apostles' time no one used any Scripture but the

Old Testament, nay, Christ himself used no other, and what controversy arose about baptism would have to be settled by its authority; but since this not even leads us to think anything but that baptism, the sign of the covenant, must be given to infants equally with circumcision, there could have been no hesitation with the apostles in approving the baptism of infants.

Origen on Romans, book v., thus testifies : " The church received from the apostles the tradition of giving baptism even to infants." *
Augustine asserts the same in his book on the baptism of infants dedicated to Marcellinus.† I do not adduce these in this place to give them the authority of Scripture, but on account of faith in history (for Origen flourished about 150 years after the ascension of Christ), that we may not ignore the antiquity of infant baptism, and at the same time that we may attain to certainty that beyond all controversy the apostles baptized infants. So the Catabaptists do nothing at all different from the false apostles in former tmes, of whom Paul thus speaks : They order you to be circumcised for this only, that they may glory in your flesh. So these men glory in mobs and their seditious, or rather heretical, church. For I assert truly that in our time no dogma, however unheard of, can so rightly be called heresy as this sect's, for they have separated themselves from the churches of believers, they have rebaptized, and have their own assemblages. Now I lay my hand to the appendix.

APPENDIX.

Though I ever expend most liberally what little talent the Lord has given me, I am compelled to restrain my hand in the appendix, not out of niggardliness, but because you are already wearied, good reader, of so great prolixity, and because I am

* Book v., chap. ix.

† *A treatise on the merits and forgiveness of sins, and on the baptism of infants.* Migne, x., col. 109 sqq. Eng. trans. *Nicene and Post-Nicene Fathers*, v., 15–200.

compelled to yield to the importunity of the Fair that presses.*
With the help of God then I will refute the foolish, impious and
absurd arguments advanced by the Catabaptists, a few passages
of Scripture being adduced, but such as that whole crowd cannot
resist.

I. The Catabaptists teach that the dead sleep, both body and
soul, until the day of judgment, because they do not know that
"sleeping" is used by the Hebrews for "dying." Then they
do not consider that the soul is a spirit, which, so far from
being able to sleep or die, is nothing but the animating principle
of all that breathes, whether that gross and sensation-possessing
spirit that quickens and raises up the body, or that celestial spirit
that sojourns in the body. That celestial spirit then that we call
soul the Greeks call entelecheia [*i. e.*, actuality]; this is so lively,
enduring, strong, tenacious and vigilant a substance that its nature
forbids the absence of action or existence. Its nature is incessant
action or motion. So that it can as little sleep as the light or the
sun can be an obscure body. Wherever you drive the sun it glows
and kindles, as Phaethon experienced.† So the soul, no matter
whither you drive it, animates, moves and impels, so that even
when united firmly to the body, which itself under its own inertia
sleeps, yet the soul sleeps not. For we recall what we have seen
in sleep. Much more when freed from the body is it incapable
of sleep, since it is a substance suited for continuous activity,
incapable of weariness. So the body sleeps, the soul never, but
when it is freed from the body this last sleeps the eternal night
Finally the Catabaptists are ignorant that by the Hebrews the
resurrection of the dead is not always received of the supreme
resurrection of the flesh, which we shall some time see; sometimes
it means this, sometimes that, continuance and existence of mind,

* Allusion to the Frankfort (on the Main) Autumnal Fair, which was the
great book mart at that time; the date of this treatise being July 31, 1527.

† He ventured to drive the chariot of the sun across the heavens, and came
so near the earth that he almost set it on fire!

by which, freed from the body, it persists and exists in life, oppressed neither by sleep nor death, for it cannot be so overcome.*

In Josh. vii. 12 the Lord says: The children of Israel could not stand (surgo) before their enemies, and a little after [verse 13]: Thou canst' not stand before thy enemies. Here in both places to rise is put for to stand fast and steady. For Jerome also translates " to stand." In Matt. xxii. 31 Christ says: Touching the resurrection of the dead have ye not read that which was spoken unto you by God, saying: I am the God of Abraham, the God of Isaac, and the God of Jacob? He is not the God of the dead, but of the living. By which reply he taught nothing else but that Abraham, Isaac and Jacob are living, though dead. Of whom the Sadducees either denied the resurrection, *i. e.*, living, or at least, after Catabaptist fashion, asserted that they [the dead] slept. For Christ's reply referred not to the resurrection of the flesh, but to the fact that Abraham, Isaac and Jacob lived, though dead. So Paul speaks in Heb. xi. 35: But others were tortured (or crucified), not accepting deliverance, that they might obtain a better resurrection. Notice here how *resurrection* is used for the life of souls, which they are to have when released from the body. In this sense they so embraced the life that follows this that they would not accept the present life even when it was offered. So firm was their faith that they were sure the life that followed would be better. Whence also the saying of Christ in John vi. 40: I will raise him up at the last day, ought not to be distorted to any sense other than: " I will preserve him in life when he dies who trusts in me." So he either implies

* The theory here rejected is known as " Psychopannychia," the doctrine of the sleep of the soul. It received very elaborate refutation from the youthful Calvin: *Psychopannychia, qua refellitur quorundam imperitorum error, qui animas post mortem usque ad ultimum judicium dormire putant. Libellus ante septem annos compositus, nunc tamen primum in lucem aeditus.* Reprinted in *Calvini Opera*, ed. Baum et al., v., col. 165-232; Eng. trans., *Calvin's Tracts*, vol. iii., 413-490.

that they who trust him will never die or will ever live most joyously. For that "last day" here is not so much that final day of all things of the present world as the final day of each when he leaves this world. This is easily understood from John v. 24: He cometh not into judgment, but hath passed from death unto life. In 1 Cor. xv. the apostle, speaking of the resurrection, makes this which is understood as continuance or persistence in life, so to speak superior, of which he speaks in general, until he comes to the passage: How do the dead rise, or with what body do they come? There finally he reaches the discussion of that resurrection of the flesh which is to come at length. Do you, reader, that you may see that I assert nothing rashly, come to this passage, dismissing the rest. Notice how "From man came death, and from man the resurrection from the dead, for as in Adam all die, so in Christ all are made alive," pertains not only to the resurrection of the flesh, but to that life which follows this at once. For through Adam we die, but through Christ we are preserved in life. For he says: He who believeth in me shall live even though he die. Then consider what follows: Else what shall they do who are baptized for the dead if the dead rise not at all? Why are they then baptized for the dead? You see the ancients had a custom of baptizing themselves in behalf of the dead, not that this is approved by Paul or us (it was a foolish thing which followed the faithful out of unbelief even unto belief, for some things cling which perversely have the appearance of piety, especially toward parents and relatives). But the apostle acutely employed the foolish abuse of bapitism—which in my judgment was nothing else than the sprinkling with lustral water the graves of their dead, as some do to-day—against those who denied that the soul lived after it left the body until it was raised for judgment. And he thus catches them: If then the soul sleeps, why do you, too, moisten with lustral water the graves of the dead? What benefit do you do those who do not live, but are either nothing or asleep? You may note here in passing, reader, that this argument is used partly in behalf of infant baptism. For if they supposed that with baptismal or lustral water they accomplished something for the dead, much less would they refuse it to children. For they would do this according to the Lord's word, for that they would have no document. Third, consider this, which he adds: And why stand we in jeopardy every hour? I die daily, etc. For this, too, tends hither. Paul means: If either no life follows this, or a sleep more than Epimenidean,* I should be foolish to undergo every danger daily. But it is very different. Eternal life follows this immediately, for otherwise I would not expose myself rashly to dangers of this kind. Fourth, he says: Let us eat, etc., and even "Perverse communications corrupt good manners" points this way. For nothing equally corrupts manners with teaching that the soul dies, or, as the Catabaptists now blaspheme, sleeps till the last day, and then they affirm that the devil and all are saved. What penalty then awaits the faithless and criminal? This corruption would not spread so widely if they only denied that the flesh would live again. Fifth, consider this, too: Eknepsate dikaiōs, *i. e.*, be vigilant. These words reflect Paul's keenness. For when they, pressed in the sleep of ignorance, suppose (like the wolf which believes that all animals eat raw flesh because it does so itself) that souls sleep, he says therefore wake up. And when because of their keenness these little scholars seem to themselves by no means to sleep, he rightly says wake up. For you think that you are awake and have hit the nail on the head when you are dreaming so somnolently about sleep. After this weigh carefully the following, reader, and when you see that the apostle at first is speaking in general about the life of the soul after this life, and thence comes to the resurrection of the flesh, return to this and you will see that the Catabaptists are oppressed not so much by sleep as by evil, and teach whatever occurs to them.

* According to the tale Epimenides slept fifty-seven years.

II. The Catabaptists teach this, too, that the devil and all impious will be blessed. Why then do they threaten us with eternal damnation unless we join them? See how consistent is their teaching! When we die we shall sleep till the last day, then we shall be cleared in the judgment. So the lower world is done away with, and Gehenna, and the inextinguishable fire, and the flames which devour the tares gathered into bundles. But they have learned that לעלם, *i. e.*, the Hebrew word meaning forever, does not mean interminable duration. Here they do just as they do everywhere. When they have learned one thing, what they either are ignorant of or will not see they turn aside and reject. Let them therefore take Luke i. 33 : He shall reign over the house of Jacob forever. Is this *forever* used for *some ages?* Another witness is Matt. xxv. 41 : Depart from me, ye cursed, into eternal fire, prepared for the devil and his angels. Tell me here, when will that fire have an end if *eternal* is always a definite time? How many ages, I ask, will there be when this age shall be finished? So that you are able to say how long that fire will endure before it is extinguished. But why do I ask, as if you said anything but what is most vain! And so do you, O reader, listen: In that last judgment, after which there shall be no other, after which there shall be no age but sheer eternity, Christ will say: Depart hence from me into eternal fire. What end will that have that can find no end? For if that " eternal " were temporary, as it cannot be, for then all time ceases, then the salvation of the blessed would be temporary. But the foolish talk foolishness.

III. Catabaptists assume to themselves all, the office of preaching, and of others who are legitimately set apart by Christian churches they inquire, Who elected you? For they are not sent even by their evil church. But here they do not regard Scripture. It has no force. We do not read that any of the true apostles assumed to himself the ministry of the word. So no one ought to assume it to himself. When Paul asks: How shall they preach unless they are sent? let him hear, Catabaptists. By what authority, pray? That of the father of lies and strife.

IV. Wherever it suits, the Catabaptists deny Scripture and assert their own spirit. But we know that Scriptures are to be interpreted by the spirit, but not by that contentious and rash spirit which the Catabaptists excite, rather by the true, eternal, peaceful and self-consistent spirit. We know also that Christ appealed to Scripture, who yet gave by sign and teaching sufficient proof whether he spoke from God, so that neither a Catabaptist nor any other should dare to demand credence for himself when he speaks without Scripture authority. So that very wonderful is the effrontery with which they dare to demand Scripture proof for infant baptism, rather from non-Scripture. For they have nothing by which they may trust in Scripture, but only a negative basis alone when they say: We do not read that the apostles baptized infants, therefore they should not be baptized. They ward off all Scripture by the boss of an asserted spirit. Spurn not prophecy, they say, and do not extinguish the spirit. Right enough! But what is added? Prove all things. We shall then prove the spirit, for the divine John warns not to trust every spirit, but to prove them whether they are of God. You deny that Christ is by nature the Son of God, the propitiation for the sins of all the world. Your spirit is then not of God by John's test. So we spurn your prophecy no otherwise than as when Saul put himself into the company of prophets. You extinguish the spirit by your rebaptism. Why not, when it is so often submerged? For it is not that spirit which at the foundation of the world brooded over the waters, but that which hurled itself into swine with the great damage of the neighbors, itself doubtless swimming out and leaving those amid the swamps of Gennesaret who ought to have solaced the winter of the poor. Attend to the allegory.

PERORATION.

I doubt not, most pious reader, that you have long missed in us that direction of Paul: Bear with one another in love, endeavoring to keep the unity of the spirit in the bond of peace. But for your missing it, we who are on the side of true baptism are not in fault. For nothing grieves us so much as their audacity. For though, as the apostle continues, we are one body and one soul or spirit, in that we are called to one and the same hope, they are unwilling to hear the apostle's warning. For secretly they have taught what is not right, doubtless not knowing "One Lord, one faith, one baptism." So it is not strange that they have left us, since they who do not see those things are not of us. It is yours meanwhile to advance in the fear of the Lord, and to guard yourself from the hypocrisy of evil men. Farewell, and pray for the victory for truth. I turn to the "Disputation at Baden," which everybody says has been distorted intentionally by the printers, but which I have not yet had time to read, so that if it requires refutation at my hands I may give it.* Be assured that all this when it was printing was snatched from the jaws of the pen.

* Baden is a town only 12 miles northwest of Zurich, but such a centre of the bitterest foes of Zwingli that he did not venture to go thither to attend the Disputation. It was the Old Church's reply to the Zurich Disputation of 1523, and lasted from May 21st to June 18th, 1526. The Acts were published at Luzern, May 18, 1527.

www.ingramcontent.com/pod-product-compliance
Lightning Source LLC
Chambersburg PA
CBHW060559230426
43670CB00011B/1887